WESTMAR COLLE

Kant

Kant

PHILOSOPHICAL CORRESPONDENCE
1759–99

Edited and translated by
ARNULF ZWEIG

THE UNIVERSITY
OF CHICAGO
PRESS

The letters in this collection are translations of correspondence contained in the Prussian Academy edition of Kant's works, *Kant's gesammelte Schriften* (Berlin and Leipzig: Walter de Gruyter & Co.), Vols. X–XII (1922) and XXIII (1955).

International Standard Book Number: 0–226–42360–3
Library of Congress Catalog Card Number: 66–23705

THE UNIVERSITY OF CHICAGO PRESS, CHICAGO 60637

THE UNIVERSITY OF CHICAGO PRESS, LTD., LONDON

Translator's Preface

This volume contains translations of virtually all of Kant's philosophical correspondence, together with some of his personal and historically interesting letters. Also included are a few of the many letters written to Kant by his students, colleagues, disciples, and critics. Some of these letters are needed in order to understand Kant's own remarks, and others have considerable interest in their own right. In some cases, the letters have been abridged, with only the significant passages translated, and sometimes a portion of a letter has been merely summarized. Such summaries, as well as other explanatory remarks by the translator, are in brackets. The Prussian Academy of Sciences edition of Kant's works, Volumes X–XII and XXIII, includes over seven hundred letters and fragments of letters, comprising about fifteen hundred pages; Volume XIII has seven hundred pages of explanatory notes and indexes. Although it was tempting to include many more than will be found in this collection, the great majority of letters not included would be of interest only to the specialist, and he presumably would want to study them in the original language.[1]

A complete citation for each letter to the second printing of the Prussian Academy edition will be found under the headings in the text. Most of the explanatory footnotes are derived from the Academy edition Volume XIII or from K. Vorländer's definitive biography of Kant, *Immanuel Kant, der Mann und das Werk* (Leipzig: Felix Meiner, 1924), though I have not attempted to reproduce in even a limited way the enormous scholarly achievement of those volumes. In one or two letters Kant himself wrote a footnote, and these are so designated. I have sometimes given a German or Latin expression in brackets following the translation.

---

[1] Only one of the letters, to my knowledge, has ever been published in its entirety in English. It is Kant's letter of February 21, 1772, to Marcus Herz, which appeared in the *Philosophical Forum* (Boston University), XIII (1955), and was reprinted in L. W. Beck, *Studies in the Philosophy of Kant* (Indianapolis: Bobbs-Merrill Co., 1965). My translation of this letter differs only insignificantly from that of the previous translator, Arne Unjhem.

Two people above all deserve thanks for their help in this work. The first is Professor Lewis White Beck, whose writing and teaching first stimulated my interest in Kant and who gave me many valuable suggestions and much friendly advice on translating the correspondence. The other is my wife, who not only encouraged and aided me but who also made many critical suggestions for improving the manuscript. I would also like to express my thanks to the University of Oregon for granting me sabbatical leave during 1962–63, to the Research Committee of the Graduate School of the University of Oregon for two summer research grants, and to the American Philosophical Association for a grant in support of this volume. Because of these sources of assistance, I was able to spend the academic year 1962–63 in Germany and Austria. I would like particularly to express my pleasure at the hospitality extended to me and to my family by my colleagues in the Universities of Vienna and Bonn during that year.

Arnulf Zweig

Eugene, Oregon

Contents

viii · *Contents*

Introduction

Introduction

Although most of Kant's letters were written reluctantly, sometimes hastily, and never with a view to publication,[1] they provide a
great deal of information about his life and attitudes, the development of his philosophical ideas, and the impact of his thought and
character on his contemporaries. We do not find the wit and
liveliness that Kant the conversationalist was reputed to have or,
with one or two exceptions, the warmth and passion that Kant's
correspondents reveal in their own letters to him. Direct, humor-
less, unadorned by any flights of literary imagination, Kant's
letters invariably reflect some specific business or obligation and
seldom if ever manifest any sense of enjoyment or delight on the
part of their author, who obviously regarded letter-writing as a
chore and a distraction from more serious work. Nevertheless,
there are great rewards for the reader. The firsthand reports of the
evolution in Kant's thinking, the replies to criticisms and questions from his disciples and foes—and sometimes the very failure
to reply to such inquiries—are invaluable aids to our understanding of Kant's philosophy. Metaphysics, theology, mathematics, education, political theory, astronomy, applied ethics—almost
all of Kant's intellectual interests are discussed and surveyed, and
at the same time a picture of Kant's personality and character, his
mental and physical anxieties, and an understanding of Kant's
place in the history of the late eighteenth century are made
available to us. Although many of the letters require little more
explanation than is provided in the footnotes, it may be useful to
review the topics discussed, identify some of the issues and person-
alities involved, and mention a few of the letters not included in
this collection.

[1] Kant expressed himself on this point when he declined to include his letters
in the published correspondence of Lambert and again in that of Mendelssohn.
See, for example, his remarks to J. Bernoulli, November 16, 1781 [172], and
to Marcus Herz, April 7, 1786 [267].

I. 1759–70

Kant's career up to 1770, the year of his promotion to the professorship of logic and metaphysics in the University of Königsberg, is not very well represented in the correspondence. Of the fifty odd letters and fragments in the Prussian Academy of Sciences edition, only the correspondence with Lambert, Hamann, and Mendelssohn is of genuine importance.[2]

Lambert. J. H. Lambert (1728–77) was a mathematician, physicist, and philosopher whose renown, at the time of his correspondence, exceeded that of Kant. A member of the Berlin Academy, Lambert, in his *Cosmological Letters* (1781), supported an astronomical theory somewhat similar to that of Kant's *General Natural History of the Heavens* (*Allgemeine Naturgeschichte und Theorie des Himmels* [1755]).[3] Lambert's *New Organon,* his philosophy of science, appeared in 1764. In his first letter to Kant, November 13, 1765 [33], he takes note of their common interests and the similarity of their ideas in philosophy and in science. Lambert here makes mention of the need for "an analysis of the

---

[2] A letter to J. G. Lindner in 1759 has some biographical interest; it reveals how depressed Kant was with his teaching position and perhaps with life in general: "I sit daily at the anvil of my lectern and guide the heavy hammer of my repetitious lectures, always beating out the same rhythm. Now and then a nobler sort of inclination stirs in me somewhere, a desire to expand beyond these narrow spheres; but in truth the threat of that feeling always drives me back to hard work without delay. . . . In this town where I find myself and with the modest prosperity for which I allow myself to hope, I make do finally with the applause I receive and the benefits I derive from that, dreaming my life away." What the "nobler inclination" might have been, or what it was that broke Kant out of his despondent mood, we do not know. There are other miscellaneous letters of 1759–70 that may deserve mention. A tantalizing note from a certain Frau Maria Charlotte Jacobi in 1762 hints very faintly at romance; she and her girl friend send Kant a kiss. A letter to a Fräulein Charlotte von Knobloch, in 1763, contains some amusing anecdotes concerning Swedenborg's alleged feats of clairvoyance and communication with ghosts together with Kant's skeptical comments on these stories. An exchange of letters with Herder in 1768 mentions Kant's progress on "the metaphysics of morals," a work Kant hoped to complete within a year. (In fact the *Foundations of the Metaphysics of Morals* did not appear until 1785, the *Metaphysics of Morals* until 1797.)

[3] Some people erroneously believed, after Lambert's death, that Kant's own theory derived from Lambert. In his letter to Biester, June 8, 1781 [168], Kant explained that he wrote his *Natural History of the Heavens* before Lambert published a similar cosmological hypothesis and that Lambert had remarked on this similarity in his letter of 1765 [33]. Kant's letter to J. F. Gensichen, April 19, 1791 [466], also discusses the matter. Kant there explains that his own theory of the Milky Way was formulated six years earlier than Lambert's *Cosmological Letters.* This was in fact accurate.

elements of human knowledge," which should discuss "the universal and necessary possibilities of synthesizing and uniting of simple concepts." He had read Kant's essay, "Only Possible Proof of the Existence of God" (1763) and knew that Kant was working on a reconstruction of the method of metaphysics analogous to one which he himself advocated. Lambert suggests that they exchange letters on their research, a proposal which must have flattered Kant (who called Lambert "the greatest genius in Germany"), for he replied to Lambert with unusual alacrity. Lambert's letter is amusing also for its uncharitable observations (a prefiguration of C. P. Snow's "two cultures") on Greek scholars, antiquarians, art critics, and literati.

Kant's reply self-confidently announces that he has finally found "the proper method for metaphysics and thereby also for the whole of philosophy"; but he is not yet prepared to publish his findings for, as he candidly admits, he lacks examples of propositions that can be demonstrated by means of this method. He has therefore put aside the project in order to devote himself to other essays, the subject of two of these being the metaphysical foundations of natural philosophy and the metaphysical foundations of practical philosophy.[4] Lambert awaited these books impatiently, as he states in his next letter, but as it turned out, in vain. We can only guess what Kant had in mind in 1765, though many scholars regard this as the beginning of Kant's investigations leading to the *Critique of Pure Reason*. It becomes clear that the discovery of the problem to which Kant's letter of 1772 to Herz is devoted was one cause of Kant's repeated postponement of his project, though undoubtedly the heavy burden of his teaching duties (Kant lectured up to twenty-eight hours a week, in addition to private seminars) was also important.

Lambert's reply, February 3, 1766 [37], describes his own methodology at considerable length, utilizing the distinction between "formal" and "material" knowledge, a distinction that became an important part of Kant's analysis of metaphysics in the inaugural dissertation (1770) and also in his later critical writings. Formal knowledge, Lambert suggests, is expressed in "simple concepts" a priori; it is concerned only with the organization of non-formal or material knowledge. Complex, synthesized concepts

---

[4] As a matter of fact, Kant published nothing under these titles until twenty years later, when the *Metaphysical Foundations of Natural Science* appeared (1786).

must be derived from simple concepts. The latter type of concepts, such as space and time, require direct acquaintance, that is, intuition. The extent of Kant's indebtedness to Lambert is expressed in his letter to Bernoulli, November 16, 1781 [172].

Hamann. Kant's correspondence with J. G. Hamann (1730–88) does not discuss any technical questions of philosophy but reveals very strikingly the conflicting attitudes and convictions of these philosophers. Hamann, the "wizard (or Magus) of the North" as he was called, was the most improbable friend one could imagine for Kant. Passionate, mystical, intellectually and physically untidy, he was the antithesis of all that Kant and the Enlightenment represented. His flamboyant style of writing is a language all its own, using a veritable stream of consciousness technique full of classical and biblical allusions along with copious, often brilliant neologisms. Though at one time a deist, Hamann had undergone a sudden conversion to an intensely fundamentalist and emotional type of Christianity.[5] The long letter of July 27, 1759, expresses Hamanns' astonishment, rage, and amusement at the efforts of Kant and J. C. Berens, a long-time friend of Hamann's, to convert him away from zealotry back to what these men regarded as rational deism. It is a brilliant letter, powerful and sarcastic.[6]

Less theatrical but nonetheless entertaining was Hamann's second letter of 1759 (not included here), and the circumstances that prompted it are again interesting for what they reveal about Kant. Apparently Kant and Hamann had discussed collaborating on a natural science textbook for children. (Kant's interest in education and his views on that topic are also shown in his letter to Wolke, March 28, 1776 [109].) Hamann lampoons the idea that Kant is capable of this and argues that a book by a philosopher, written for children, would have to be as ostensibly simple and babbling as a book by God, written for mere human beings. Hamann suggests basing physics on the biblical account of creation, presenting physical phenomena with a view to showing their divine origin. This suggestion could hardly have pleased Kant, and it is not surprising that he failed to reply to this or to Hamann's subsequent effusions on the subject.

---

[5] Kierkegaard must have recognized Hamann as a prefiguration of himself. He quotes Hamann on the title page of *Fear and Trembling.*

[6] An English translation of some parts of the letter may be found in R. G. Smith, *J. G. Hamann* (New York: Harper & Bros., 1960). The translation in the present volume is new and complete.

Kant's only extant letters to Hamann were written in 1774. They contained a tedious discussion of Herder's *Älteste Urkunde des Menschengeschlechts,* which appeared anonymously in that year. The main topic concerned Herder's intention in discussing the occurrence of common symbols in both the biblical account of creation and the literature of pagan antiquity, and Herder's claim that this similarity reflected God's effort to instruct the human race. The letters do include some pleasant academic gossip concerning the promotion of a man of dubious piety—Hamann calls him a "Roman-apostolic-catholic-heretic-crypto-Jesuit"—to the professorship of theology, but they are otherwise rather boring. The most interesting remark made in them is Kant's concluding plea to Hamann (April 6, 1774 [86]) to communicate his further ideas "if possible, in the language of men. For I, poor earthling that I am, have not been properly trained to understand the divine language of an Intuitive Reason."

Mendelssohn and the Popular Philosophers. Moses Mendelssohn (1729–86) was the most distinguished of the so-called popular philosophers of the German Enlightenment. A group of somewhat unsystematic intellectuals, more or less Leibnizian in outlook though often opposed to learned discourse and technical arguments, they preferred to appeal instead to common sense, the *gesunder Menschenverstand,* or healthy human understanding. The men usually included under this heading were J. G. H. Feder, C. Meiners, C. Garve, J. J. Engel, C. F. Nicolai, and J. E. Biester. Feder and Meiners taught at Göttingen, where they later founded the *Philosophische Bibliothek,* a journal specifically devoted to combatting Kant's "critical philosophy." The journal survived only four volumes. Garve, a more sensitive man (his letters to Kant are genuinely moving), worked in Breslau. It was Garve's review of the *Critique of Pure Reason* (a review edited and distorted by Feder before its publication in January, 1782, in the *Göttinger Gelehrte Anzeigen*) that provoked Kant's wrath [7] and stimulated him to write certain parts of the *Prolegomena to Any Future Metaphysics* (the appendix of that work refers to the review). Nicolai, a friend of Mendelssohn's and of Lessing's, was editor of the *Bibliothek der schönen Wissenschaften* (1757–58), then of the *Briefe, die neueste Litteratur betreffend* (1759–65) and, most important, of the *Allgemeine deutsche Bibliothek*

[7] See his letter to Garve, August 7, 1783 [205].

(1765–1805), a propaganda organ of the Enlightenment.[8] Opposed to prejudice, superstition, orthodoxy, pietism, mysticism, and Jesuitism, he was, for all his zeal, platitudinous and shallow. Kant, who was for a time on cool but friendly terms with Nicolai, directed one of his last essays, *Über die Buchmacherei* (1798), against him, and Nicolai also became a target for Fichte, Goethe, and Schiller. Biester, who published the *Berliner Monatsschrift*, to which Kant contributed, was secretary to the minister of education, von Zedlitz, as well as librarian in the Royal Library. As one of Kant's chief ambassadors in the capital, his correspondence with Kant during the period 1792–94 tells us much about Kant's difficulties with the censorship of unorthodox religious views. The French Revolution is also touched upon in these letters.

Of all these men, it was Mendelssohn for whom Kant had the greatest respect and affection. Unlike most of the popular philosophers, Mendelssohn did not disapprove of careful arguments and rigorous demonstration. Like Kant, he deplored the fall of philosophy, once the "queen of the sciences," to the shabby status of a facile, diverting parlor game. In 1763, Mendelssohn and Kant competed for the Berlin Academy Prize. Mendelssohn's *Treatise on Evidence in the Metaphysical Sciences* won, but the judges praised Kant's essay, *An Inquiry into the Distinctness of the Fundamental Principles of Natural Theology and Morals* (*Untersuchung über die Deutlichkeit der Grundsätze der natürlichen Theologie und der Moral*), and the two works were to have been published together. The topic proposed for this competition was the question: "Whether metaphysical truths generally, and in particular the fundamental principles of natural theology and morals, are capable of proofs as distinct as those of geometry." [9] Mendelssohn maintained that metaphysics can be as certain as geometry, though it is not as easily comprehended. Kant insisted that there are fundamental differences between metaphysics and mathematics, especially with regard to the role of definition or concept formation. Mathematics arrives at its concepts synthetically, *from* definitions; its concepts are constructed figures, from which

---

[8] Nicolai is known also for a parody on Goethe's *Sorrows of Werther: The Joys of Young Werther* (*Freuden des jungen Werthers* [1775]).

[9] A translation of Kant's essay is included in *Kant's Critique of Practical Reason and Other Writings in Moral Philosophy* (Chicago: University of Chicago Press, 1949), translated and edited by L. W. Beck.

we can derive only what we have originally put into them.[10] Validity is here independent of what exists in nature. Philosophy, however, cannot produce its own objects but must take them as given and try to see them as they are. Definitions are thus the end of philosophy rather than the beginning. "Metaphysics is without doubt the most difficult of human insights; but none has ever been written."

The disagreement with Mendelssohn did not inhibit the start of a warm friendship. Mendelssohn must have written a cordial letter early in 1766 to which Kant's letter of February 7 [38] is a reply. In this letter he expresses his pleasure at the prospect of a correspondence with Mendelssohn, chats about a Jewish student whom Mendelssohn had recommended to Kant, and asks Mendelssohn to forward copies of Kant's *Dreams of a Ghost-Seer Explained by Dreams of Metaphysics* to various gentlemen (including Lambert). Kant refers to it as *einige Träumerey* ("some reveries") and adds: "It is, as it were, a casual piece, containing not so much a working out of such questions as a hasty sketch of the way they should be treated."

Evidently the work estranged Mendelssohn by what the latter took to be an insincere tone, "between jest and earnest." In his answer to Mendelssohn (the latter's critical letter is not extant), April 8, 1766 [39], Kant forcefully defends his own character. In addition to this extended self-evaluation, unique in Kant's writings, he also indicates his view of the worth of current metaphysics, whose "chimerical insights" lead to folly and error. An exposure of dogmatism is needed, says Kant, an organon, on which he is now at work. Kant speaks of having already reached "important insights" that will define the proper procedure for metaphysics.

The discussion of the soul, in this letter, gives us a brief statement of the position Kant defended in his *Dreams of a Ghost-Seer*. He is concerned with the relationship of material and spir-

---

[10] It is interesting to see how Kant remained true to this early thesis throughout his critical writings. Indeed, the claim is generalized in the *Critique of Pure Reason: all* a priori knowledge depends on "what we have originally put into" our judgments. See *Critique* A xx, B ix, B xii, B xiii, B 130. I am grateful to Professor Samuel Todes for pointing out the similarity of these passages to me. See also Kant's letters on mathematics in this collection, as listed in the Index.

itual substances but is not optimistic about solving such metaphysical problems. What are the powers of spiritual substances, and how can we discover the precise way in which souls are joined to material substances? Our philosophical fabrications are completely unhindered by any data when we discuss theories that purport to answer these questions. Kant suggests that there are matters (birth, life, and death) that we can never hope to understand by means of reason. The main theme of the *Dreams of a Ghost-Seer,* to which Kant is referring in this letter, is the parallel between the dreams and visions of Swedenborg, on the one hand, and the speculations of allegedly scientific metaphysics, on the other. Kant's essay tries to show how a clever manipulation of concepts can produce ostensible knowledge of the supersensible. He shows that such structures are mere airy possibilities of thought, undeserving of serious attention. The metaphysician's theories are "dreams of reason," whereas those of the ghost-seer are "dreams of sensation." He writes: "I do not know whether there are spirits; yes, what is more, I do not even know what the word 'spirit' means." Philosophy "excites the suspicion that it is found in bad company" when serious efforts are devoted to explaining the whims of fantastic persons.

Kant's attitude toward traditional metaphysics as shown in this work and in the letter to Mendelssohn was, in 1766, quite close to Hume's. The philosopher's task should be to survey the nature and limits of our cognitive powers. Speculative metaphysics offers no possibility of scientific certainty, its principles being based on mere wish fulfilment. The tone of the critical philosophy is there, though Kant had not yet developed the major theses, nor even formulated the main questions, of the *Critique of Pure Reason.*

II. 1770–81

Kant's position in the dissertation of 1770. In 1770 Kant received the appointment he had long awaited, the professorship of logic and metaphysics. He sent copies of his inaugural dissertation, *The Form and Principles of the Sensible and Intelligible Worlds,* to various scholars whose opinions he respected, among them Mendelssohn [11] and Lambert. In the accompanying letter to Lam-

[11] Mendelssohn's response in the letter of December 25, 1770 [63], offers a number of significant criticisms of the dissertation, for example, of Kant's interpretation of Shaftesbury as a follower of Epicurus. Mendelssohn's criti-

bert, Kant states some of the main theses of the dissertation. Again, Kant is concerned with the need for a transformation of metaphysics, a program that the separation of non-empirical from empirical principles will help to realize. His position at this time, partly influenced by Leibniz' *Nouveaux Essais* (1765), involved the separation of a "sense world" and an "intellectual world," with a corresponding schism in the structure of our cognitive faculties. In order to reconcile the independence of mathematics from experience with the applicability of mathematics to reality, Kant propounds the theory that space and time are forms of intuition, invariant characteristics of immediate experience.[12] This is essentially the position taken in the transcendental aesthetic of the *Critique of Pure Reason*. The Newtonian view, that space and time are "real beings" existing independently of objects, events, and observers, Kant argued, makes unintelligible how geometry (the science of space) can be known a priori to be valid for everything in space and time. Geometry, on Newton's view of space, would have to have the status of a merely empirical science. Ultimately, Kant attempts to mediate between this absolute theory of space and time and the theory of Leibniz. Though independent of what fills them, space and time are not independent of knowing minds. But Kant believed the consequence of his theory—that space and time are supplied by our own faculty of sensibility—to be that the objects that we perceive in space and time are only phenomenal images of noumenal realities, and such noumenal entities, if they are to be known at all, would have to be reached by some non-empirical means, viz., pure thought. Thus we have two "worlds": the world of our sensibility is "appearance," and that of our understanding is genuine, "intelligible" reality. As against Leibniz, the distinction between sensibility and understanding is made to be one of kind and not of degree—sensibility is passive; understanding is active or "spontaneous." In addition, along with the Platonic distinction of two worlds, Kant followed

cisms of Kant's theory of time, and similar objections by Lambert, are answered in Kant's letter to Herz, February 21, 1772 [70] and again in the *Critique of Pure Reason* A 36–B 53 ff. Kant thought that his view had been misinterpreted as a version of the subjective idealism of Berkeley.

[12] Kant was led to this view particularly by the problem of space. His essay *On the First Ground of the Distinction of Regions in Space* (1768) defended the thesis that conceptually incongruent but symmetric figures (for example, mirror images) cannot be distinguished without assuming, contrary to Leibniz but in agreement with Newton, an absolute space independent of all matter existing in it.

Leibniz in assuming that the categories or non-empirical concepts of the intellect (causality, substance, necessity, and so on) have not only a "logical use," that is, in the organization of experience, but also a "real use," in which they provide knowledge of the world of true Being.

It is this "dogmatic" position (in contrast to the skeptical view of metaphysics in *Dreams of a Ghost-Seer*) against which Kant reacted in the decade between 1770 and the appearance of the *Critique of Pure Reason* in 1781. The change is recorded primarily in Kant's letters to Marcus Herz (1747–1803). Along with Kant's later correspondence with his apostatic disciples, these letters comprise perhaps the most significant philosophical material to be found in Kant's letters.[13]

Herz and the letter of 1772. Herz studied in Königsberg from 1755 to 1770 and acted as "respondent" or "public defender" for Kant's inaugural dissertation, a fact indicative of Kant's respect for him. After studying medicine in Halle, Herz returned to Berlin in 1774 to begin his medical practice. By 1776, he was also giving public lectures on the philosophy of Kant; several letters of 1778 deal with Herz's request for lecture notes from Kant. One of the most distinguished members of Herz's audience was von Zedlitz, the minister of spiritual affairs (which included education) to whom Kant later dedicated the *Critique of Pure Reason*. But Kant's confidence in Herz stemmed not only from the latter's philosophical talents; Herz was a physician, and Kant a hypochondriac. Most of Kant's letters to Herz make mention of symptoms and ailments, sometimes very extensively described, with discussions of possible treatments and requests for advice. Though Kant was never seriously ill, he constantly complained about his health and the adverse effects of his indisposition (mainly gastric and intestinal) on his work.[14]

[13] For a discussion of Herz and Kant, see L. W. Beck, "Kant's Letter to Marcus Herz," in *Studies in the Philosophy of Kant* (Indianapolis: Bobbs-Merrill Co., 1965), an essay that appeared originally in *Philosophical Forum* (Boston University), XIII (1955). For another recent discussion of this letter, see R. P. Wolff, *Kant's Theory of Mental Activity* (Cambridge, Mass.: Harvard University Press, 1963). Virtually all of the standard commentaries on Kant make some mention of the letter. Some scholars (for example, Norman Kemp Smith) see it as supporting the "patchwork theory" of the deduction of the categories, whereas others (for example, H. J. Paton) oppose this interpretation. There is a good discussion of the letter in T. D. Weldon, *Kant's Critique of Pure Reason* (London: Oxford University Press, 1958).

[14] In one of his last works, *The Strife of the Faculties*, Kant blamed his lifelong hypochondria on the narrowness of his chest.

The letter of February 21, 1772, shows Kant's thinking at the point at which the Leibnizian aspects of the theory in his inaugural dissertation first became suspect to him. Suddenly he is troubled by the uncritical assumption he had made, that categories or "intellectual representations," which Kant had characterized only negatively as "ideas we employ that are not derived from our experience of objects," could nevertheless be supposed to agree with those objects and thus to represent things as they are. How can concepts that do not *produce* their objects (like God's thinking) and that are not produced in us *by* the objects to which they refer (like empirical concepts) be applicable a priori to an independent reality? In other words, Kant is asking for a justification or "deduction" of the "real use" of pure concepts when these concepts are to apply not simply to mathematical "objects" that we ourselves construct but to things existing independently of our minds. He wants to know how we can tell that a concept "spontaneously" created by the mind actually corresponds to anything. Kant says that he has found a way to classify these concepts "following a few fundamental laws of the understanding" and that in three months he will be ready with his solution—an extraordinarily sanguine prediction, as it turned out. For by the time Kant had completed the *Critique of Pure Reason,* the "recollection of David Hume," as he characterizes it in the Introduction to the *Prolegomena,* had "interrupted [his] dogmatic slumbers. . . . ," and the problem stated as it is in this letter to Herz was found to be incapable of solution. The categories could not be shown to agree with the nature of things, if "thing" is taken to refer to noumenal entities in a non-empirical world.

Though Kant had not yet arrived at the most distinctive argument of his critical position, the transcendental deduction, he had evidently reached a form of the table of categories and, more important, a formulation of what was to become the central problem of the *Critique of Pure Reason,* viz., how are synthetic a priori judgments possible. Here in the letter to Herz he mentions that work for the first time by name. It was this momentous work that took up most of Kant's attention in the "silent decade" of the seventies.

Kant published very little between 1770 and 1781, and the number of letters he wrote is also small. His correspondence with Hamann in 1774 has already been mentioned. A few letters to Herz tell of his progress or lack of progress on the *Critique,* along with some very detailed discussion of his physical debilities, and these letters are not only biographically important but help us to see how intimate the friendship of these two men must have been. The correspondence with Lavater and Wolke, however, presents us with an entirely different side of Kant's intellectual interests.

Lavater. J. C. Lavater (1741–1801) was a Swiss poet, mystic, and a renowned physiognomist, a man who influenced Goethe and who was also close to Hamann. Lavater was an ardent reader of Kant, his *Lieblingsschriftsteller.* His letters to Kant indicate that the literary and learned world was awaiting Kant's new writings with great eagerness. "Are you dead to the world?" Lavater asks. "Why is it that so many scribble who cannot write, while you who write so well are silent?" Lavater tells Kant that he and his countrymen are anxious to see the *Critique.* In one letter he asks Kant to evaluate his own book, on faith and prayer, somehow imagining that Kant would approve of it. One can imagine how Lavater's enthusiasm for Kant must have been tempered by the latter's reply (April 28, 1775 [99] and [100]) for Kant's views were already those of *Religion within the Limits of Reason Alone.* The letters are in fact a clear and eloquent summary of Kant's position. A certain cooling off on Lavater's part is confirmed by his failure to reply to Kant for almost a year, although the two men afterward remained on good terms and Lavater later once wrote to Kant of his joy at having found someone to talk with "to satiety and still not to satiety" about Kant's ideas. Though the correspondence between them ended, Kant mentions Lavater a number of times in various works, critically but not disrespectfully. He had no patience for the Lavaterian attempt to analyze character by means of the study of facial lines, calling it "indistinct concepts without any order," and in his lectures on anthropology in 1785 Kant maintained that physiognomists are correct in their analyses of character only when they know the people they are supposedly analyzing. Elsewhere Kant refers to Lavater as a *Schwärmer*—a fanatic or enthusiast inspired by a delusion—but Kant did not always use this word abusively.[15]

Letters on Education: Wolke. Kant's interest in education was always intense, to such an extent that he was even willing to interrupt his work on the *Critique* in order to write and speak in

---

[15] Cf. his reference to Maria von Herbert as *die kleine Schwärmerin* in a letter to Elisabeth Motherby, February 11, 1793 [559].

support of the educational reforms of an experimental school, the Philanthropin. This institution was founded in Dessau in 1774 by J. B. Basedow, a man whose views on education Kant regarded highly. Kant used Basedow's *Methodenbuch* as the text in his lectures on practical pedagogy in the winter semester of 1776–77. The Philanthropin was based more or less on the liberal principles of Rousseau's *Émile*.[16] From the very beginning, the school was in serious financial difficulties, for which Basedow's enthusiasm failed to compensate. Kant's correspondence with Basedow and the men who replaced him, C. H. Wolke and J. H. Campe, reflects Kant's efforts to keep the Philanthropin in business.[17] The most important of these letters, for a view of Kant's ideas on education and especially on religious instruction, is the letter to Wolke of 1776 [109]. Kant believed that a child "must be raised in freedom, but in such a way that he will allow others to be free as well" (*Reflexionen zur Anthropologie,* No. 1473). In the letter to Wolke, he makes explicit his opposition to traditional methods of education and especially to customary religious education. Kant urges that a child not even be introduced to prayer until his understanding has matured to such a degree that he can understand (what Kant regards as) the true purpose of devotional acts, viz., to apprehend his duties as if the latter were divine commands.

III. Letters in the 1780's and 1790's

Reactions to the Critique of Pure Reason: *Mendelssohn and Garve.* Readers of Kant who find him difficult to understand may be reassured by the response of Kant's own contemporaries to the publication of the *Critique of Pure Reason*. Mendelssohn, on whom Kant had counted heavily to help disseminate the new philosophy, called it *dieses Nervensaftverzehrendes Werk*—"this nerve-juice-consuming book"! Garve, too, proved disappointingly

---

[16] The "natural" method of education at the Philanthropin insisted on treating children as children. Powdered hair, swords, gilded coats, and makeup were forbidden. The children had short haircuts and wore sailor jackets. They learned languages in a sort of "Berlitz" program. The curriculum included Latin, German, French, mathematics, geography, physics, music, dancing, drawing, and physical education. Religion was taught in such a way that sectarian distinctions in theology were completely avoided.

[17] To this end, Kant published several appeals for subscriptions in the *Königsberger gelehrte und politische Zeitung*.

unsympathetic. To Mendelssohn and to Garve Kant wrote in 1783, carefully setting forth some of the main theses of the *Critique* and defending himself against various criticisms, especially that of "unpopularity" in style of writing. Kant challenges Garve to compose a deduction of the categories that will make pleasant reading, or to try to construct a "whole new science" without the difficult arguments and distinctions in the *Critique* (to Garve, August 7 [205]; to Mendelssohn, August 16 [206]).

These letters taken together provide not only a nice introduction to those theses but also show Kant's view (in 1783) on two matters which his critics have frequently debated and about which it must be admitted Kant himself was never entirely clear: the distinction between appearance and thing-in-itself, on the one hand, and the distinction between sensible and supersensible objects. Talking about the first distinction, Kant says to Garve that it is a difference between two concepts or ways of talking about all *given* objects. Viewed in this light, the distinction does not commit Kant to the two "worlds" theory of the dissertation. In the letter to Mendelssohn, however, Kant speaks of the existence of two radically different kinds of *entities*. The *Critique,* he says, does not aim to deny the existence of objects (*Gegenstände*) that are not objects of possible experience; in fact, the existence of such entities is required by it! It would seem, then, that the claim that there exist supersensible objects (*übersinnliche Gegenstände*) must be distinguished from the appearance versus thing-in-itself dualism, for, as Kant had indicated only a week earlier, in distinguishing appearances from things as they are in themselves, the phrase "thing-in-itself" refers not to some object other than the object we encounter in experience but to that same object considered apart from its relation to a knowing subject. In the decades following, the problem of the status of the Kantian thing-in-itself became one of the main targets for Kant's critics. Discussion centered around the question whether Kant's theory of perception entails the claim that unknowable things in themselves are the cause of our sense impressions. Kant's ablest student, J. S. Beck, attempted to save him from inconsistency by interpreting his theory to mean that "thing-in-itself" is just another way of talking about the object that appears and that it is this phenomenal object, not some mysterious supersensible entity, that affects our senses. Kant's answers to Beck's letters do not positively endorse this interpretation—by then Kant was old and, as he told his followers, no longer equipped for overly subtle discussions—but the letter to Garve may be taken as one piece of evidence in support of Beck's interpretation.

Disciples and Critics. The sudden profusion of letters after 1783 attests to the impact of the *Critique of Pure Reason* on the intellectual life of Germany and Europe. Though Kant's reputation in the learned world was already high, his fame now became extended well beyond the sphere of the universities. Kant's philosophy was the topic of discussion in literary salons and court gatherings. Young ladies wrote to him for moral guidance, and religious zealots and political absolutists, deploring the popularity of his liberal ideas, wrote to him to try to convert him. Kant was hailed as the benefactor of mankind, liberator of the human spirit and defender of freedom. Journals were founded to spread the critical philosophy, and several of Kant's students wrote popularizations of his work to make him understandable to the general reading public. The progress of Kant's philosophy did not go unchallenged, however. An upsurge of fanaticism, religious reaction, and political interference in the form of censorship and loyalty oaths was about to begin. As early as 1783 Kant heard from his friend F. V. L. Plessing that the enemies of the Enlightenment were gathering strength, a lament which Plessing repeated in his letter of March 15, 1784 [226]. Rumor had it that "a Protestant king is supposed secretly to be a J-s-t!" wrote Plessing. The Jesuits, "those hellish spirits," had poisoned the hearts of princes. But as far as the government was concerned, Plessing's dire warnings were a few years premature. Kant's most vocal enemies, at this time, were not political figures but the old guard philosophy professors who defended Leibniz and Wolff.

Although Kant was attacked and misunderstood by popular philosophers, empiricists (who assailed Kant for subscribing to synthetic a priori judgments), and rationalists (who assailed him for limiting knowledge to the domain of experience), the favorable reactions of younger men more than compensated for these hostile opinions. The spread of Kantianism was aided by the dedication of Kant's new disciples at the University of Jena, especially C. G. Schütz, C. F. Schmid, and K. L. Reinhold. The *Allgemeine Literaturzeitung,* to which Kant contributed, did much to promote the critical philosophy. Schütz, whose correspondence with Kant is of interest in tracing the progress of Kant's writings after the *Critique of Pure Reason,* was the author of the first sensible review of the *Critique,* and it was he who persuaded Kant to write a review of Herder's *Ideen* (1785) for the *A.L.Z.*[18] (Schütz was moved to tears by Kant's refusal of the generous honorarium offered by the journal.) Schmid's support of Kantianism came in the form of an elucidatory dictionary of Kantian terminology, *Wörterbuch zum leichteren Gebrauche der Kantischen Schriften* (1788), and Reinhold's *Letters concerning the Kantian Philosophy* (1786/87 in the *Deutsche Merkür;* 1790 as a book) was most important in popularizing Kant.[19] By 1787, when Reinhold was professor of philosophy at the University of Jena, people spoke of the "Kant-Reinhold" philosophy—a phrase that lost its cogency, however, when Reinhold later became a follower of Fichte.[20]

Reinhold's letters to Kant, in 1787 and 1788, are rhapsodic in praising the critical philosophy and its creator. They also contain some nice academic gossip, including some anecdotes about Kant's enemy at Jena, a Professor Ulrich, who made a practice of inviting Reinhold's students to dinner in order to seduce them away from the study of Kant! Kant's letter to Reinhold, in 1788, expresses his opinion of various contemporaries and states his approval of Reinhold's work. Of greater philosophical interest, however, are Kant's letters in the following year, in which he gives a lengthy account of his objections to the Wolffian philosopher, Eberhard.

J. A. Eberhard, professor of philosophy at Halle, was founder of the *Philosophisches Magazin,* a periodical dedicated to destroying Kant's philosophy. He denied the originality of Kant's analytic/synthetic distinction, rejected the "Copernican revolution" with its consequent limitation of the understanding to objects of sensible

[18] In February, 1785, Schütz wrote to Kant saying that Herder ought to take pride in Kant's discussion of his book—the review was generally recognized as Kant's even though it appeared unsigned. But Herder's reaction to it was not what Schütz predicted, as can be seen from a letter Herder wrote to Hamann in which he expresses his vexation and accuses Kant of being bitter toward him for having decided not to follow the path of his former teacher's "verbal juggling." Herder objects especially to being treated like a schoolboy now that he is forty years old and a thinker in his own right.

[19] Reinhold, who was born in Vienna in 1758, started his career as a Jesuit. Stirred by the Enlightenment under Emperor Josef, he came to reject most orthodox dogmas and eventually he abandoned the Jesuit order and was converted to Protestantism. In 1783, in Weimar, Reinhold became the son-in-law of C. M. Wieland, the famous novelist.

[20] Reinhold's uncommon candor is shown by his public pronouncement, while still at the height of his fame, that Fichte had refuted him. He died, virtually forgotten, in 1823.

intuition, and argued that reason, being capable of intellectual intuitions, can furnish its own "material" without the aid of the senses. Kant, in his letters to Reinhold, is especially critical of Eberhard's attempt to use the principles of contradiction and sufficient reason as devices for achieving knowledge of objects. Some of the material in these letters was later incorporated into Kant's polemical essay against Eberhard, *On a Discovery according to Which All New Critique of Pure Reason Is Supposed To Be Obviated by an Earlier One (Ueber eine Entdeckung nach der alle neue Kritik der reinen Vernunft durch eine ältere entbehrlich gemacht werden soll* [1790]), in which Kant attacks the meta-sensible use of reason, refutes Eberhard's objections to his notion of synthetic judgments, and offers an interpretation of Leibniz that contains the argument that Leibniz's theory requires completion by Kant's own philosophy. The main points in this essay against the philosophical *ancien régime* may be found in the letters to Reinhold of 1789.

Other Opposition: Marburg and Berlin. Eberhard's controversy with Kant was by no means the only occasion on which the entrenched partisans of competing philosophies did battle with Kant and his followers. In Marburg the conflict came to a head earlier than elsewhere. At the probable instigation of the Wolffians, Kant's theories were investigated for alleged impiety or skepticism, and in 1786 lecturers were actually forbidden to discuss his philosophy.[21] Apparently Kant's critic Feder, still stung by the untoward aftereffects of his hostile review of the *Critique,* was one of the main forces behind the ban.

Meanwhile in Berlin, the death of Frederick the Great (1786) and the accession of Frederick William II created a climate that proved to be hostile not only to Kant but to all the Enlightenment, including some of Kant's bitter opponents. Whereas the Wolffians regarded Kant as insufficiently rationalistic, the inspired irrationalists who now came to power could see him only as the embodiment of rationalism and as the enemy of orthodox, historical Christianity, an intractable critic of every form of mysticism and zealotry. The actual suppression of heresy did not get seriously started until 1788. As late as December, 1787, Kant learned from J. C. Berens that the new king was still allowing the same freedom

[21] See notes to Kant's letter to J. Bering, April 7, 1786 [266].

of the press enjoyed under his predecessor (Berens to Kant, December 5, 1787 [310]). But one year later, the troubles had begun (Berens to Kant, October 25, 1788 [338]). It was suspected in some quarters that since Kant had claimed that reason was incapable of providing theoretical knowledge of the supersensible, he must be secretly sympathetic to the religious reactionaries. His friends implored him to make his position emphatically clear so as to stop the fanatics. The bookdealer Meyer wrote from Berlin (September 5, 1788 [333]) asking Kant to compose an essay on freedom of the press to fight the growing suppression. Kiesewetter and Biester kept Kant informed of developments in the capital, where, for a time, the liberal theologians and clerics paid little attention to the government's edicts on religion. In the decade that followed, the antics of Frederick William II and his pious counselors were to become more than the joking matter they first appeared to be. The king's mystical visions and sexual escapades are reported in a number of Kiesewetter's gossipy letters of 1790 and after, a few samples of which have been included in this collection. The heretic-hunting mood reached its climax, for Kant's career, in 1793–94, when Kant's publications on religion were brought under the censorship of the royal Commission on Spiritual Affairs. In 1792, Fichte had sought Kant's advice on how to get his own *Critique of Revelation* approved by the censor of theology in the University of Halle. Thus, it was not only the government that sought to suppress freedom of thought but some of the theological faculties in the universities themselves. Kant explained to Stäudlin (May 4, 1793 [574]) what he had tried to do in his *Religion within the Limits of Reason Alone* and how he had presented the book to the theological faculty in Königsberg to avoid conflict with the authorities. In the fall of 1794, however, the order condemning Kant's book, and any further expression of his unorthodox views, was issued by the king's minister, Woellner. Kant was obedient, though his response to the king (letter [642]) is in no way obsequious. Kant's religion of "rational faith" is given a powerful statement here.

Granting the forcefulness of Kant's letter to Frederick William II, we must admit nevertheless that Kant was a constitutionally timid person. Even twenty years earlier Kant had shown something of this character when, in considering an opportunity for a better position, he confessed to Herz that "all change frightens me" (early April, 1778 [134]). Now in his old age Kant was unwilling to spend his remaining energy on political (or for that matter philosophical) disputes. His letters of 1789 and after speak repeatedly of his advancing age and increasing frailty. Again and again he excuses himself for failing to act vigorously against his various opponents. Biester respectfully but disappointedly accepted Kant's decision to comply with the royal decree commanding Kant's silence (December 17, 1794 [646]). Only after the death of Frederick William II in 1797 did Kant feel himself freed from his promise (on the rather casuistic grounds that the pronoun in "Your Majesty's servant" referred specifically to that monarch, so that the obligation to remain silent had been undertaken only to him). Though Kant took a lively interest in the public controversies and political turbulence of the decade following 1789, he devoted himself as much as possible to the completion of his philosophical system. Only on rare occasions did he allow himself to be distracted from this work. One such occasion was the famous Mendelssohn-Jacobi feud in the 1780's. Two others, of more personal than literary or philosophical interest, were the Plessing affair and the tragic case of Maria von Herbert. Each of these three topics requires some explanation.

Mendelssohn, Lessing, and Jacobi. The literary quarrel between Mendelssohn and Jacobi [22] dominated the discussions of German intellectuals for several years, until finally Kant himself was drawn into the dispute. (Kant's essay, *What Is Orientation in Thinking?* contains his answer to the disputants, both of whom had attempted to gain his support.) The story of this controversy is somewhat complicated. F. H. Jacobi (1743–1819), the "philosopher of faith," had maintained that Spinoza's philosophy contained the only logically acceptable system of metaphysics. Since this system was monistic, however, it entailed the denial of any genuine theism. To accept Spinozism was therefore to become an atheist. Hume, according to Jacobi, had performed an important service by exposing the pretensions of natural theology, for he had made it clear that God is an affair of the heart, not of reason, and that philosophy (that is, Spinozism) must be given up in the name of faith. Jacobi also argued for the possibility of immediate intuitions of a supersensible reality. Like Kant, however, he held that

[22] See also n. 1 to the letter from Marcus Herz, February 27, 1786 [260].

the field of knowledge is restricted to objects of possible experience. Reason is incapable of penetrating beyond the sensible.[23] So much the worse for reason.

Now Lessing's position was not altogether opposed to Jacobi's. Lessing had published some works of the deist H. S. Reimarus (1694–1768) (under the title *Wolffenbüttel Fragments*) but unlike the deists, Lessing did not believe religious truths capable of proof. A pioneer of the "higher criticism," Lessing believed that faith rests on inner experience and that religious ideas are to be judged by their effect on conduct. Lessing died in 1781, just after he had admitted to Jacobi that Spinoza's theory seemed to him to be correct. This is what Jacobi wrote to Mendelssohn in 1783, and from this disclosure arose their furious controversy, a controversy on which some were even to put the blame for Mendelssohn's death in 1786.[24] Since pantheism seemed to Jacobi indistinguishable from atheism, he was shocked at Lessing's confession. Mendelssohn, however, took Jacobi's attack on Lessing to be also an attack on himself, and even though Mendelssohn was not a pantheist he felt called upon to defend Spinoza and Lessing. In his book *Morning Lessons* (1785), Mendelssohn challenged Jacobi, who replied by publishing his answer to Mendelssohn and their letters to each other. Herder and Goethe were drawn into the argument, and both of them rejected Jacobi's equation of Spinozism with atheism.

What Lessing had said to Jacobi was that orthodox ideas about God were of no utility to him. God is One and All, and if Lessing had to name anyone as philosophically sound, it would have to be Spinoza. Like Spinoza, Lessing believed human actions to be determined. God is the ultimate cause of the world order, and everything that exists is a part of him. "Why should not the ideas that God has of real things be these real things themselves?"

---

[23] Unlike Kant, Jacobi maintained that we perceive things as they are in themselves. He also rejected Kant's formalism in ethics and defended the possibility of immediate moral intuitions. Jacobi's criticism of Kant's theory of the thing-in-itself became famous and was later repeated by various critics: the affirmation of things-in-themselves, he argued, can be justified only by using the causal principle, which principle is supposed to be subjectively grounded and applicable only intraphenomenally. An epigrammatic remark of Jacobi's was often quoted: "Without it [the assumption of things-in-themselves] I could not get into the system; with it, I could not stay."

[24] See notes to the letter from Marcus Herz, February 27, 1786 [260].

asked Lessing.[25] One consequence of the *Pantheismusstreit,* as it came to be called, was the revival of interest in the study of Spinoza. Another, as has been mentioned, was Kant's essay on orientation. The main letters mentioning the feud are those from Mendelssohn (October 16, 1785), Biester (June 11, 1786), and Herz (February 27, 1786 [260]) [26] and Kant's letter to Herz (April 7, 1786 [267]). In the last of these, Kant condemns Jacobi as guilty of a frivolous and affected "inspiration" (*Genieschwär-merey*) and goes on to speak of "the excellent Moses," so that it is clear where Kant's sympathies lay.

L'affaire Plessing. When the editors of Kant's correspondence were assembling their manuscripts, it was with considerable reluctance that an indelicate letter of Plessing's (April 3, 1784 [228]) was included in the Prussian Academy edition of Kant's correspondence. Plessing's friendship with Kant is a significant counterexample for any theory that pictures Kant the "stern moralist" as utterly inflexible, prudish, or inhuman. F. V. L. Plessing (1749–1806) was a fascinating and unstable person who figured not only in Kant's life but also in Goethe's (whose *Harzreise im Winter* deals with Plessing). In his youth, Plessing studied at one university after another, unable to settle on any one subject or in any one place. His life was beset with neurotic and financial difficulties involving his family. In 1782 he came to know Kant and Hamann in Königsberg and decided that it might still be possible to make something of himself, whereupon he studied for the doctorate with Kant. Plessing did in fact become a philosopher,[27] and some of his correspondence with Kant is concerned with his philosophy of history. He was a brooding, troubled man who found himself able to accept Kant's negative doctrines, though he remained basically dissatisfied with Kant's faith grounded on morality.

As Plessing's letters to Kant make clear, Plessing had become involved in (and had lost) a paternity suit, and Kant had helped him by acting as intermediary in transmitting Plessing's maintenance payments. Kant's willingness to become involved in such an unprofessional and undignified problem seems to reveal a less

[25] "On the Reality of Things outside God," an essay for Mendelssohn.

[26] These are not of any intrinsic interest and have not been included here.

[27] In 1788 he accepted a professorship at Duisberg, one of the smallest universities in Germany, far removed from the frontiers of intellectual debate, which was just as he wished.

rigoristic attitude on his part than one might have expected. A careful reading of the letter will disclose that Kant's tolerance of Plessing's human failings did not, however, extend to a condoning of the "unnatural" and calculated practice of birth control. Plessing's arguments against Kant on this matter show a lively wit. It is unfortunate that Kant's answer to Plessing is not available to us. (Kant's highly puritanical attitude toward sex is made very explicit, however, in another letter, where even marital sexual relations are viewed as unsavory and the sexual libertine likened to a cannibal! [To C. G. Schütz, July 10, 1797 (761)])

Maria von Herbert. Whatever difficulties Kant's philosophy may have encountered in Prussia and other northern German states, the spread of Kantian ideas in Austria and southern Germany aroused even more opposition. (This may be seen in the letters of M. Reuss [699] and C. Stang [715], two Benedictine followers of Kant.) In the town of Klagenfurt in southern Austria, however, there lived a Baron Franz Paul von Herbert, one of the few people in reactionary Austria who was interested in the philosophy of Kant. The extent of his dedication is shown by the fact that in 1789, "driven by a philosophical itch" (as K. Vorländer puts it),[28] he left his lead factory, wife, and child to journey to Weimar, then to Jena, for the sake of studying Kant's philosophy. In 1791 he returned to Klagenfurt, bringing with him some of the revolutionary spirit of the critical philosophy. Herbert's house then became a center for the passionate discussion of Kant's philosophy. It was, in the words of one of Fichte's students, "a new Athens," dedicated to, among other things, the improvement of religion, a task that required replacing piety with morality.

Maria, the young sister of Franz Paul, who participated in these discussions, was born in 1769. In family circles she was called "Mizza" and her face was said to be very beautiful. If her physical appearance is somewhat a matter of conjecture to us, the intensity of her emotions and the sensitivity of her mind (notwithstanding her charmingly bad spelling) are not. In 1791 she wrote her first letter to Kant, a letter full of despair, which impressed him so deeply that he showed it to his friend Borowski and prepared a careful preliminary draft of his answer to her plea. Erhard, a friend of her brother's and of Kant's, explained in a letter that she had thrown herself into the arms of a certain man "in order to realize

[28] K. Vorländer, *Immanuel Kant, der Mann und das Werk* (Leipzig: Felix Meiner, 1924), II, p. 116.

an idealistic love." Evidently the man turned out to be a cad for, as Erhard says, he "misused her." Maria fell in love a second time, and for a while she deceived her new lover about her previous relationship. When she finally disclosed her earlier affair to him, his love for her cooled. In her letter, she begs Kant for guidance. Kant's answer is interesting for what it reveals about his own sensitivity to the nuances of emotional and moral problems and about his views on love. He presents his statement in the manner of a sermon, and there is a gently didactic tone throughout. Kant seems willing to make some concessions to the natural weaknesses of human beings. He says in effect that, although we have a duty to abstain from lying and from insincerity, we are to be forgiven for failing to pour out every secret of our hearts to someone we love. An ideal love would consist in mutual esteem and a totally uninhibited sharing, but the inability to be utterly open with another person is a sort of reticence that lies in human nature and does not constitute a weakness of character. These consoling remarks are followed, however, by some more characteristically Kantian moralizing: Maria is not to have any moral credit for confessing her earlier deception, if the motive of her disclosure was a desire to achieve peace of mind rather than true repentence for having lied. Nor should she brood over the new lover's change of heart; if his affection does not return, it was probably only sensual in the first place. Besides, the value of one's life does not depend on whether or not one achieves happiness.

The second and third letters Maria sent to her "spiritual physician" are less agitated than the first, but it is not so much resignation as a deeper despair and a sense of overwhelming apathy that breathes through them. The inner emptiness she expresses, the sense of being "almost superfluous" to herself, of being incapable of significant action (even morality has become uninterestingly easy for her, since she feels no temptation to transgress its laws), suggest a beautiful personality destroying itself by the very clarity of its self-awareness. Maria tells Kant, in her third letter (sometime early in 1794 [614]) that she had in fact been on the point of suicide but that though death would please her she will not take her own life out of consideration for morality and the feelings of her friends. Kant did not answer either of these letters but sent them to Elizabeth Motherby, the daughter of an English friend, as a warning to the young woman (whose "good training had, however, made such a warning unnecessary," Kant said) of what happens to ladies when they think too much and fail to control their fantasies! For all his perceptiveness and liberalism, Kant was not enthusiastic about women's rights or greatly concerned about the frustrations suffered by intelligent ladies in a society that regarded them as merely useful or decorative ornaments.[29] In 1803, nine years after her last letter, Maria did in fact commit suicide.

From Kant to Fichte. Although Kant's philosophical letters in the 1790's touch on a great number of topics, some of the most interesting letters are those that show the gradual defection of Kant's once ardent admirers and that enable us to see the development of Kant's own thinking in response to their criticisms. It is a pity that there are no very serious philosophical exchanges with Fichte in the correspondence.[30] However, the correspondence with S. Maimon, J. S. Beck, and J. H. Tieftrunk provides a wealth of discussion of just those issues (principally the problems concerning the *Ding an sich,* the "affecting" of sensibility, and the primary significance of synthesis, or *Zusammensetzung*) that make the transition from Kant to Fichte comprehensible.

In 1789 Salomon Maimon (1753–1800) sent Kant the manuscript of his *Essay on the Transcendental Philosophy* (*Versuch über die Transzendentalphilosophie* [1790]). Their mutual friend Herz described Maimon to Kant as "formerly one of the rawest Polish Jews" who by virtue of his brilliance and perseverance had miraculously managed to educate himself in all the sciences. (See Herz's letter, April 7, 1789 [351].) Herz had read the book, and it was on his advice that Maimon asked for Kant's opinion of it. Kant answered Maimon's criticisms in a letter to Herz (May 26,

[29] The limitations of Kant's sympathy for egalitarianism is shown also in his attitude toward the rights of servants. See his letter to C. G. Schütz, July 10, 1797 [761], in which he discusses the right to possess another person (a household servant) as if the latter were a thing.

[30] Kant's letter of February 2, 1792 [504] containing his advice to Fichte on how to deal with the censorhip authorities in Halle is included in this collection; it contains a good statement of Kant's religious beliefs. A number of other letters in 1792 concern Kant's efforts to help Fichte publish his *Critique of Revelation* (*Versuch einer Kritik aller Offenbarung*) and, with the subsequent confusion as to its authorship, Fichte's explanation and apologies for the confusion, and so on. (See notes to the letter to Fichte of February 2, 1792 [504].) The book was attributed to Kant himself, partly because it came from his publisher, Hartung. Hartung had inadvertently left out the Preface, in which Fichte spoke of the work as "my first venture before the public," a phrase that would have made clear that the anonymous author was not Kant.

1789 [362]), and called his work a book full of "the most subtle investigations" written by an astute critic who had understood him better than any other. Maimon wrote again in July, 1789, expressing his gratitude for Kant's rejoinder, though he was not satisfied with Kant's reply. He wrote several times in 1790, again in 1791 (see his letter of September 20 [486]), 1792, and 1793, but Kant did not answer him.[31] Maimon's criticism of Kant in 1789 already pointed the way to Fichte and the idealist movement that was soon to take hold. He denied Kant's basic distinction between passive sensibility and the active, spontaneous understanding. He maintained that the human mind is part of an infinite world soul that produces not only the form but also the content of experience. The understanding is intuitive, not merely discursive. Maimon accepted the negative, antidogmatic part of Kant's theory as correct but rejected the positive theory of the thing-in-itself (which he interpreted to mean the claimed existence of a thinkable entity without any determinate characteristics) as inconceivable. We cannot form a clear concept of either an object-in-itself or of a subject-in-itself. The thing-in-itself loses its character of thinghood, in Maimon's philosophy, and becomes merely an irrational limit of rational cognition, the idea of an endless task whose completion is constantly retreating as knowledge advances. The self-contradictory assumption of the existence of things independent of all consciousness arose in the attempt to explain the origin of the "content" of appearances; but there is in fact no content or material of experience independent of form. The distinction between the matter and form of knowledge is only a contrast between a complete and an incomplete consciousness of what is present to us, the incomplete consciousness being what we refer to as the given, that irrational residue that we distinguish from the a priori forms of consciousness. The contrast is only one of degree; form and matter are the terminal members of an infinite series of gradations of consciousness. The given is therefore only an idea of the limit of this series.

[31] In 1794, Kant spoke disparagingly of Maimon, in a letter to Reinhold on March 28 [620]. It is one of the few places where Kant makes an anti-Semitic remark. Perhaps it should be forgiven, on the grounds that Kant was extremely sensitive to criticism and to the apostasy of his followers, and 1794 was a bad year for him not only on these two accounts but also because of his troubles with the official proscription of his work on religion. The persecution from which Kant suffered seemed serious enough to Kant's friends to warrant an offer of asylum from one of them (the educator J. H. Campe).

While on some issues Maimon took Hume's position against Kant's (for example, he maintained that the concept of causality is the product of habit, not a pure concept of the understanding), his indebtedness to Leibniz is also evident. For some reason Maimon called himself a skeptic, but his rejection of Kant's account of things-in-themselves and the given, along with his conception of the human understanding as part of the divine understanding, clearly foreshadows Fichte and the development of "absolute idealism." In fact, Fichte wrote to Reinhold, in 1795, "My esteem for Maimon's talent is boundless. I firmly believe and am ready to prove that through Maimon's work the whole Kantian philosophy, as it is understood by everyone including yourself, is completely overturned. . . . All this he has accomplished without anyone's noticing it and while people even condescend to him. I think that future generations will mock our century bitterly." [32]

Kant's correspondence with Jakob Beck (1761–1840) contains not only some of the most penetrating criticisms of Kant's theory but also an indication of how Kant was himself being influenced by the men he denounced as "my hypercritical friends." By 1799, the seventy-five-year-old Kant (who complained to Garve, September 21, 1798 [820] that his condition was reduced to that of a vegetable) was so saddened by the independent line that his former students had taken that he angrily criticized the position of Fichte (whose books he had not read) and Beck (whose position he had virtually adopted as his own) in an "Open letter on Fichte's *Wissenschaftslehre*" (the last letter in this collection, August 7, 1799). There he charged that his *Critique of Pure Reason* had not been intended as a propaedeutic to any future system of metaphysics, that it was in fact the complete statement of pure philosophy, and that no "standpoint" (the allusion is to Beck's *Only Possible Standpoint from which the Critical Philosophy Must Be Judged*) of any interpreter or commentator is required in order to comprehend it.

All of these remarks are either false or misleading. The occasion of the open letter was a challenge put to Kant by a reviewer in the *Erlanger Literaturzeitung,* January 11, 1799, who asked Kant whether his theories were really meant to be taken literally

[32] There is a fairly lengthy discussion of Maimon's importance in Richard Kroner's *Von Kant bis Hegel* (Tübingen: J. C. B. Mohr [Paul Siebeck], 1921–24). A more recent work devoted entirely to Maimon is Samuel Atlas' *From Critical to Speculative Idealism: The Philosophy of Solomon Maimon* (The Hague: Martinus Nijhoff, 1964).

(*buchstäblich*) or as interpreted by Fichte or Beck. Kant's personal attack on Fichte as a "treacherous friend" may have been encouraged by his overly zealous disciple Johann Schultz, on whom Kant relied for an account of Fichte's position and whom Kant had earlier (see the letter to J. A. Schlettwein, May 29, 1797 [752]) endorsed as his most reliable expositor. Certainly, neither Fichte nor Beck had done anything to deserve it. Fichte's official reply, in the form of an open letter to Schelling, was temperate. Privately, however, he declared Kant's theory to be "total nonsense" unless given a Fichtean interpretation; he even called Kant "no more than three-quarters of a mind" who had "mightily prostituted himself." [33] That the *Critique* was supposed to be a propaedeutic to a reconstruction of metaphysics was not only asserted by Kant himself in numerous passages in the *Critique* but clearly implied by him in his references to the system of metaphysics he intended to compose when "the critical part of [his] task" was finished. This is what he had written to L. H. Jakob [303] and to Reinhold [322] in 1787 and 1788 in connection with his completion of the third *Critique*.[34] A sketch of Kant's planned system of metaphysics was even included in a letter to Beck in 1792 [500], and the outline Kant gives there agrees with the reorganized form of the *Critique* that Beck recommended in his own letters. It would seem then that the doctrinal gulf between Kant and his erstwhile disciples was not at all as wide as Kant seems to suggest in the declaration against Fichte.

Like Maimon, Beck denied the positive role that Kant's theory of perception seemed to have given to the thing-in-itself. Beck argued that when Kent spoke of objects affecting our sensibility it could only be phenomenal objects that he had meant, not an

---

[33] K. Vorländer, *op. cit.*, II, 265.

[34] Kant's statement to Jakob that on completion of the critical part of his plan he could proceed to the dogmatic is puzzling if one recalls Kant's customary use of the word "dogmatic" to stigmatize the philosophical method he rejected, viz., one that proceeds without a prior investigation of reason's competence to answer the questions it is asking. But perhaps Kant was thinking of "dogmatic" in the sense in which he distinguished "dogmata" from "mathemata" in the *Critique of Pure Reason* A 736–B 764 and not in the derogratory sense. In the *Critique,* a dogma is one sort of non-analytic apodeictic proposition, viz., a synthetic proposition that can be "directly derived from concepts." Mathemata are the other sort of synthetic a priori proposition, not found in philosophy, which can be "directly obtained through the construction of concepts." There are no dogmata "in the whole domain of pure reason, in its merely speculative employment," Kant argued (*loc. cit.*).

unknowable thing-in-itself acting on an unknowable subject-in-itself. The self that is affected and the object that acts on it must both be viewed as products of a more basic activity of the understanding, an activity that we presuppose when we regard our experiences as produced in us either by an independent object or by our own power of thinking. This most basic activity Beck equated with the function of producing the transcendental unity of apperception in Kant's deduction of the categories, and it is this "standpoint" one needs to attain in order to understand Kant's theory. It is a unique act of synthesizing a priori, an act whereby the subject constitutes himself as a conscious thinker.

Kant's agreement with Beck is shown most clearly in his willingness to make the activity of synthesis (*Zusammensetzung*) the basic condition of all cognition. Beck used the phrase "original attribution" (*ursprüngliche Beylegung*), which Kant at first (and with justification) found unintelligible; Beck's colleague J. H. Tieftrunk spoke of an act of *Setzen* ("positing") [787]; and in Fichte's *Wissenschaftslehre* the ego "posits" the non-ego in an original *Tathandlung*. Although each of these men found his own views to be either subtly or dramatically different from those of the others (Beck, for example, tried to convince Kant that he was radically opposed to Fichte), they agreed that Kant's theory of affection must be reconsidered. But Kant himself had certainly already modified his position when he wrote to Beck, as early as January, 1792 [500]: "The content [of a representation] must thus . . . be *created* [*gemacht*] by an inner activity . . . that precedes a priori the manner in which the manifold is given." Beck thought that Kant's method of exposition in the *Critique* was only a concession to the uninitiated reader who had not yet arrived at the "standpoint" of seeing "objects" as the product of that original activity of the understanding. He and Tieftrunk, both of them perhaps reiterating the criticisms of G. E. Schulze, argued that it was inconsistent of Kant to make an unknowable thing-in-itself that which *affects* us—inconsistent because "affecting" is a causal relation and the concept of cause is supposed to be meaningful only intraphenomenally and because Kant seems to know a great deal about unknowables here, for example, that they are real (another category illegitimately used) and efficacious. Beck's suggested reconstruction of Kant's theory, which would begin with the "standpoint," that is, the original activity of mind that first produces the "I think" expressed in the categories, was, as has already been pointed out, not at all uncongenial to Kant, and the extent of Beck's influence on Kant may be seen in Kant's *Opus Postumum.*[35]

The apostasy of Kant's ablest disciples may give the impression that Kant's final years were spent in friendless isolation. This was not the case, although Kant was not on very warm terms with his family. His sisters and their husbands were too far removed from him in education and social position; his nieces must have been illiterate (they signed Kant's will with X's).·Nor was Kant very close to his brother Johann, whom he had not seen since 1758.

The love and esteem of his friends and former students, however, continued throughout their lives and his, and the respect of men like Schiller must have been very pleasing to Kant's old age.[36] Kiesewetter kept him supplied with his favorite turnips,[37] along with the latest gossip from Berlin. J. Richardson, who published an English translation of Kant's *Essays and Treatises,* kept him informed on the progress of his philosophy in England.[38] J. H. I. Lehmann sent sausages from Göttingen (along with gossip and Feder's belated apologies to Kant), as did F. Nicolovius,[39] and Herz wrote movingly to his old friend and mentor.[40] In 1798 Kant spoke of a work that would fill the last gap in his system, the transition from the metaphysical foundations of natural science to

[35] For a discussion of this, see Herman-J. de Vleeschauwer, *The Development of Kantian Thought,* translated by A. R. C. Duncan (London: Thomas Nelson & Sons, Ltd., 1962). This book is an altogether invaluable study for an understanding of Kant's relationship to his contemporaries. Kant's *Opus Postumum* is also discussed at some length in F. Copleston's *History of Philosophy,* Vol. VI (London: Burns & Oates, Ltd., 1960), though Copleston attributes to Fichte the influence I believe to be Beck's. Since Kant had not read Fichte's *Wissenschaftslehre* and knew it only from a review and from what Johann Shultz told him of it, Copleston's conjecture seems mistaken.

[36] Kant's correspondence with Schiller deals with the latter's request that Kant contribute an article to the journal *Die Horen.* Kant declined. The letters are respectful on both sides. It is not clear whether Kant was aware of Schiller's poetry and dramas.

[37] Gourmet readers may be interested in Kiesewetter's advice on how to cook these turnips (November 25, 1798 [827]). They must be washed in warm water, dropped at once into boiling water, and then cooked for no more than fifteen minutes. They must be stored in a dry place.

[38] The translation was published in two volumes in London, 1798–99. Richardson sent a letter June 21, 1798 [808] (not included in this collection) along with the first volume of the translation.

[39] Friedrich Nicolovius (1768–1836) had a publishing firm in Königsberg (1790–1818).

[40] December 25, 1797 [791].

physics. Until 1801, his seventy-seventh year, he devoted what energy he had to this project. But in April of 1802 he wrote,[41] "My strength diminishes daily, my muscles vanish, and even though I have never had any actual illness and have none now, it is two years since I have been out of the house. Nevertheless I view all changes that are in store for me with calm." In April, 1803, he celebrated his last (seventy-ninth) birthday with his dinner companions. In October of that year he became ill (after eating his favorite English cheese) but recovered sufficiently to entertain his usual dinner guests later that month. From December until the following February, however, he grew much weaker and his death came on the twelfth of February, "a cessation of life and not a violent act of nature," said his friend and biographer, Wasianski.[42]

---

[41] To the fiancé of his brother's daughter, Pastor K. C. Schoen, April 28, 1802 [892].

[42] Quoted in K. Vorländer, *Immanuel Kants Leben* (2d ed.; Leipzig: Felix Meiner, 1921), p. 207.

The Letters

From J. G. Hamann, July 27, 1759

- 11 -   VOL. X, pp. 7–16

Honored tutor,

I do not hold it against you that you are my rival or that you have enjoyed your new friend [Berens] for weeks during all of which I only saw him for a few scattered hours, like a phantom or even more like a clever scout.[1] I shall however bear this grudge against your friend, that he ventured to introduce you yourself into my very own seclusion; and that he not only tempted me to let you see my sensitivity, wrath, and jealousy but even exposed you to the danger of getting quite close to a man whom the disease of his passions has given an intensity of thinking and of feeling that a healthy person does not possess. This is what I wanted to say to *your sweetheart right in the ear* when I thanked you for the honor of your first visit.

If you are Socrates and your friend wants to be Alcibiades, then for your instruction you need the voice of a *genius*. And that role is one I was born for; nor can I be suspected of pride in saying this —an actor lays aside his royal mask, no longer walks and speaks on stilts, as soon as he leaves the stage—allow me therefore to be called "genius" and to speak to you as a genius out of the clouds, as long as I am writing this letter. But if I am to speak as a genius, I beg that you give me at least the patience and attentiveness with which an illustrious, handsome, clever, and informed public recently heard the farewell address of a mortal concerning the fragments of an urn on which one could with effort decipher the

[1] This letter from Hamann to Kant was written shortly after Kant and J. C. Berens (1729–92) visited Hamann in Königsberg. The point of the visit was to convert Hamann away from the orthodox Christianity he had recently embraced. Before Hamann's trip to London in 1757 and his sudden conversion, he and Berens had both been enamored of deism and world citizenship. In an effort to restore him to what Berens and Kant regarded as sanity, Kant tried to persuade Hamann to translate some articles from the French *Encyclopédie*. As is obvious from this letter, the efforts of Kant and Berens were in vain.

letters BIBLIOTEK.[2] The "project" was to learn to think of beautiful bodies. Only a Socrates can do that, never a count; no legislature will create a genius out of a Watson, through the power of its governing offices and the authority of its election.

I write in epic style since you do not yet understand how lyric language must be read. An epic author is a historian of unusual creatures and their still more unusual lives. A lyric author is the historian of the human heart. Self-knowledge is hardest and highest; the easiest and most disgusting, natural history, philosophy, and poetry. It is pleasant and profitable to translate a page of Pope —into the fibers of the brain and of the heart—but vanity and a curse to leaf through a part of the *Encyclopédie*.[3] I finished the work you proposed to me only last night. The article concerning beauty is a piece of chattering and a summarizing of Hutchinson [*sic*].[4] The article about *art* is less harsh and thus sweeter than the Englishman's discourse concerning nothing but a word. So only one article remained that really deserved translation. It had to do with forced labor.[5] Every perceptive reader of my heroic letter will appreciate from experience the effort required to be calm about such people but will also have the sympathy for all forced laborers that the writer of my article has for them and will look for the amelioration of the abuses that make it impossible for them to be good forced laborers. Since I, however, have no desire to become one and hold no office of that sort on this earth, where I have to be dependent on the mood of those who are lower than I, this article will find enough other translators who have a calling for that job. A man of the world who knows the art of making *visits* will always put *enterprises* in charge of a good *superintendent*.

To return to our dear cousin [Berens]. You cannot love this old man out of inclination; the motive must be vanity or selfish egotism. You should have known him when I loved him. In those days he thought the way you do, most honorable tutor, about

[2] The allusion is to the academic farewell address of Matthias Friedrich Watson, professor of poetry in Königsberg, 1756–59. Hamann thought the speech incredible. Evidently it consisted largely of autobiographical anecdotes, together with extracts from a book entitled *Critical Outline of a Selected Library* [*Bibliothek*] *for Friends of Philosophy and Belles-Lettres*.

[3] The famous *Encyclopédie ou Dictionnaire Raisonée des Sciences, des Arts et des Métiers* (1751).

[4] The article, "Beau," is by Diderot. In its historical introduction, there is a discussion of Francis Hutcheson's aesthetics.

[5] N. A. Boulanger's article, "Corvée."

natural rights; he knew nothing but generous tendencies in himself and in me.

You have it, this final contempt is a leftover bit of love for you. Let yourself be warned and let me parrot Sappho:

> Ah, send me back my wanderer,
> Ye Nisaean matrons and Nisaean maids,
> Nor let the lies of his bland tongue deceive you! [6]

I think your acquaintance with him is still innocent and that you are merely passing the long summer and August evenings. Could you not see me as a girl, confused and shamed, a girl who has sacrificed her honor to her friend, who entertains his company with her weaknesses and nakedness, of which she has made no secret to him, privately.

France, the life of the court, and his present association with a pack of Calvinists, these are responsible for all the trouble. He loves the human race as a Frenchman loves a woman, for his mere personal enjoyment and at the expense of her virtue and honor. In friendship as in love, he casts aside all secrets. But that means that he denies the god of friendship; and when Ovid, his heart's poet, writes to a corrupt friend, he is still tender enough to prefer to her love-making the intimacy of *another* person.

> Those kisses are common to you with me,
> And common to me with you—why does
> Any third attempt to share those goods? [7]

That he thinks differently than he talks, writes differently than he talks, I shall be able to show you more clearly when we have occasion to talk and walk. Yesterday everything was supposed to be open, and in his last little note he wrote me: "I beg you not to make us a laughingstock by misusing in any way what I, as an honest friend, am writing to you—our domestic affairs are none of your business now—we live quietly here, cheerful, human, and Christian." I have lived up to this condition so scrupulously that I have plagued my conscience over innocent words that escaped my lips and that no one could have understood. Now everything is supposed to be public. But I shall keep to what he has written.

We are not going to reach an understanding. I am not going to

---

[6] Ovid *Heroides,* Epis. XV, v. 53–56 (trans. by Grant Showerman; Cambridge, Mass.: Loeb Classical Library, 1914).

[7] Ovid *Amores* 2, 5, 31 f. (trans. by Grant Showerman; Cambridge, Mass.: Loeb Classical Library, 1914).

put up with having to justify myself. Because I cannot justify myself without damning my judges, and these are the dearest friends I have on earth.

If I had to justify myself, I would have to argue:

1) that my friend [Berens] has a false conception of himself,
2) an equally false conception of all his fellow men,
3) has had and still has a false conception of me,
4) has wrongly and one-sidedly judged the issue between us as a whole and in its context,
5) has not the slightest conception or feeling as to what he and I have heretofore done and are still doing.

Because I know all the principles and motivations of his actions, I can forgive what I know and don't know that he has done and still does, since he, according to his own confession, cannot make head or tail of anything I say or do. This must seem like bragging to you and happens quite naturally in the course of events. I am still too modest, but I can certainly boast with my bleary red eyes against one with cataracts.

It would be a simple matter, compared with all my work and effort, to get myself acquitted. But to be condemned to the poison cup while innocent! Acquittal is what all Xantippes and Sophists think of—but not Socrates; for to him it was more a matter of the innocence of his conscience than of its reward, staying alive.

So that sort of Apology is out of the question for me. The God I serve, whom scoffers take to be clouds, fog, "vapeurs and Hypochondrie," will not be appeased by means of rams' blood and calves' blood; otherwise I could prove very quickly that your friend's reason and wit, as my own, is a lascivious calf and his noble intentions a ram with horns.

What your friend doesn't believe is as little my affair as what I believe is his affair. On this subject we are thus divided, and the talk remains simply a matter of trade. A whole world full of handsome and profound minds, were they nothing but morning stars and Lucifers, could be neither judge nor expert witness here, and such a world is not the public of a lyric poet, who smiles at the applause of his eulogy and remains silent at its faults.

Peter the Great was called upon by the gods to have his own people imitate the handsome spirit of other nations in certain petty details. But do we get younger by shaving off our beards? The truth is not found in mere sensuous judgments.

A subject of a despotic government, says Montesquieu, mustn't know what is good and evil.[8] Let him be afraid, as if his prince were a god who could cast down his body and soul into hell. Were he to have insights, he would be an unhappy subject for his state; if he has any virtue, he is a fool to let it be noticed.

A patrician in a Greek republic could not have connections with the Persian court, if he were to avoid being rebuked as a traitor to his fatherland.

Are the laws of the vanquished proper for the conqueror? Was the subject repressed by those laws? Do you grant your fellow citizens a similar fate?

Abraham is our father—do we work according to Peter's plan? as the ruler of a little free state in Italy learned to babble of "commerce" and "the Public"—do your father's works understand what you say, use your knowledge judiciously, and put your "alas!" in the right place. We can do more harm with truths than with errors, if we use the former absurdly and are able to modify the latter by luck or by habit. That is why many an orthodox soul can ride to the devil, in spite of the truth, and many a heretic gets to heaven, despite excommunication by the ruling church or public.

How far a man can be effective in the order of the world is a task for you, a task, however, to which one dare not turn until one understands how the soul may be effective in the system of its little world. Whether "pre-established harmony" is not at least a *happier sign* of this miracle than *"influxus physicus"* manages to express, you may decide for yourself. Meanwhile I am content to deduce from that, that the Calvinistic church is as little in a position to make an adherent of your friend as is the Lutheran.

These impressions are nothing but apples that I toss as Galatea did to tease her lover. I am as little concerned with truth as is your friend; like Socrates, I believe everything that others believe—but I aim to disturb other people in their beliefs. That is what the wise man had to do, because he was surrounded with Sophists and priests whose sound reason and good works existed only in the imagination. There are people who imagine themselves healthy and honorable, just as there are *malades imaginaires*.

If you want to judge me from Mr. B's critique and my writings, that is as unphilosophical a judgment as if one were to survey Luther from head to toe by reading one brochure to the duke of Wolfenbüttel [*sic*].

[8] See Montesquieu, *De l'Esprit des Lois,* Bk. III, chap. 9, and Bk. IV, chap. 3.

He who trusts another man's reason more than his own ceases to be a man and stands in the front ranks of the herd of mimicking cattle. Even the greatest human genius should seem to us unworthy of imitation. Nature, said Batteux; [9] one mustn't be a Spinozist in matters of fine arts or in those of government.

Spinoza led an *innocent mode of life,* too timid in reflection; had he gone farther, he would have expressed the truth better than he did. He was incautious in whiling away his time and occupied himself too much with spider webs; this taste revealed itself in his thinking, which can only entangle small vermin.

Of what use are the archives of all kings and of all centuries, if a few lines out of this great fragment, a few notes out of this chaos, can give us knowledge and power. How happy is the man who can visit daily the archives of him who can guide the hearts of all kings like brooks,[10] who does not desire in vain to inspect his marvelous economy, the laws of his kingdom, and so on. A pragmatic author says about this: "The statutes of the Lord are more precious than gold, than much fine gold, sweeter than honey and the dripping honey comb." [11] "The law of thy mouth is better unto me than thousands of gold and silver." "I have more understanding than all my teachers, for Thy testimonies are my meditation. I understand more than the ancients, because Thou through Thy commandments hast made me wiser than mine enemies, for they are ever with me."

What do you think of this system? I want to make my neighbors happy. A rich merchant is happy. So that you might become rich —you need insight and moral virtues.

In my mimicking style, a sterner logic prevails and a connection more coherent than in the concepts of lively minds. Your ideas are like the playing colors of shot silk, says Pope.

At this instant I am a leviathan, the monarch or prime minister of Ocean, on whose breath depends the ebb and flow of the tides. The next instant I see myself as a whale, created by God, as the mightiest poet says, to sport in the sea.

I must almost laugh at the choice of a philosopher to try to change my mind. I look upon the finest logical demonstration as a

[9] Charles Batteux, *Les Beaux Arts Réduits à un Même Principe* (Paris, 1747), p. 9: "The spirit which is father to the arts must imitate nature."
[10] Prov. 21:1.
[11] Ps. 19:10–11.
[12] Ps. 119: 72, 99–100, 98.

sensible girl regards a love letter and upon a Baumgartian explanation as a witty courtesan.

I have been imposed upon with dreadful lies, most honored tutor. I wonder whether your reading so many travel books has made you credulous or incredulous. One forgives the original authors, since they do it unaware and, like a comic hero, "speak prose without knowing it."[13] Lies are the mother tongue of our reason and wit.

One mustn't believe what one sees—let alone what one hears. When two people are in different situations, they must never fight about their sense impressions. A stargazer can tell a person on the fourth story a great deal. The latter must not be so stupid as to claim the other man's eyes are sick. Come on down: then you'll be convinced that you didn't see anything. A man in a deep ditch without water can see stars at bright noon. The man on the surface does not deny the stars—but all he can see is the lord of the day. Because the moon is closer to the earth than the sun is, you tell your moon fairy tales about the glory of God. It is God's glory to conceal a thing; it is the glory of kings to search out a matter.[14]

As one knows the tree by its fruits, so I know that I am a prophet from the fate that I share with all witnesses: slander, persecution, contempt.

All at once, my dear tutor!, I want to deprive you of the hope of bargaining with me about certain matters that I can judge better than you. I have more *data,* I base myself on *facts,* and I know my authors not out of journals but by carefully and repeatedly wallowing in them; I have not read extracts but the Acts themselves, wherein the "interests" of the king as well as that of the country are discussed.

Every animal has its characteristic gait in its thinking and writing. One proceeds in sentences and pages like a grasshopper; the other, in a cohesive connection like a slow worm in its track for the sake of security, which his construction may need. The one straight, the other crooked. According to Hogarth's system, the snake line is the basis of all beautiful painting, as I read in the vignette on the title page.[15]

The Attic philosopher, Hume, needs faith if he is to eat an egg

---

[13] Monsieur Jourdain, in Moliere's *Le Bourgeois Gentilhomme,* Act II, scene 6.

[14] Prov. 25:2.

[15] William Hogarth's *The Analysis of Beauty* (London, 1753).

and drink a glass of water.[16] He says: Moses, the law of reason, to which the philosopher appeals, condemns him. Reason is not given to you to make you wise but to make you aware of your folly and ignorance, just as the Mosaic law was given to the Jews, not to make them righteous, but rather to make their sins more sinful to them.[17] If he needs faith for food and drink, why does he deny faith when he judges of matters that are higher than sensuous eating and drinking.

To explain something by means of *custom*—custom is a composite thing consisting of monads. Custom is called "second nature," and its phenomena are just as perplexing as nature itself, which it imitates.

If Hume were only sincere, consistent with himself——. All his errors aside, he is like Saul among the prophets.[18] I only want to quote one passage that will prove that one can preach the truth in *jest,* and without awareness or desire, even if one is the greatest doubter and, like the serpent,[19] wants to doubt even what God said. Here it is: "The Christian religion not only was at first attended with miracles, but even at this day cannot be believed by any reasonable person without one. Mere reason is insufficient to convince us of its veracity. And whoever is moved by *Faith* to assent to it, is conscious of a continued miracle in his own person, which subverts all the principles of his understanding, and gives him a determination to believe what is most contrary to *custom* and *experience* . . ." ["custom" and "experience" italicized by Hamann].[20]

Beg your friend that it becomes him least to laugh at the eyeglasses of my aesthetic imagination, for I must arm the naked eyes of my reason with those same glasses.

A tender lover never worries about his expenses, when an affair breaks up. So if perhaps, according to the new "right of nature" of old people, the question were one of money, tell him that I have nothing and must myself live on my father's generosity; that nevertheless everything belongs to him that God may want to give me—which, however, I do not follow, because I might then lose the blessing of the fourth commandment. If I should die, I want to

[16] See Hume's *Treatise of Human Nature,* Bk. I, Pt. III, secs. vi and vii.
[17] Rom. 7:7–8.
[18] I Sam. 10:11; 19:24.
[19] Gen. 3:1–5.
[20] Hume's *Enquiry concerning Human Understanding,* Sec. X, concluding paragraph.

bequeath my corpse to him, which he can then, like the Egyptians, treat as a forfeit, as is supposedly written in the pleasant *Happelio* of Greece, Herodotus.[21]

The lyre for lyric poetry is the *tireli* of the lark. If only I could sing like a nightingale sings. So there will at least have to be art critics among the birds, who always sing, and boast of their incessant diligence.

You know, most honored tutor, that genii have wings and that they sound just like the applause of the multitude.

If one is permitted to mock God with grace and strength, why shouldn't one be able to amuse oneself with idols?

Mother Lyse sings: Make mockery of idols false.[22] A philosopher however looks at poets, lovers, and visionaries as a man looks at a monkey, with pleasure and pity.

As soon as men can understand one another, they can work. He who confused the languages—who punished the exemplars of pride out of love and also for the sake of political ends, for the good of the populace as a friend of humanity—joined them together again on the day that they slandered men with tongues of fire, as if intoxicated by sweet wine.[23] The truth did not want highway robbers to get too close to her; she wore dress upon dress, so that they had misgivings about ever finding her body. How terrified they were when they had their wish and saw the truth, the terrible ghost, before them.

I shall come and pick up this letter in person at the earliest possible date.

From J. H. Lambert, November 13, 1765

- 33 -   VOL. X, *pp. 51–54*

Dear sir:

I believe that the similarity of our ways of thinking will excuse this letter, its frankness, and the omission of customary

[21] The allusion is to Herodotus' story concerning the treasure of Rhampsinitos. See his *History,* Bk. II, chap. 121.

[22] From the eighth stanza of the song, "Sei Lob und Ehr' dem Höchsten Gut," by the famous Johann Schütz (1640–90).

[23] Gen. 11:7–9.

circumlocutions. I need no such artificial mannerisms, since Professor and Pastor Reccard's [1] trip to Königsberg gives me such a fine opportunity to express to you the pleasure I feel at our agreement on so many new thoughts and investigations. You may already have learned from the Reverend Dr. Reccard, dear sir, that he lives for the sake of astronomy, and finds his pleasure in the depths of the firmament. I need not recommend him further.

A year ago Professor Sulzer [2] showed me your "Only Possible Proof of the Existence of God." I found in it my own thoughts and even the phrases I would choose to express them, and I decided at once that if you were to see my *Organon* [3] you too would find your own likeness in most of my book. Since then, I have worked out my *Architectonic,* [4] and the book has been ready for the printer for a year now. But now I see, dear sir, that you are going to publish a *Proper Method for Metaphysics* this coming Easter. What could be more natural than my desire to see whether what I have done is in accord with the method you propose? I have no doubts as to the correctness of the method. The only difference will be that I do not count under "architectonic" all the things heretofore treated in metaphysics and that, on the other hand, a complete metaphysics must include more than has previously been the case. I take "architectonic" to include all the *simple* and *primary* parts of human knowledge and not only the *principia,* which are principles [*Gründe*] derived from the *form* of knowledge, but also the *axiomata* and *postulata. Axiomata* must be derived from the *matter* of knowledge and actually only appear in simple concepts, thinkable in themselves and not self-contradictory, whereas *postulata* state the universal and necessary possibilities of the synthesis [*Zusammensetzung*] and uniting [*Verbin-*

---

[1] Gotthilf Christian Reccard (1735–98) came to Königsberg as professor of theology in 1765.

[2] Johann Georg Sulzer (1720–79), aesthetician, member of the Berlin Academy of Sciences, and one of the men to whom Kant sent his inaugural dissertation for review. His letter to Kant of December 8, 1770 [62], contains some interesting remarks on space and time, but for some reason Kant did not take his criticisms as seriously as he did those of Lambert and Mendelssohn.

[3] *Neues Organon oder Gedanken über die Erforschung und Bezeichnung des Wahren und dessen Unterscheidung vom Irrthum und Schein* ("New Organon, or Thoughts on the Discovery and Designation of Truth and its Differentiation from Error and Appearance") (Leipzig, 1764).

[4] *Anlage zur Architectonic oder Theorie des Einfachen und des Ersten in der philosophischen und mathematischen Erkenntniss* ("Outline of Architectonic, or Theory of the Simple and Primary Elements of Philosophical and Mathematical Knowledge") (Riga, 1771).

dung] of the simple concepts. We do not get to any material knowledge from the form alone; we shall remain in the realm of the *ideal,* stuck in mere nomenclature, if we do not look out for what is primary and thinkable in itself, the matter or *objective* stuff of knowledge.

If the *Architectonic* were a novel, I think it would already have found numerous publishers, so true is it that booksellers and readers corrupt each other, both of them wanting to avoid any thorough thinking. Hereabouts one philosophizes exclusively about so-called belles-lettres. Poets, painters, and musicians find the vocabulary of their own arts too lowly, and each one therefore borrows the artistic terms of the other. The poet speaks of nothing but coloration, the mixing of hues, brush strokes, composition and design, style, shade, and so on. The musician speaks of coloration, expression, wording, the fiery and witty "ideas" expressed by the notes, the "pedantry" of the fugue, and so on. He has, just like the painter, a "style" in which he can sound sublime, moderate, middle-class, heroic, crawling, and so on. It is such metaphors, which no one understands or explains, that give these arts their refined and elevated character; and just for that reason one ac-quires a learned and "sublime" appearance when one uses them. Since no one has yet troubled to sift out what is intelligible in such expressions and restate it in its proper terms, one can use them all the more boldly. Explication cannot be carried out to the point where colors become comprehensible to the blind or sounds to the deaf. Yet this is evidently the intention of such metaphors.

But I come back to the *Architectonic.* I see from various indica-tions that Mr. Kanter [5] is a man who will also publish philosophy and larger works, and for this reason I wanted to give him a number of things to print, though at the moment I have no other manuscript. Whether it would be advantageous or all the same, because of the costs, to have it printed in Leipzig would depend on the difference in prices and the freight charges. If it could be done in Leipzig, there are various other reasons why that would be best. In my ignorance I take the liberty of forwarding the enclosed sheet, in case Mr. Kanter might be inclined to publish the work and could deliver it by Easter. The honorarium would be around two hundred thalers and is the more moderate because the work will necessarily create a stir.

I can tell you with confidence, dear sir, that your ideas about the

[5] Johann Jakob Kanter, (1738–86), bookdealer and publisher in Königs-berg.

origin of the world, which you mention in the preface [6] to *Only Possible Proof* . . . were not known to me before. What I said on page 149 of the *Cosmological Letters* [7] dates from 1749. Right after supper I went to my room, contrary to my habit then, and from my window I looked at the starry sky, especially the Milky Way. I wrote down on a quarto sheet the idea that occurred to me then, that the Milky Way could be viewed as an ecliptic of the fixed stars, and it was this note I had before me when I wrote the *Letters* in 1760. In 1761 I heard in Nürnberg that an Englishman had had similar thoughts a few years before,[8] which he had had printed in letters to another Englishman, but that these ideas were quite undeveloped and the translation that someone in Nürnberg had begun had not been completed. I answered that the *Cosmological Letters* would not arouse interest until perhaps some future astronomer discovers something in the sky that cannot be explained in any other way. And when the system will have been verified a posteriori, then the lovers of Greek literature will labor without rest until they can prove that the whole system was already known to Philolaus or Anaximander or some Greek wise man or other and that it has only been rediscovered and polished up in more recent times. For these people can find everything among the ancients, as soon as you tell them what to look for. I am more surprised, however, that Newton did not stumble on the idea, since he did know of the difficulty about the fixed stars.

I have a number of wishes, dear sir. One of them I shall not express, since I don't know whether and how far the present constitution of things will let it be so. However, I can say that the wish is not mine alone. The other thing is that it would be very

[6] See Kant's *Werke*, II, 68 f., for the preface to Kant's *Only Possible Proof of the Existence of God*, in which a footnote refers to his earlier *General Natural History and Theory of the Heavens* (*Allgemeine Naturgeschichte und Theorie des Himmels*) and to Lambert's agreement with ideas on the formation of the world, the Milky Way, and the fixed stars, as expressed in Lambert's *Cosmological Letters* of 1761. Kant's *General Natural History* was published in 1755, but the publisher went bankrupt just as the book came out. As a result, Kant's theories, specifically the nebular hypothesis, were not well known to Lambert and other physicists. Laplace, forty-one years later, does not mention Kant's book.

[7] *Cosmological Letters on the Establishment of the Universe* (*Cosmologische Briefe über die Einrichtung des Weltbaues* [Augsburg, 1761]).

[8] *An Original Theory and New Hypothesis of the Universe*, by Thomas Wright of Durham (1750). Kant credits this work with stimulating his own composition of the *General Natural History*. Kant knew of Wright's ideas from a 1751 review of his book in a Hamburg newspaper.

pleasant, if time and your affairs allow it, to exchange letters with you. Cosmology, metaphysics, physics, mathematics, belles-lettres, and their principles, and so on, in short, every quest of new ideas, and every occasion that I might be of service to you. We have heretofore hit upon almost the same investigations without knowing it. Would we not make better progress by advising one another in advance? How easily one reaches agreement in the consequences when one is agreed in the starting points, and how emphatic one can then be. Wolf has brought approximately half of the method of mathematics into philosophy. The other half remains to be done, so we know what to strive for.

I am honored to be, with sincere respect, dear sir,

J. H. LAMBERT
Professor and member of the
Royal Academy of Sciences

Berlin

To J. H. Lambert, December 31, 1765

- 34 - VOL. X, *pp. 54–57*

Dear sir:

Nothing could have been more welcome and pleasant for me than to receive the letter with which you have honored me; for, in all sincerity, I hold you to be the greatest genius in Germany, a man capable of important and enduring contributions to the investigations on which I too am working. I beg you also not to think me negligent for my delay in answering. Mr. Kanter, whom I informed of your proposal, asked me to postpone my letter until he might indicate his final decision to you in a letter of his own. He recognizes very well the significance of an association with such a distinguished writer as you, and he is willing enough to undertake the publication. But he would like to postpone it, since he does not have enough time before the Easter book fair and he is overwhelmed with other commitments. He has gone into partnership with his former employee, Mr. Hartknoch, who managed his affairs in Riga till now, and he has assured me that he will send you his explanation of the matter just mentioned right away.

It is no small pleasure for me that you have noticed the fortunate agreement of our methods, an agreement that I have often observed in your writings. It has served to increase my confidence, since it is a logical confirmation that shows that our methods satisfy the touchstone of universal human reason. I value greatly your invitation to share our plans with each other, and since I feel highly honored by this proposal I shall not fail to make use of it. For unless I deceive myself I think I have finally reached some conclusions I can trust. But the talent one sees in you, dear sir, combining an exceptional acuteness for details with a breadth of vision of the whole, is universally admitted, so that your willingness to unite your powers with my small endeavors allows me to hope for important instruction, for myself and perhaps for the world as well.

For a number of years I have carried on my philosophical reflections on every earthly subject, and after many capsizings, on which occasions I always looked for the source of my error or tried to get some insight into the nature of my blunder, I have finally reached the point where I feel secure of the method that has to be followed if one wants to escape that delusion of knowledge that has us constantly expecting to reach a conclusion, yet just as constantly makes us retrace our steps, a delusion from which the devastating disunity among supposed philosophers also arises. For we lack a common standard with which to procure agreement from them. Now, whatever the nature of the investigation before me, I always look to see what it is I have to know in order to solve a particular problem, and what degree of knowledge is possible for a given question, so that the judgment I make is often more limited but also more definite and secure than is customary in philosophy. What I am working on is mainly a book on the proper method of metaphysics (and thereby also the proper method for the whole of philosophy). Apropos, I must tell you, dear sir, that Mr. Kanter, in true bookseller's fashion, did not hesitate to announce the title in the Leipzig catalog when he heard from me that I might have a work with that title ready for the next Easter fair. I have, however, departed so widely from my original plan that I now want to postpone this book a little while, for I regard it as the culmination of my whole project. My problem is this: I noticed in my work that, though I had plenty of examples of erroneous judgments to illustrate my theses concerning mistaken procedures, I did not have examples to show *in concreto* what the proper procedure should be. Therefore, in order to avoid the accusation that I am merely hatching new philosophical schemes, I must first publish a few little essays, the contents of which I have already worked out. The first of these will be the "Metaphysical Foundations of Natural Philosophy" and the "Metaphysical Foundations of Practical Philosophy." [1] With the publication of these essays, the main work will not have to be burdened excessively with detailed and yet inadequate examples.

The moment for ending my letter has arrived. I shall in the future have the honor of presenting you, dear sir, with parts of my project, and I shall request your very respected judgment.

You complain with reason, dear sir, of the eternal trifling of punsters and the wearying chatter of today's reputed writers, with whom the only evidence of taste is that they talk about taste. I think, though, that this is the euthanasia of false philosophy, that it is perishing amid these foolish pranks, and it would be far worse to have it carried to the grave ceremoniously, with serious but dishonest hair-splitting. Before true philosophy can come to life, the old one must destroy itself; and just as putrefaction signifies the total dissolution that always precedes the start of a new creation, so the current crisis in learning magnifies my hopes that the great, long-awaited revolution in the sciences is not too far off. For there is no shortage of good minds.

Professor Reccard, who pleased me with his kind visit and also with your honored letter, is well liked here and universally respected as he deserves to be, though certainly there are few people able to appreciate his full worth. He sends his regards, and I am, with the greatest respect, dear sir,

Your most devoted servant,

I. KANT

P.S. As I had finished this letter, Mr. Kanter sent over the letter he owes you, which I am enclosing.

---

[1] Kant's *Metaphysiche Anfangsgründe der Naturwissenschaft* did not in fact appear until twenty years later, 1786. No "metaphysical foundations of practical philosophy" was ever published by Kant. See L. W. Beck's *Commentary on Kant's Critique of Practical Reason* (Chicago: University of Chicago Press, 1960), chap. i, for a full account of Kant's plans, and changes of plans, for a book on the foundations of ethics.

From J. H. Lambert, February 3, 1766

- 37 -   VOL. X, *pp. 62–67*

Dear sir,

I am in every way obliged to you for your most treasured letter of December 31 and should like especially to render my sincerest thanks for your efforts in connection with Mr. Kanter. If it suits him I should be very pleased to see him here at Easter and to make the necessary appointments with him. I shall also have various matters to discuss with him in connection with the calender revision that I have undertaken for the Academy. Might I beg you, sir, to inform Mr. Kanter of all this when you have time. I have nothing else to say in answer to his letter. But do think up ways in which, perhaps because of my location [in Berlin], I can be of service to you, so that I shall not remain your debtor.

There is no denying it: whenever a science needs methodical reconstruction and cleansing, it is always metaphysics. The universal, which is supposed to reign in that science, leads us to suppose ourselves omniscient, and thus we venture beyond the limits of possible human knowledge. I think this shows that if we want to avoid omissions, premature inferences, and circular reasoning, we had better work piecemeal, demanding to know at every step only what is capable of being known. I think it has been an unrecognized but perennial error in philosophy to force the facts and, instead of leaving anything unexplained, to load up with conjectures, thus actually delaying the discovery of the truth.

The method that your writings exhibit, sir, is undeniably the only method that one can use with security and progress. I see it approximately as follows (and this is also how I set it forth in the last part of my *Dianoiologie* [*Neues Organon I,* 386–450]). . . . [Lambert's account of his method is lengthy and not very interesting. He warns against hasty generalization and the overlooking of ambiguities and urges that philosophical investigations begin with "simple" rather than "complex" things.]

But I wanted to make some more general remarks. The first concerns the question whether or to what extent knowing the *form* of knowledge leads to knowing the *matter*. This question is important for several reasons. First, our knowledge of the form, as in logic, is as incontestable and right as is geometry. Second, only that part of metaphysics that deals with form has remained undisputed, whereas strife and hypotheses have arisen when material knowledge is at issue. Third, the basis of material knowledge has not, in fact, been adequately shown. Wolf assumed nominal definitions and, without noticing it, shoved aside or concealed all difficulties in them. Fourth, even if formal knowledge does not absolutely determine any material knowledge, it nevertheless determines the ordering of the latter, and to that extent we ought to be able to infer from formal knowledge what would and what would not serve as a possible beginning. Fifth, a knowledge of form can also help us to determine what belongs together and what must be put into distinct categories, and so on.

In thinking over these relationships of form and matter, I arrived at the following propositions, which I only want to list here.

1. Form gives us *principles,* whereas matter gives us *axioms* and *postulates.*

2. Formal knowledge must begin with simple concepts, which cannot be internally self-contradictory, since they are simple in themselves and conceivable and independent in themselves.

3. Axioms and postulates actually contain only simple concepts. For synthesized concepts [*zusammengesetze Begriffe*] are not conceivable a priori in themselves. The possibility of synthesizing must first of all be derived from the principles [*Grundsätzen*] and postulates.

4. Either no synthesized concepts are conceivable or the possibility of synthesizing must already be conceivable in the simple concepts.

5. The simple concepts are *individual* concepts. For genera and species contain the *fundamenta divisionum et subdivisionum* within them and, just for that reason, are more highly synthesized the more abstract and universal they are. The concept of "thing," *ens,* is of all concepts the most synthesized.

6. According to the Leibnizian analysis, which proceeds by way of abstraction and analogies, one arrives at more highly synthesized concepts the more one abstracts, and for the most part, at *nominal* relational concepts that concern the form more than the matter.

7. On the other hand, since form consists of nothing but relational concepts, it can give an account of nothing but simple relational concepts.

8. Accordingly, the really objectively simple concepts must be found by a direct intuition [*Anschauen*] of them, that is, we must, in good anatomical fashion, assemble all the concepts and let each one pass through inspection, in order to see whether, when we ignore all the relations of a given concept to other concepts, there are several concepts included in it or whether it is indeed simple [*einformig*].

9. Simple concepts are like space and time, that is to say, totally different from one another, easily recognizable, easy to name, and practically impossible to confuse, if we abstract from their degrees and concentrate only on their kinds [*quale*]. And thus I believe that not a single one of those concepts remains unnamed in our language.

With these propositions in mind I have no hesitation in saying that Locke was on the right track when he sought the simple elements in our knowledge. But we need to eliminate the distortions caused by linguistic usage. For example, there is an undeniably individual, simple something in the concept of *extension*—something that is not found in any other concept. There is something simple in the concepts of *duration, existence, movement, unity, solidity,* and so on, something belonging uniquely to each of these concepts, that can readily be distinguished in thought from the many relational concepts that may accompany them. Axioms and postulates that lay the groundwork for scientific knowledge are also indicated by these simples and are all of the same type as Euclid's.

The other remarks I wanted to make concern the comparison of philosophical and mathematical knowledge. I realized that where mathematicians have succeeded in opening up a new field that philosophers previously thought they had entirely completed, the mathematicians not only had to reverse everything the philosophers had done but also had to reconstruct everything on simple foundations, so much so that philosophy was entirely useless and contemptible to them. The single condition that only homogeneous elements can be added implies that all philosophical propositions whose predicates do not apply uniformly to their subjects are rejected by the mathematician. And there are entirely too many such propositions in philosophy: A watch is called "gold" when even the casing is hardly made of gold. Euclid does not derive his elements from either the definition of space or that of geometry but begins instead with lines, angles, and so on, the simple elements in the dimensions of space. In mechanics, we make little use of the definition of motion; rather, we immediatly consider what accompanies motion, viz., a body, the direction, velocity, time, force, and space, and these elements are *compared* with one another in order to discover *principles*. I have been led to the conclusion that as long as a philosopher does not carry his analysis of measurable objects to the point where the mathematician can find unities, measures, and dimensions he must surely still be hanging on to some confusion, or at least the predicates of his propositions do not apply uniformly to the subjects.

I await impatiently the publication of both your "First Principles of Natural Philosophy and of Practical Philosophy" and I agree entirely that a genuine method commends itself most effectively when displayed in actual examples, since one can then illustrate it with individual cases, whereas it might well be too abstract when expressed logically. But once the examples are there, logical remarks about them become highly serviceable. Examples perform the same job that figures do in geometry, for the latter, too, are actually examples or special cases.

I close now and want to assure you that our continued correspondence would be exceptionally pleasing to me. I remain most eagerly at your service, sir,

Your most devoted servant,
J. H. Lambert

Berlin
At the corner of Cronenstrasse and
Schinkenbrücke in the Bethgenschen house

To Moses Mendelssohn, April 8, 1766

- 39 -   VOL. X, *pp. 69–73*

Dear sir,

For your kind efforts in forwarding the writings I sent you, I again send my sincerest thanks and my readiness to reciprocate in any way that I might be of service.[1]

The unfavorable impression you express concerning the tone of my little book proves to me that you have formed a good opinion of the sincerity of my character, and your very reluctance to see that character ambiguously expressed is both precious and pleasing to me. In fact, you shall never have cause to change this opinion. For though there may be flaws that even the most steadfast determination cannot eradicate completely, I shall certainly never become a fickle or fraudulent person, after having devoted the largest part of my life to studying how to despise those things that tend to corrupt one's character. Losing the self-respect that stems from a sense of honesty would therefore be the greatest evil that could, but most certainly shall not, befall me. Although I am absolutely convinced of many things that I shall never have the courage to say, I shall never say anything I do not believe.

I don't know whether, in reading this rather untidily completed book, you noticed certain indications of my reluctance to write it. For I saw that my prying inquiry into Swedenborg's "visions" would make a great stir among people who knew him personally

---

[1] The letter is a reply to Mendelssohn's letter, not extant, of some time between February 7 and April 8. On the former date, Kant replied to another letter of Mendelssohn's (also not extant). He expressed his pleasure at the prospect of a correspondence with Mendelssohn and asked him to forward some copies of Kant's *Dreams of a Ghost-Seer Explained by Dreams of Metaphysics* (*Träume eines Geistersehers, erläutert durch Träume der Metaphysick* [1766]) to various gentlemen (including Lambert). Kant referred to the book as *einige Träumerey* ("some reveries") and added: "It is, as it were, a casual piece, containing not so much a working out of these questions as a hasty sketch of the way they should be decided." He asked for Mendelssohn's opinion. As is evident from Kant's reply, the opinion was not what Kant had hoped. Mendelssohn was offended by what he took to be the tone of Kant's essay, "between jest and earnest."

or from his letters and published works and that I would never be at peace from their incessant questions until I had got rid of the alleged cognitions mentioned in all these anecdotes.

It was in fact difficult for me to devise the right style with which to clothe my thoughts, so as not to expose myself to derision. It seemed to me wisest to forestall other people's mockery by first of all mocking myself; and this procedure was actually quite honest, since my mind is really in a state of conflict on this matter. As regards the spirit reports, I cannot help but be charmed by stories of this kind; but as regards the rational bases of such reports, I cannot rid myself of one or two suspicions of their correctness—leaving aside the absurdities, fancies, and unintelligible notions that undermine their value.

As to my expressed opinion of the value of metaphysics in general, perhaps here and again my words were not sufficiently careful and qualified. But I cannot conceal my repugnance, and even a certain hatred, toward the inflated arrogance of whole volumes full of what are passed off nowadays as insights; for I am fully convinced that the path that has been selected is completely wrong, that the methods now in vogue must infinitely increase the amount of folly and error in the world, and that even the total extermination of all these chimerical insights would be less harmful than the dream science itself, with its confounded contagion.

I am far from regarding metaphysics itself, objectively considered, to be trivial or dispensable; in fact I have been convinced for some time now that I understand its nature and its proper place in human knowledge and that the true and lasting welfare of the human race depends on it—an appraisal that would seem fantastic and audacious to anyone but you. It befits brilliant men such as you to create a new epoch in this science, to begin completely afresh, to draw up the plans for this heretofore haphazardly constructed discipline with a master's hand. As for the stock of knowledge currently available, which is now publicly up for sale, I think it best to pull off its dogmatic dress and treat its pretended insights skeptically. My feeling is not the result of frivolous inconstancy but of an extensive investigation. Admittedly, my suggested treatment will serve a merely negative purpose, the avoidance of stupidity [*stultitia caruisse*], but it will prepare the way for a positive one. Although the innocence of a healthy but uninstructed understanding requires only an *organon* in order to arrive at insight, a *propaedeutic* [*catarcticon*] is needed to get rid of the pseudo insight of a spoiled head. If I may be permitted to mention something of my own efforts, I think I have reached some important insights in this discipline since I last published anything on questions of this sort, insights that will establish the proper procedure for metaphysics. My notions are not merely general ones but provide a specific criterion. To the extent that my other distractions permit, I am gradually preparing to submit these ideas to public scrutiny, but principally to yours; for I flatter myself that if you could be persuaded to collaborate with me (and I include in this your noticing my errors) the development of the sciences might be significantly encouraged.

It suffices for my not inconsiderable pleasure that my superficial little essay will have the good fortune to entice "Basic Reflections"[2] from you on this point, and I regard it as useful enough if it occasions deeper investigations in others. I am sure that the main point of all these considerations will not escape you, though I could have made it more clear if I had not had the paper printed one page at a time. I could not always foresee what would lead to a clearer understanding of later pages; moreover, certain explanations had to be left out, because they would have occurred in the wrong place. In my opinion, everything depends on our seeking out the *data* of the problem, how is the soul *present in the world, both in material and in non-material things.* In other words, we need to discover the nature of that power of external agency, and the nature of that *receptivity* or capacity of being affected by an external agency, of which the union of a soul with a human body is only a special case. Since we have no experience through which we can get to know such a subject in its various relationships (and experience is the only thing that can disclose the subject's external power or capacity), and since the harmony of the soul with the body discloses only the counterrelationship of the *inner* condition (thinking or willing) of the soul to the *outer* condition of the material body (not a relation of one external activity to another external activity) and consequently is not at all capable of solving the problem, the upshot of all this is that one is led to ask whether it is intrinsically possible to determine these powers of spiritual substances by means of a priori rational judgments. This investigation resolves itself into another, namely, whether one can by means of rational inferences discover a *primitive* power, that is, the

[2] A reference to Mendelssohn's *Phaedon* (1767). In the second dialogue, Mendelssohn argues that a material thing cannot think.

primary, fundamental relationship of cause to effect. And since I am certain that this is impossible, it follows that, if these powers are not given in experience, they can only be invented. But this invention, an heuristic fiction or hypothesis, can never even be proved to be possible, and it is a mere delusion to argue from the mere fact of its conceivability (which has its plausibility only because no impossibility can be derived from the concept either). Such a delusion is Swedenborg's reverie [*Träumerei*], though I myself would try to defend it if someone were to argue it impossible. My analogy between a spiritual substance's actual moral influx and the force of universal gravitation is not intended seriously; but it is an example of how far one can go in philosophical fabrications, completely unhindered, when there are no *data*, and it illustrates how important it is, in such exercises, first to decide what is required for a solution of the problem and whether the necessary *data* for a solution may be lacking. If, for the time being, we put aside arguments based on propriety or on the divine purposes and ask whether it is ever possible to attain such knowledge of the nature of the soul from our experience—a knowledge sufficient to inform us of the manner in which the soul is present in the universe, in relation both to matter and to beings of its own sort—we shall then see whether *birth* (in the metaphysical sense), *life,* and *death* are matters we can ever hope to understand by means of reason. Here we must decide whether there really are not limitations established by the bounds of our reason, or rather, the bounds of the experience that contains the *data* for our reason. But I shall stop now and commend myself to your friendship. I beg also that you convey to Professor Sultzer my particular respect and the desire to hear from him. I am, most respectfully,

Your most devoted servant,
I. KANT

Königsberg

To J. H. Lambert, September 2, 1770

- 57 -   VOL. X, *pp. 96–99*

Noble sir,
Honored professor,

I am taking advantage of the opportunity I have of sending you my [inaugural] dissertation by way of the respondent of that work, a capable Jewish student of mine. At the same time, I should like to destroy an unpleasant misunderstanding caused by my protracted delay in answering your valued letter. The reason was none other than the striking importance of what I gleaned from that letter, and this occasioned the long postponement of a suitable answer. Since I had spent much time investigating the science [metaphysics] on which you focused your attention there, for I was attempting to discover the nature and if possible the evident and immutable laws of that science, it could not have pleased me more that a man of such discriminating acuteness and universality of insight, with whose method of thinking I had often been in agreement, should offer his services for a united testing and pursuit of the plan for the secure construction of this science. I could not persuade myself to send you anything less than a clear summary of how I view this science and a definite idea of the proper method for it. The carrying out of this intention entangled me in investigations that were new to me and, what with my exhausting academic work, necessitated one postponement after another. For perhaps a year now, I believe I have arrived at a position that, I flatter myself, I shall never have to change, even though extensions will be needed, a position from which all sorts of metaphysical questions can be examined according to wholly certain and easy criteria. The extent to which these questions can or cannot be resolved will be decidable with certainty.

I could summarize this whole science, as far as its nature, the sources of its judgments, and the method with which one can progress in it are concerned; and this summary could be made in a rather small space, namely, in a few letters, to be submitted to your thorough and knowledgeable judgment. It is that judgment for which I beg here, anticipating the most excellent results from your criticism. But since in a project of such importance a little expenditure of time is no loss at all, if one can thereby produce something complete and lasting, I must beg you again to believe my good intentions to be unaltered but again to grant me more time to carry them out. In order to recover from a lengthy indisposition that has bothered me all summer, and at the same time to keep busy during odd hours, I have resolved this winter to put in order and complete my investigations of pure moral philosophy, in which no empirical principles are to be found, the "Metaphysics of Morals." It will in many respects pave the way for the most important views involved in the reconstruction of metaphysics and seems to be just as necessary in view of the current state of the practical sciences, whose principles are so poorly defined. After I have completed this work I shall make use of the permission you gave me, to present you with my essays in metaphysics, as far as I have come with them. I assure you that I shall take no proposition as valid which does not seem to you completely warranted. For unless this agreement can be won, the objective will not have been reached, viz., to ground this science on indubitable, wholly incontestable rules. For the present it would please and instruct me to have your judgment of some of the main points in my dissertation, since I intend to add a few pages to it before the publisher presents it at the coming book fair. I want both to correct the errors caused by hasty completion and to make my meaning more determinate. The first and fourth sections can be scanned without careful consideration; but in the second, third, and fifth, though my indisposition prevented me from working them out to my satisfaction, there seems to me to be material deserving more careful and extensive exposition. The most universal laws of sensibility play an unjustifiably large role in metaphysics, where, after all, it is merely concepts and principles (*Grundsätze*) of pure reason that are at issue. A quite special, though purely negative science, general phenomenology (*phaenomologia generalis*), seems to me to be presupposed by metaphysics. In it the principles of sensibility, their validity and their limitations, would be determined, so that these principles could not be confusedly applied to objects of pure reason, as has heretofore almost always happened. For space and time, and the axioms for considering all things under these conditions, are, with respect to empirical knowledge and all objects of sense, very real; they are actually the *conditions* of all appearances and of all empirical judgments. But extremely mistaken conclusions emerge if we apply the basic concepts of sensibility to something that is not at all an object of sense, that is, something thought through a universal or a pure concept of the understanding as a thing or substance in general, and so on. It seems to me, too (and perhaps I shall be fortunate enough to win your agreement here by means of my very inadequate essay), that such a *propaedeutic discipline,* which would preserve metaphysics proper from any admixture of the sensible, could be made usefully explicit and evident without great strain.

I beg your future friendship and kind interest in my modest scientific efforts. I hope I may be permitted to commend to you Mr. Marcus Herz, who is delivering this letter and who would like your help with his studies. He is a young man of excellent character, industrious and capable, who adheres to and profits from every piece of good advice.

I am, most respectfully,

Your most devoted servant,
I. Kant

Königsberg

From J. H. Lambert, October 13, 1770

- 61 -   VOL. X, *pp. 103–10*

Dear sir,

Your letter and also your dissertation concerning the sensible and intellectual world gave me great pleasure, especially because I regard the latter as a sample of how metaphysics and ethics could be improved. I hope very much that your new position may occasion more of such essays, since you have not decided to publish it separately.

You remind me of my suggestion of five years ago, of a *possible future collaboration.* I wrote to Mr. Holland [1] about it at that time, and would have written to some other scholars, too, had not the book catalogs shown me that belles-lettres are displacing everything

---

[1] Georg Jonathan Holland (1742–84), mathematician and philosopher.

else. I think that the fad is passing, however, and that people are ready to take up the serious disciplines once more. I have already heard from some people who never read anything but poems, novels, and literary things at the universities that, when they had to get down to business, they found themselves in an entirely new country and had to start their studies all over again. These people are in a position to know what needs to be done at the universities.

In the meantime I planned to write some little treatises myself, to invite the collaboration of some scholars with similar views, and thus to create a private society where all those things that tend to ruin public learned societies would be avoided. The actual members would have been a small number of selected philosophers, who would, however, have had to be at home in physics and mathematics as well, since in my view an *authentic metaphysician* is like a man who lacks one of his senses, as the blind lack sight. . . . The members would have expressed their opinions on difficult matters in the form of questions, or in such a manner that room would have been left for rejoinders and objections. . . .

But I turn now to your excellent dissertation, since you particularly wanted to have my thoughts about it. If I have correctly understood the matter, certain propositions are basic, and these are, briefly, as follows:

The first main thesis is that *human knowledge,* by virtue of being *knowledge* and by virtue of *having its own form,* is divided in accordance with the old *phaenomenon* and *noumenon* distinction and, accordingly, arises out of two entirely different and, so to speak, *heterogeneous* sources, so that what stems from the one source can never be derived from the other. Knowledge that comes from the senses thus is and remains sensible, just as knowledge that comes from the understanding remains peculiar to the understanding.

My thoughts on this proposition have to do mainly with the question of *universality,* namely, to what extent these two ways of knowing are so completely *separated* that they *never* come together. If this is to be shown a priori, it must be deduced from the nature of the senses and of the understanding. But since we first have to become acquainted with these a posteriori, it will depend on the classification and enumeration of [their] *objects* [*obiecte*].

This seems also to be the path you take in the third section. In this sense it seems to me quite correct to say that truths that integrally involve *space* and *location* [*Ort*] are of an entirely different sort from those that must be regarded as eternal and immutable. I merely mentioned this in my *Alethiology*, No. 81.87 [in Lambert's *Neues Organon* (1764)], for it is not so easy to give the reason why truths integrally involve time and location in this way and in no other, even though the question is extremely important.

But there I was talking only of *existing* things. The truths of geometry and chronometry, however, involve time and location essentially, not merely accidentally; and in so far as the concepts of space and time are eternal, the truths of geometry and chronometry belong to the class of eternal, immutable truths also.

Now you ask whether these truths are sensuous? I can very well grant that they are. The difficulty seems to lie in the concepts of time and location and could be expressed without reference to this question. The first four statements in your No. 14 seem to me quite correct; [2] and it is especially good that you insist on the true concept of *continuity,* which metaphysics seems to have completely forgotten,[3] since people wanted to bring it in as the idea of a set of connected simple entities [*Complexus Entium Simplicium*] and therefore had to alter the concept. The difficulty actually lies in the fifth statement. You do not offer the statement, time is the subjective condition [*Tempus est subiectiva conditio*], and so on, as a definition.[4] It is nevertheless supposed to indicate something peculiar and essential to time. Time is undeniably a *conditio sine qua non* and belongs therefore to the representation of every sensible

[2] The propositions are as follows: (1) The idea of time does not originate in, but is presupposed by, the senses. (2) The idea of time is singular, not general. (3) The idea of time, therefore, is an intuition . . . not a sensuous but a *pure* intuition. (4) Time is a continuous quantity. . . . (Kant's *Werke,* II, 398 ff.)

[3] In discussing the fourth proposition (see n. 2), Kant argues: "A *continuous* quantity is one that does not consist of simple parts. . . . The metaphysical [Leibnizian] law of continuity is this: All changes are continuous or flowing, that is, opposite states succeed each other only by an intermediate series of different states." Lambert is criticising the Wolffian metaphysics, which maintained that "if in a composite the parts are arranged next to each other in turn in such an order that it is absolutely impossible that others be placed between them in some other order, then the composite is called a continuum. By the agency of God, continuity precludes the possible existence of a distinct part intermediate between two adjoining parts." (See Christian Wolff, *Philosophia prima, Sive Ontologia* [1736], No. 554, and *Cosmologia Generalis* [1731], Nos. 176 ff.)

[4] "Time is the subjective condition necessary, because of the nature of the human mind, for co-ordinating any sensible objects among themselves by means of a certain law." (Kant's *Werke,* II, 400.)

object and of every object integrally involving time and location. Time is also particularly necessary in order that any human being have such representations. It is also a pure intuition [*Intuitus purus*], not a substance, not a mere relation. It is distinct [*sie differiert*] from *duration* [*dauer*] in the way *location* is distinct from *space*. It is a particular determination of duration. Moreover, it is not an *accident* that perishes along with substances, and so on. These propositions are all correct. They lead to no definition, and the best definition will always be that time is time, since we do not want to involve ourselves in logical circularity by defining it in terms of its relations to things that are in time. *Time* is a more determinate concept than *duration*, and for that reason, too, it leads to more negative propositions. For example, whatever is in time has some duration [*dauert*]. But the reverse does not hold, in so far as one demands a beginning and an end for "being in time." Eternity is not in time, since its duration is absolute. Any substance that has absolute duration is likewise not in time. Everything that exists has duration, but not everything is in time, and so on. With a concept as clear as that of *time*, we do not lack propositions. The trouble seems to lie only in the fact that one must simply think time and duration and not define them. All changes are bound to time and are inconceivable without time. *If changes are real, then time is real*, whatever it may be. *If time is unreal, then no change can be real*. I think, though, that even an idealist must grant at least that changes really exist and occur in his representations, for example, their beginning and ending. Thus time cannot be regarded as something *unreal*. It is not a substance, and so on, but a finite determination of duration, and like duration, it is somehow real in whatever this reality may consist. If this cannot be identified without danger of confusion, by means of the words we use for other things, it will either require the introduction of a new primitive term or it will have to remain unnamed. The reality of time and of space seems to have something so simple and peculiar about it that it can only be thought and not defined. Duration appears to be inseparable from existence. Whatever exists has a duration that is either absolute or of a certain span, and conversely, whatever has duration must necessarily, while it lasts, exist. Existing things that do not have absolute duration are temporally ordered, in so far as they begin, continue, change, cease, and so on. Since I cannot deny reality to changes, until somebody teaches me otherwise, I also cannot say that time (and this is true of space as well) is only a helpful device for human representations. And as for the colloquial phrases in use that involve the notion of time, it is always well to notice the ambiguities that the word "time" has in them. For example,

A long time is an interval of time or of two moments [*intervallum temporis vel duorum momentorum*] and means "a definite duration."

At this or that time, and so on, is either a definite moment, as in astronomy, the time of setting, of rising [*tempus immersionis, emersionis*], and so on, or a smaller or larger interval preceding or following a moment, an indefinite duration or point in time, and so on.

You will gather easily enough how I conceive location [*Ort*] and space [*Raum*]. Ignoring the ambiguities of the words, I propose the analogy,

Time : Duration = Location : Space

The analogy is quite precise, except that space has three dimensions, duration only one, and besides this each of these concepts has something peculiar to it. Space, like duration, has absolute but also finite determinations. Space, like duration, has a reality peculiar to it, which we cannot explain or define by means of words that are used for other things, at least not without danger of being misleading. It is something simple and must be thought. The whole intellectual world [*Gedankenwelt*] is non-spatial; it does, however, have a counterpart [*Simulachrum*] of space, which is easily distinguishable from physical space. Perhaps this bears a still closer resemblance to it than merely a metaphoric one.

The theological difficulties that, especially since the time of Leibniz and Clarke,[5] have made the theory of space a thorny problem have so far not confused me. I owe all my success to my preference for leaving undetermined various topics that are impervious to clarification. Besides, I did not want to peer at the succeeding parts of metaphysics when working on ontology. I won't complain if people want to regard time and space as mere pictures and appearances. For, in addition to the fact that constant appearance is for us truth, though the foundations are never discovered or only at some future time; it is also useful in ontology to take up

[5] The Leibniz-Clarke correspondence of 1715 and 1716 was published in London, 1717, and in German translation, Frankfurt, 1720. For a recent discussion of the controversy, see Robert Paul Wolff, *Kant's Theory of Mental Activity* (Cambridge, Mass.: Harvard University Press, 1963), pp. 4–8.

concepts borrowed from appearance, since *the theory must finally be applied to phenomena again.* For that is also how the astronomer begins, with the phenomenon; deriving his theory of the construction of the world from phenomena, he applies it again to phenomena and their predictions in his *Ephemerides* [star calendars]. In metaphysics, where the problem of appearance is so essential, the method of the astronomer will surely be the safest. The metaphysician can take everything to be appearance, separate the empty from the real appearance, and draw true conclusions from the latter. If he is successful, he shall have few contradictions arising from the principles and win much favor. It only seems necessary to have time and patience.

I shall be brief here in regard to the fifth section. I would regard it as very important if you could find a way of showing more deeply the ground and origin of truths integrally involving space and time. As far as this section is concerned with method, however, I would say here what I said about time. For if *changes,* and therefore also *time* and *duration,* are something real, it seems to follow that *the proposed division in section five must have other, and in part more narrow, intentions;* and according to these, the classification might also be different. This occurred to me in Nos. 25–26. In regard to No. 27, the "whatever exists, exists in some place and at some time" [*Quicquid est, est alicubi et aliquando*], is partly in error and partly ambiguous, if it is supposed to mean located at a time and in a place [*in tempore et in loco*]. Whatever has *absolute* duration is not in time [*in tempore*], and the intellectual world is only "located in" [*in loco*] the aforementioned counterpart [*Simulachri*] of space or in the "place" [*loco*] of intellectual space [*Gedankenraums*].

What you say in No. 28, and in the note on pages 2–3 concerning the mathematical infinite, that it has been ruined by the definitions in metaphysics and that something else has been substituted for it, has my full approval. In regard to the "being and not being at the same time" [*Simul esse et non esse*] mentioned in No. 28, I think that a counterpart of time [*Simulachrum temporis*] exists in the intellectual world as well, and the phrase "at the same time" [*Simul*] is therefore used in a different sense when it occurs in the proofs of absolute truths that are not tied to time and place. I should think that the counterpart of space and time [*Simulacrum spatii et temporis*] in the intellectual world could also be considered in the theory you have in mind. It is an imitation of actual space and actual time and can readily be distinguished from them. Our symbolic knowledge is a thing halfway between sensing and actual pure thinking. If we proceed correctly in the delineation of the simples and in the manner of our synthesizing, we thereby get reliable rules for constructing signs of things that are so highly synthesized that we need not review them again and can nevertheless be sure that the sign represents the truth. No one has yet formed himself a clear representation of all the members of an infinite series, and no one is going to do so in the future. But we are able to do arithmetic with such series, to give their sum, and so on, by virtue of the laws of *symbolic* knowledge. We thus extend ourselves far beyond the borders of our actual [*wirklichen*] thinking. The sign $\sqrt{-1}$ represents an unthinkable non-thing. And yet it can be used very well in finding theorems. What are usually regarded as specimens of the pure understanding can be viewed most of the time as specimens of symbolic knowledge. This is what I said in No. 122 of my *Phaenomenology* with reference to question No. 119.[6] And I have nothing against your making the claim quite general, in No. 10.

But I shall stop here and let you make whatever use you wish of what I have said. Please examine carefully the sentences I have underlined and, if you have time, let me know what you think of them. Never mind the postage. Till now I have not been able to deny all reality to time and space, or to consider them mere images and appearance. I think that every change would then have to be mere appearance too. And this would contradict one of my main principles (No. 54, *Phaenomenology*). If changes have reality, then I must grant it to time as well. Changes follow one another, begin, continue, cease, and so on, and all these expressions are temporal. If you can instruct me otherwise, I shall not expect to lose much. Time and space will be *real* appearances, and their

[6] "Phänomenologie oder Lehre von dem Schein" is a part of Lambert's *Neues Organon*. The claim made by Kant, to which Lambert refers, is that man is "incapable of any intuition of intellectual concepts," so that our cognition must be "symbolical." Since "all the material of our cognition is given only by the senses, but the noumenon, as such, is not conceivable by representations drawn from sensations, the intellectual concept is destitute of all data of human intuition." (*Werke*, II, 396.) In Lambert's book, the question is raised "to what extent it is possible for us to have a distinct representation of truths without any sensuous images?" He argues that words and signs must be used as substitutes for images and that by means of them it is possible to transcend the imagination. Algebra is said to be a perfect example of this.

foundation is an existent something that truly conforms to time and space just as precisely and constantly as the laws of geometry are precise and constant. The language of appearance will thus serve our purposes just as precisely as the unknown "true" language. I must say, though, that an appearance that absolutely never deceives us could well be something more than mere appearance. . . .

I have the honor of being, very respectfully,

Your most devoted servant,
J. H. Lambert

Berlin

From Moses Mendelssohn, December 25, 1770

- 63 - VOL. X, *pp. 113–16*

Noble sir,
Distinguished professor,

Mr. Marcus Herz, who is indebted to you for your instruction and even more for the wisdom you imparted to him in your personal association, continues gloriously on the path that he began under your tutelage. I endeavor to encourage his progress a little through my friendship. I am sincerely fond of him and have the pleasure of almost daily conversations with him. Nature has truly been generous to him. He has a clear understanding, a gentle heart, a controlled imagination, and a certain subtlety of mind that seems to be peculiar to that race. But how lucky for him that these natural gifts were so early led on the path of truth and goodness. How many people, without this good fortune, left to themselves in the immeasurable region of truth and error, have had to consume their valuable time and best energies in a hundred vain attempts, so that they lacked both time and power to follow the right road when at last, after much groping about, they found it. Would that I might have had a Kant for a friend before my twentieth year!

Your dissertation has now reached my eager hands, and I have read it with much pleasure. Unfortunately my nervous infirmities make it impossible for me of late to give as much effort of thought to a speculative work of this stature as it deserves. One can see that this little book is the fruit of long meditation and that it must be viewed as part of a whole system, the author's own creation, of which he has only shown us a sample. The ostensible obscurity of certain passages is a clue to the practiced reader that this work must be part of a larger whole with which he has not yet been presented. For the good of metaphysics, a science that, alas, has fallen on sad days, it would be a shame for you to keep your thoughts in stock for long without offering them to us. Man's life is short. How quickly the end overtakes us, while we still cherish the thought of improving on what we have. And why do you so carefully avoid repeating what you have said before? Old ideas are seen in another light, suggesting new and surprising views, when they appear in the context of your new creations. Since you possess a great talent for writing in such a way as to reach many readers, one hopes that you will not always restrict yourself to the few adepts who are up on the latest things and who are able to guess what lies undisclosed behind the published hints.

Since I do not quite count myself as one of these adepts, I dare not tell you all the thoughts that your dissertation aroused in me. Allow me only to set forth a few, which actually do not concern your major theses but only some peripheral matters.

Pages 2–3 [*Werke,* II, 388]. You will find some thoughts concerning infinite extension, similar though not as penetratingly expressed, in the second edition of my *Philosophische Schriften,* now in press. I shall be honored to send you a copy. Mr. Herz can testify that everything was ready for the printer before I received your book, and I told him of my pleasure at finding that a man of your stature should agree with me on these points.

Page 11 [*Werke,* II, 396]. You regard Lord Shaftesbury as at least a distant follower of Epicureanism. But I have always thought that one must distinguish carefully between Shaftesbury's "moral instinct" and the feeling of pleasure [*Wollust*] of Epicurus. The former, for Shaftesbury, is merely an innate faculty for distinguishing good from evil by means of the mere feeling [of pleasure or displeasure] that these arouse. For Epicurus, on the other hand, the feeling of pleasure is not only a criterion of goodness [*criterium boni*] but is itself supposed to be the highest good [*summum bonum*].[1]

---

[1] In No. 9 of the dissertation, Kant attributed to Shaftesbury and Epicurus the view that the feelings of pleasure or displeasure are the criteria of morality.

Page 15 [*Werke*, II, 399], *Quid significet vocula post. . . .*[2] This difficulty seems to demonstrate the poverty of language rather than the incorrectness of the concept. The little word "after" [*post*] originally signifies a chronological order; but it is possible to use it to indicate any order in general where A is possible only when or in case B does not exist. In short, the order in which two absolutely (or even hypothetically) contradictory things can exist. You will object that my unavoidable words "when or in case" presuppose the idea of time. Very well, then, let us shun those little words, too, if you like. I begin with the following explication:

If A and B are both real and are the immediate (or even the remote) consequences [*rationata*] of a ground, C, I call them hypothetically compatible things [*compossibilia secundum quid*]: if they are unequally remote consequences, or *rationata,* I call them hypothetically incompatible. I continue:

Hypothetically compatible things (things that in this world are *compossibilia*) are simultaneous; hypothetically incompatible real things [*Actualia*], however, are successive, to wit, the nearer *rationatum* precedes, and the more remote one follows.

Here, I hope, there occurs no word presupposing the idea of time. In any case, it rests more with language than with the thoughts.

For several reasons I cannot convince myself that time is something merely subjective. Succession is after all at least a necessary condition of the representations that finite minds have. But finite minds are not only subjects; they are also objects of representations, both those of God and those of their fellows. Consequently it is necessary to regard succession as something objective.

Since we have to grant the reality of succession in a representing creature and in its alterations, why not also in the sensible objects, which are the models and protoypes of representations in the world?

On page 17 [*Werke,* II, 401], the way you find a fallacious circularity in this way of conceiving time is not clear to me. Time is (according to Leibniz) a phenomenon and has, as do all appearances, an objective and a subjective aspect. The subjective is the *continuity* we attribute to it; the objective is the succession of

[2] "For I understand what the word 'after' means only by means of the previous concept of time." Kant argues that time therefore cannot be defined by reference to the series of actual things existing one *after* the other.

alterations that are equidistant consequences [*rationata*] of a common ground.

On page 23 [*Werke*, II, 406], I don't think the condition *eodem tempore* [at the same time] is so necessary in the law of contradiction. In so far as something is the same subject, it is not possible to predicate the A and non-A of it at different times. The concept of impossibility demands no more than that the *same* subject cannot have two predicates, A and non-A. Alternatively, one could say it is impossible that non-A be a predicate of the subject A.

I would not have been so bold as to criticize your book with such abandon had not Mr. Herz made known to me your true philosophical spirit and assured me that you would never take offense at such frankness. This attitude is so rare, among imitators, it frequently serves as a distinguishing mark of men who think for themselves. He who has himself experienced the difficulty of finding the truth, and of convincing himself that he has found it, is always more inclined to be tolerant of those who differ from him. I have the honor of being, noble sir and revered professor, most respectfully,

Your most devoted servant,
MOSES MENDELSSOHN

To Marcus Herz, February 21, 1772

- 70 - VOL. X, *pp. 129–35*

Noble sir,
Esteemed friend,

You do me no injustice if you become indignant at the total absence of my replies; but lest you draw any disagreeable conclusions from it, let me appeal to your understanding of the way I think. Instead of excuses, I shall give you a brief account of the kind of things that have occupied my thoughts and that cause me to put off letter-writing in my idle hours. After your departure from Königsberg I examined once more, in the intervals between my professional duties and my sorely needed relaxation, the project that we had debated, in order to adapt it to the whole of philosophy and other knowledge and in order to understand its extent and limits. I had already previously made considerable progress in the effort to distinguish the sensible from the intellectual in the field of morals and the principles that spring therefrom. I had also long ago outlined, to my tolerable satisfaction, the principles of feeling, taste, and power of judgment, with their effects—the pleasant, the beautiful, and the good—and was then making plans for a work that might perhaps have the title, "The Limits of Sense and Reason." I planned to have it consist of two parts, a theoretical and a practical. The first part would have two sections, (1) general phenomenology and (2) metaphysics, but this only with regard to its nature and method. The second part likewise would have two sections, (1) the universal principles of feeling, taste, and sensuous desire and (2) the basic principles of morality. As I thought through the theoretical part, considering its whole scope and the reciprocal relations of all its parts, I noticed that I still lacked something essential, something that in my long metaphysical stud-ies I, as well as others, had failed to pay attention to and that, in fact, constitutes the key to the whole secret of hitherto still obscure metaphysics. I asked myself: What is the ground of the relation of that in us which we call "representation" to the object? If a representation is only a way in which the subject is affected by the object, then it is easy to see how the representation is in conformity with this object, namely, as an effect in accord with its cause, and it is easy to see how this modification [*Bestimmung*] of our mind can *represent* something, that is, have an object. Thus the passive or sensuous representations have an understandable relationship to objects, and the principles that are derived from the nature of our soul have an understandable validity for all things insofar as those things are supposed to be objects of the senses. In the same way, if that in us which we call "representation" were active with regard to the object, that is, if the object itself were created by the representation (as when divine cognitions are conceived as the archetypes of all things), the conformity of these representations to their objects could be understood. Thus the possibility of both an *intellectus archetypi* (on whose intuition the things themselves would be grounded) and an *intellectus ectypi* (which would derive the data for its logical procedure from the sensuous in-tuition of things) is at least intelligible. However, our under-standing, through its representations, is not the cause of the object (save in the case of moral ends), nor is the object [*Gegenstand*] the cause of the intellectual representations in the mind (*in sensu reali*). Therefore the pure concepts of the understanding must not be abstracted from sense perceptions, nor must they express the reception of representations through the senses; but though they must have their origin in the nature of the soul, they are neither caused by the object [*Obiect*] nor bring the object itself into being. In my dissertation I was content to explain the nature of intellectual representations in a merely negative way, namely, to state that they were not modifications of the soul brought about by the object. However, I silently passed over the further question of how a representation that refers to an object without being in any way affected by it can be possible. I had said: The sensuous representations present things as they appear, the intellectual representations present them as they are. But by what means are these things given to us, if not by the way in which they affect us? And if such intellectual representations depend on our inner activity, whence comes the agreement that they are supposed to have with objects— objects that are nevertheless not possibly produced thereby? And the axioms of pure reason concerning these objects—how do they agree with these objects, since the agreement has not been reached with the aid of experience? In mathematics this is possible, because the objects before us are quantities and can be represented as quantities only because it is possible for us to produce their mathematical representations (by taking numerical units a given number of times). Hence the concepts of the quantities can be spontaneous and their principles can be determined a priori. But in the case of relationships involving qualities—as to how my understanding may form for itself concepts of things completely a priori, with which concepts the things must necessarily agree, and as to how my understanding may formulate *real* principles concerning the possibility of such concepts, with which principles experience must be in exact agreement and which nevertheless are independent of experience—this question, of how the faculty of the understanding achieves this conformity with the things themselves, is still left in a state of obscurity.

Plato assumed a previous intuition of divinity as the primary source of the pure concepts of the understanding and of first principles. Mallebranche [*sic*] believed in a still-continuing perennial intuition of this primary being. Various moralists have accepted precisely this view with respect to basic moral laws. Crusius believed in certain implanted rules for the purpose of forming judgments and ready-made concepts that God implanted in the human soul just as they had to be in order to harmonize with things. Of these systems, one may call the former the *influxus hyperphysicus* and the latter the *harmonia praestabilita intellectualis*. But the *deus ex machina* is the greatest absurdity one could hit upon in the determination of the origin and validity of our knowledge. It has—besides its deceptive circle in the conclusion concerning our cognitions—also this additional disadvantage: it encourages all sorts of wild notions and every pious and speculative brainstorm.

While I was searching in such ways for the sources of intellectual knowledge, without which one cannot determine the nature and limits of metaphysics, I divided this science into its naturally distinct parts, and I sought to reduce the transcendental philosophy (that is to say, all concepts belonging to completely pure reason) to a certain number of categories, but not like Aristotle, who, in his ten predicaments, placed them side by side as he found them in a purely chance juxtaposition. On the contrary, I arranged them according to the way they classify themselves by their own nature, following a few fundamental laws of the understanding. Without going into details here about the whole series of investigations that has continued right down to this last goal, I can say that, so far as my essential purpose is concerned, I have succeeded and that now I am in a position to bring out a "Critique of Pure Reason" that will deal with the nature of theoretical as well as practical knowledge—insofar as the latter is purely intellectual. Of this, I will first work out the first part, which will deal with the sources of metaphysics, its methods and limits. After that I will work out the pure principles of morality. With respect to the first part, I should be in a position to publish it within three months.

In mental preoccupation of such delicate nature, nothing is more of a hindrance than to be occupied with thoughts that lie outside the scope of the field. Even though the mind is not always exerting itself, it must still, both in its relaxed and happy moments, remain uninterruptedly open to any chance suggestion that may present itself. Encouragements and diversions must serve to maintain the mind's powers of flexibility and mobility, whereby it is kept in readiness to view the subject matter from other sides all the time and to widen its horizon from a microscopic observation to a universal outlook in order that it may adopt all conceivable positions and that views from one may verify those from another. There has been no other reason than this, my worthy friend, for my delay in answering your pleasant letters—for you certainly don't want me to write you empty words.

With respect to your discerning and deeply thoughtful little work, several parts have exceeded my expectations.[1] However, for reasons already mentioned, I cannot let myself go in discussing details. But, my friend, the effect that an undertaking of this kind has on the status of the sciences among the educated public is such that when, because of the indisposition that threatens to interrupt its execution, I begin to feel anxious about my project (which I regard as my most important work, the greater part of which I have ready before me)—then I am frequently comforted by the thought that my work would be just as useless to the public if it is published as it would be if it remains forever unknown. For it takes a literary man with more reputation and eloquence than I have to stimulate his readers in such a way that they exert themselves to meditate on his writing.

I have found your essay reviewed in the Breslau paper and, just recently, in the Göttingen paper. If the public judges the spirit and principal intent of an essay in such a fashion, all effort is in vain. If the reviewer has taken pains to grasp the essential points of the effort, his criticism is more welcome to the author than all the excessive praise resulting from a superficial evaluation. The Göttingen reviewer dwells on several applications of the system that in themselves are trivial and with respect to which I myself have since changed my views—with the result, however, that my major purpose has only gained thereby. A single letter from Mendelssohn or Lambert means more to an author in terms of making him re-examine his theories than do ten such opinions from superficial pens. Honest Pastor Schultz, the best philosophical brain I know in this neighborhood, has grasped the points of the system very well; I wish that he might get busy on your little essay, too. There are two mistaken interpretations in his evaluation of the system that he is examining. The first one is the criticism that space, instead of being the pure form of sensuous appearance, might very well be a true intellectual intuition and thus might be objective. The obvious answer is that there is a reason why space is not given in advance as objective or as intellectual, namely, if we analyze fully the representation of space, we have in it neither a repre-

[1] Herz's *Betrachtungen aus der spekulativen Weltweisheit* (1771).

sentation of things (as capable of existing only in space) nor a real connection (which cannot occur without things); that is to say, we have no effects, no relationships to regard as grounds, consequently no real representation of an object or anything real, nothing of what inheres in the thing, and therefore we must conclude that space is nothing objective.

The second misunderstanding leads him to an objection that has made me reflect considerably, because it seems to be the most serious objection that can be raised against the system, an objection that seems to occur naturally to everybody, and one that Mr. Lambert has raised.[2] It runs like this: Changes are something real (according to the testimony of inner sense). Now, they are possible only on the assumption of time; therefore time is something real that is involved in the determination of the things in themselves.

Then I asked myself: Why does one not accept the following parallel argument? Bodies are real (according to the testimony of outer sense). Now, bodies are possible only under the condition of space; therefore space is something objective and real that inheres in the things themselves. The reason lies in the fact that it is obvious, in regard to outer things, that one cannot infer the reality of the object from the reality of the representation, though in the case of inner sense the thinking or the existence of thought and the existence of my own self are one and the same. The key to this problem lies herein. There is no doubt that I must think my own state under the form of time and that therefore the form of the inner sensibility does give me the appearance of changes. I do not deny that changes are real, any more than I deny that bodies are real, even though by *real* I only mean that something real corresponds to the appearance. I can't even say that the inner appearance changes, for how would I observe this change if it doesn't appear to my inner sense? If one should say that it follows from this that everything in the world is objectively and in itself unchangeable, then I would reply: Things are neither changeable nor unchangeable. Just as Baumgarten states in his *Metaphysics,* paragraph 18: "The absolutely impossible is neither hypothetically possible nor impossible, for it cannot be considered under any condition," so also here, the things of the world are objectively or

[2] See Lambert's letter of October 13, 1770 [61].

in themselves neither in one and the same state at different times nor in different states, for thus understood they are not in time at all.

But enough about this. It appears that one doesn't obtain a hearing by stating only negative propositions. One must rebuild on the plot where one has torn down, or at least, if one has cleared away the brainstorms, one must make the pure insights of the understanding dogmatically intelligible and delineate their limits. With this I am now occupied, and this is the reason why, often contrary to my own intent of answering friendly letters, I withhold from such tasks what free time my very frail constitution allows me for contemplation and give myself over to the net of my thoughts. And so long as you find me so negligent in replying, you should also give up the idea of repaying me and suffer me to go without your letters. Even so, I would count on your constant affection and friendship for me just as you may always remain assured of mine. If you will be satisfied with short answers then you shall have them in the future. Between us the assurance of the honest concern that we have for each other must take the place of formalities.

I await your next delightful letter as a token of your sincere reconciliation. And please fill it up with such accounts as you must have aplenty, living as you do at the very seat of the sciences, and please excuse my taking the liberty of asking for this. Greet Mr. Mendelssohn and Mr. Lambert, likewise Mr. Sultzer, and convey my apologies to these gentlemen for similar reasons.

Do remain forever my friend, just as I am yours!

I. KANT

Königsberg

To Marcus Herz [toward the end of 1773]

- 79 -   VOL. X, pp. 143–46

Noble sir,
Esteemed friend,

It pleases me to receive news of the good progress of your endeavors, but even more to see the signs of kind remembrance and of friendship in the communications imparted to me. Training in the practice of medicine, under the guidance of a capable teacher, is exactly what I wish. The cemetery must in the future not be filled before the young doctor has learned how to attack the disease properly. Do make many careful observations. Here as elsewhere, theories are often directed more to the relief of the idea than to the mastery of the phenomenon. Macbride's *Systematic Medical Science*[1] (I believe you are already acquainted with it) appealed to me very much in this regard. In general, I now feel much better than before. The reason is that I now understand better what makes me ill. Because of my sensitive nerves, all medicines are without exception poison for me. The only thing I very occasionally use is a half teaspoonful of fever bark with water, when I am plagued by acid before noon. I find this much better than any absorbentia. But I have given up the daily use of this remedy, with the intention of strengthening myself. It gave me an irregular pulse, especially toward evening, which rather frightened me, until I guessed the cause and, adjusting it, relieved the indisposition. Study the great variety of constitutions. My own would be destroyed by any doctor who is not a philosopher.

You search industriously but in vain in the book fair catalog for a certain name beginning with the letter *K*. After the great effort I have made on the not inconsiderable work that I have almost completed, nothing would have been easier than to let my name be paraded therein. But since I have come this far in my projected reworking of a science that has been so long cultivated in vain by half the philosophical world, since I see myself in possession of a principle that will completely solve what has hitherto been a riddle and that will bring the misleading qualities of the self-alienating understanding under certain and easily applied rules, I therefore remain obstinate in my resolve not to let myself be seduced by any author's itch into seeking fame in easier, more popular fields, until I shall have freed my thorny and hard ground for general cultivation.

I doubt that many have tried to formulate and carry out to completion an entirely new conceptual science. You can hardly imagine how much time and effort this project requires, considering the method, the divisions, the search for exactly appropriate

---

[1] David Macbride (1726–78), a physician in Dublin. A German translation of his *A Methodical Introduction to the Theory and Practice of Physic* (London, 1772) was published in 1773.

terms. Nevertheless, it inspires me with a hope that, without fear of being suspected of the greatest vanity, I reveal to no one but you: the hope that by means of this work philosophy will be given a durable form, a different and—for religion and morality—more favorable turn, but at the same time that philosophy will be given an appearance that will make her attractive to shy mathematicians, so that they may regard her pursuit as both possible and respectable. I still sometimes hope that I shall have the work ready for delivery by Easter. Even when I take into account the frequent indispositions that can always cause interruptions, I can still promise, almost certainly, to have it ready a little after Easter.

I am eager to see your investigation of moral philosophy appear. I wish, however, that you did not want to apply the concept of reality (perfection) to moral philosophy, a concept that is so important in the highest abstractions of speculative reason and so empty when applied to the practical. For this concept is transcendental, whereas the highest practical elements are pleasure and displeasure, which are empirical, and their object may thus be anything at all. Now, a mere pure concept of the understanding cannot state the laws or prescriptions for the objects of pleasure and displeasure, since the pure concept is entirely undetermined in regard to objects of sense experience. The highest ground of morality must not simply be inferred from the pleasant; it must itself be pleasing in the highest degree. For it is no mere speculative idea; it must have the power to move. Therefore, though the highest ground of morality is intellectual, it must nevertheless have a direct relation to the primary springs of the will.

I shall be glad when I have finished my transcendental philosophy, which is actually a critique of pure reason, as then I can turn to metaphysics, which has only two parts, the metaphysics of nature and the metaphysics of morals, of which I shall present the latter first. I therefore look forward to the future.

I have read your review of Platner's *Anthropologie*.[2] I would not have guessed the reviewer by myself at this time, and I was pleased by the evident progress of his skill. This winter I am giving, for the second time, a lecture course on anthropology, a subject that I now intend to make into a proper academic discipline. But my plan is quite unique. I intend to disclose the bases

[2] Herz reviewed Ernst Platner's *Anthropologie für Ärzte und Weltweise* (Leipzig, 1772) in the *Allgemeine deutsche Bibliothek*, XX (1773), No. 1, pp. 25–51.

of all sciences, the principles of morality, of skill, of human intercourse, of the method of molding and governing men, and thus of everything that pertains to the practical. I shall seek to discuss phenomena and their laws rather than the possibility of modifying universal human nature. Hence the subtle and, to my view, eternally futile inquiries as to the manner in which bodily organs are connected with thought I omit entirely. I include so many observations of ordinary life that my listeners have constant occasion to compare their ordinary experience with my remarks and thus, from beginning to end, find the lectures entertaining and never dry. In my spare time, I am trying to prepare a preliminary study for the students out of this very pleasant empirical study, an analysis of the nature of skill (prudence) and even wisdom that, along with physical geography and distinct from all other learning, can be called knowledge of the world.

I saw my portrait in front of the library. It is an honor that disturbs me a little, for, as you know, I earnestly avoid all appearance of surreptitiously seeking eulogies or ostentatiously creating a stir. The portrait is well struck though not striking. I note with pleasure that this project stems from the amiable partisanship of my former students.

The review of your work that appears in the same issue [3] proves what I feared: that it takes quite a long time to put new thoughts into such a light that a reader may get the author's specific meaning and the weight of his arguments, until the reader may reach the point where such thoughts are fully and easily familiar.

I am, with most sincere affection and regard,

Your devoted servant and friend,
I. KANT

To J. C. Lavater, April 28, 1775

- 99 - VOL. X, pp. 176–79

. . . You ask for my opinion of your discussion of faith and prayer. Do you realize whom you are asking? A man who believes

[3] Lambert's review of Herz's commentary on Kant's dissertation. Herz's essay, *Betrachtungen aus der spekulativen Weltweisheit*, was published in 1771.

that, in the final moment, only the purest candor concerning our most hidden inner convictions can stand the test and who, like Job, takes it to be sin to flatter God and make inner confessions, perhaps forced out by fear, that fail to agree with what we freely think. I distinguish the *teachings of Christ* from the *report* we have of those teachings. In order that the former may be seen in their purity, I seek above all to separate out the moral teachings from all the dogmas of the New Testament. These moral teachings are certainly the fundamental doctrine of the Gospels, and the remainder can only serve as an auxiliary to them. Dogmas tell us only what God has done to help us see our frailty in seeking justification before Him, whereas the moral law tells us what we must do to make ourselves worthy of justification. Suppose we were ignorant of what God does and suppose we were convinced only of this: that, because of the holiness of His law and the insuperable evil of our hearts, God must have hidden some supplement to our deficiencies somewhere in the depth of His decrees, something we could humbly rely on, if only we should do what is in our power, so as not to be unworthy of His law. If that were so, we should have all the guidance we need, whatever the manner of communication between the divine goodness and ourselves might be. Our trust in God is unconditional, that is, it is not accompanied by any inquisitive desire to know how His purposes will be achieved or, still less, by any presumptuous confidence that the soul's salvation will follow from our acceptance of certain Gospel disclosures. That is the meaning of the moral faith that I find in the Gospels, when I seek out the pure, fundamental teachings that underlie the mixture of facts and revelations there. Perhaps, in view of the opposition of Judaism, miracles and revelations were needed, in those days, to promulgate and disseminate a pure religion, one that would do away with all the world's dogmas. And perhaps it was necessary to have many *ad hominem* arguments, which would have great force in those times. But once the doctrine of the purity of conscience in faith and of the good transformation of our lives has been sufficiently propagated as the only true religion for man's salvation (the faith that God, in a manner we need not at all understand, will provide what our frail natures lack, without our seeking His aid by means of the so-called worship that religious fanaticism always demands)—when this true religious structure has been built up so that it can maintain itself in the world—then the scaffolding must be taken down. I respect the reports of the evangelists and apostles, and I put my humble trust in that means of reconciliation with God of which they have given us historical tidings—or in any other means that God, in his secret counsels, may have concealed. For I do not become in the least bit a better man if I know this, since it concerns only what God does; and I dare not be so presumptuous as to declare before God that this is the real means, the only means whereby I can attain my salvation and, so to speak, swear my soul and my salvation on it. For what those men give us are only their reports. I am not close enough to their times to be able to make such dangerous and audacious decisions. Moreover, even if I could be sure, it would not make me in any way more worthy of the good, were I to confess it, swear it, and fill up my soul with it, though that may be of help to some people. On the contrary, nothing is needed for my union with this divine force except my using my natural God-given powers in such a way as not to be unworthy of His aid or, if you prefer, unfit for it.

When I spoke of New Testament dogmas I meant to include everything of which one could become convinced only through historical reports, and I also had in mind those confessions or ceremonies that are enjoined as a supposed condition of salvation. By "moral faith" I mean the unconditional trust in divine aid, in achieving all the good that, even with our most sincere efforts, lies beyond our power. Anyone can be convinced of the correctness and necessity of moral faith, once it is made clear to him. The auxiliary historical devices are not necessary for this, even if some individuals would in fact not have reached this insight without the historical revelation. Now, considered as history, our New Testament writings can never be so esteemed as to make us dare to have unlimited trust in every word of them, and especially if this were to weaken our attentiveness to the one necessary thing, namely, the moral faith of the Gospels, whose excellence consists in just this: that all our striving for purity of conscience and the conscientious conversion of our lives toward the good are here drawn together. Yet all this is done in such a way that the holy law lies perpetually before our eyes and reproaches us continually for even the slightest deviation from the divine will, just as though we were condemned by a just and unrelenting judge. And no confession of faith, no appeal to holy names nor any observance of religious ceremonies can help—though the consoling hope is offered us that, if we do as much good as is in our power, trusting in the unknown and mysterious help of God, we shall (without meritorious "works" of any sort) partake of this divine supplement. Now, it is very clear that the apostles took this biblical doctrine of divine aid as the fundamental thesis of the Gospels, and whatever might be the actual *basis* of our salvation from God's point of view, the apostles took the essential requirement for salvation to be not the honoring of the holy teacher's religious doctrine of conduct but rather the veneration of this teacher himself and a sort of wooing of favor by means of ingratiation and encomium—the very things against which that teacher had so explicitly and repeatedly preached. Their procedure was in fact more suitable for those times (for which they were writing, without concern for later ages) than for our own. For in those days the old miracles had to be opposed by new miracles, and Jewish dogmas by Christian dogmas.

Here I must quickly break off, postponing the rest till my next letter (which I enclose). My most devoted compliments to your worthy friend Mr. Pfenniger.

Your sincere friend,
I. KANT

To J. C. Lavater [after April 28, 1775]

(Enclosed in the previous letter)

- 100 - VOL. X, *pp. 179–80*

I would rather add something incomplete to my interrupted letter than nothing at all. My presupposition is that no book, whatever its authority might be—yes, even one based on the testimony of my own senses—can substitute for the religion of conscience. The latter tells me that the holy law within me has already made it my duty to answer for everything I do and that I must not dare to cram my soul with devotional testimonies, confessions, and so on, which do not spring from the unfeigned and unmistaking precepts of that law. For although statutes may bring about the performance of rituals, they cannot beget inner convictions. Because of this presupposition, I seek in the Gospels not the ground of my faith but its fortification, and I find in the moral spirit of the Gospels a clear distinction between what I am obligated to do and the manner in which this message is to be introduced into the world and disseminated, a distinction, in short, between my duty and that which God has done for me. The means of disclosure of my obligations may be what it will—nothing new is thereby provided for me, though my good convictions are given new strength and confidence. So much for the clarification of that part of my letter in which I spoke of the separation of two related but unequivalent parts of the holy scriptures and of their application to me.

As for your request that I give my opinion of the ideas on faith and prayer in your *Vermischte Schriften* ("Miscellaneous Writings" [1774]), the essential and most excellent part of the teachings of Christ is this: that righteousness is the sum of all religion and that we ought to seek it with all our might, having faith (that is, an unconditional trust) that God will then supplement our efforts and supply the good that is not in our power. This doctrine of faith forbids all our presumptuous curiosity about the manner in which God will do this, forbids the arrogance of supposing that one can know what means would be most in conformity with His wisdom; it forbids, too, all wooing of favor by the performing of rituals that someone has introduced. It allows no part of that endless religious madness to which people in all ages are inclined, save only the general and undefined trust that we shall partake of the good in some unknown way, if only we do not make ourselves unworthy of our share of it by our conduct.

To C. H. Wolke, March 28, 1776

- 109 - VOL. X, *pp. 191–94*

Noble sir,
Esteemed professor,

With sincerest pleasure I take this opportunity, while carrying out an assignment I have been given, to let you know of my great sympathy for your excellent school, the Philanthropin.

Mr. Robert Motherby, a local English merchant and my dear friend, would like to entrust his only son, George Motherby, to the care of your school. Mr. Motherby's principles agree completely with those upon which your institution is founded, even in those respects in which it is farthest removed from ordinary assumptions about education. The fact that something is unusual will never deter him from freely agreeing to your proposals and arrangements in all that is noble and good. His son will be six years old on the seventh of August this year. But though he has not reached the age you require, I believe that his natural abilities and motivations are already such as to satisfy the intent of your requirement. That is why his father wants no delay in bringing the boy under good guidance, so that his need for activity may not lead him to any bad habits that would make his subsequent training more difficult. His education thus far has been purely negative, which I regard as the best that can be done for a child in those years. He has been allowed to develop his nature and his healthy reason in a manner appropriate to his years, without compulsion, and has been restrained only from those things that might set his mind in a wrong direction. He has been brought up without inhibitions, but not so as to be troublesome. He has never experienced force and has always been kept receptive to gentle suggestions. Though his manners are not the finest, he has been taught not to be naughty, but without his being reprimanded into bashfulness and timidity. This was all the more necessary in order that a real ingenuousness might establish itself in him and especially so that he would not come to feel a need to lie. Some of his childish transgressions have therefore been excused so as not to give him the temptation to break the rule of truthfulness. Besides this, the only thing he has been taught is to write in Latin script when the letters are recited for him. He can do this (but only with a lead pencil). He is thus a blank slate on which nothing has yet been scribbled, a slate that should now be turned over to a master hand, so that the unerasable characteristics of sound reason, of knowledge and righteousness, may be inscribed upon it.

In matters of religion, the spirit of the Philanthropin agrees perfectly with that of the boy's father. He wishes that even the natural awareness of God (as the boy's growth in age and understanding may gradually make him arrive at it) should not be aimed at devotional exercises directly but only after he has realized that these are valuable merely as a means of animating an effective conscience and a fear of God, so that one does one's duties as though they were divinely commanded. For it is folly to regard religion as nothing more than a wooing of favor and an attempt to ingratiate oneself with the highest being, since this results in reducing the differences among various religions to differences of opinion as to what sort of flattery is most appealing to God. This illusion, whether based on dogmas or independent of them, is one that undermines all moral dispositions, for it takes something other than a conversion to righteousness to be the means of surreptitiously currying favor with God, as though one need not be too fastidious about righteousness since one has another exit ready in case of emergency.

It is for this reason that our pupil has been kept ignorant of religious ceremonies. It may take a certain amount of skill, therefore, to give him a clear idea of their meaning when, at your discretion, he first attends such ceremonies. But he is being placed in the charge of a man who is accustomed to finding wisdom whence it truly springs, a man whose judgment can always be trusted. It would also please the boy's father very much if in the future the Philanthropin were also to teach English according to your easy and reliable method, for the boy will be going to England when his education is completed.

The child has already had measles and the pox, and no particular care need be taken about illnesses.

The father will be happy to pay the 250 thaler annual boarding fee, according to whatever arrangements you wish.

He asks your advice about what clothes, beds, and necessary equipment are customary in your school. He hopes that it may be possible to send the boy this summer, so that the amusements you have organized for your pupils will make him like his new surroundings. If you have no one who could escort him, there is a reliable foreign merchant who can bring him along toward the end of July.

All of these are firm decisions, not just tentative plans. I therefore hope to hear from you soon, even if only a brief reply, for I realize how busy you are with your important work. I am most sympathetic to the noble labors to which you have dedicated yourself.

Your sincere admirer, friend, and servant,
IMMANUEL KANT
Professor of Philosophy

To Marcus Herz, November 24, 1776

- 112 - VOL. X, *pp. 198–200*

[Kant begs that he not be compared with Lessing. As yet he has not earned it, though he hopes to. He finds his work on "The Critique of Pure Reason" often tedious; he is tempted not to follow his plan but to work instead on something easier. Yet he is drawn back.]

. . . It must be possible to survey the field of pure reason, that is, of judgments that are independent of all empirical principles, since this lies a priori in ourselves and need not await any exposure from our experience. What we need in order to indicate the divisions, limits, and the whole content of that field, according to secure principles, and to lay the road marks so that in the future one can know for sure whether one stands on the floor of true reason or on that of sophistry—for this we need a critique, a discipline, a canon, and an architectonic of *pure reason,* a formal science, therefore, that can require nothing of those sciences already at hand and that needs for its foundations an entirely unique technical vocabulary. I do not expect to be finished with this work before Easter and shall use part of next summer for it, to the extent that my incessantly interrupted health will allow me to work. But please do not let these intentions arouse any expectations, which are sometimes likely to be disappointed.

And now dear friend, I beg of you not to be offended by my negligence in writing but hope that you will honor me with news, especially literary, from your region. My most devoted regards to Mr. Mendelssohn, and also to Mr. Engel, Mr. Lambert, and Mr. Bode, who greeted me via Dr. Reccard.

Your most devoted servant and friend,

I. KANT

To Marcus Herz, August 20, 1777

- 120 - VOL. X, *pp. 211–14*

Noble doctor,
Dearest friend,

Today Mr. Mendelssohn, your worthy friend and mine (for so I flatter myself), is departing. To have a man like him in Königsberg on a permanent basis, as an intimate acquaintance, a man of such gentle temperament, good spirits, and enlightenment —how that would give my soul the nourishment it has lacked so completely here, a nourishment I miss more and more as I grow older! For as far as bodily nourishment goes, you know I hardly worry about that and I am quite content with my share of earthly goods. I fear I did not manage to take full advantage of my one opportunity to enjoy this rare man, partly because I worried about interfering with his business here. The day before yesterday he honored me by attending two of my lectures, taking potluck, so to speak, since the table was not set for such a distinguished guest. The lecture must have seemed somewhat incoherent to him, since I had to spend most of the hour reviewing what I had said before vacation. The clarity and order of the original lecture were largely absent. Please help me to keep up my friendship with this fine man.

You have made me two presents, dear friend, that show me that both in talent and in feeling you are that rare student who makes all the effort that goes into my often thankless job seem amply rewarded.

Your book for doctors was thoroughly appealing to me and gave me genuine pleasure, though I cannot take the slightest credit for the honor it will bring you.[1] An observant, practical mind shines through the book, along with that subtle handling of general ideas that I have noticed in you before. You are sure to achieve distinction in the medical profession if you continue to practice the art not simply as a means of livelihood but as a way of

[1] *Briefe an Aerzte* (Mitau, 1777).

satisfying the curiosity of the experimental philosopher and the conscientiousness of the humanitarian within you.

Of the various indispositions that constantly plague me and often make me interrupt my intellectual endeavors (heartburn seems to be the general cause, though I seem to all my acquaintances just as healthy as I was twenty years ago), there is one complaint you may be able to help me with: I am not exactly constipated, but I have such a difficult and usually insufficient evacuation every morning that the remaining feces that accumulate become the cause, as far as I can tell, not only of that gas I mentioned but also of my clouded brain. To counteract this, I have sought relief in the past three weeks (when nature did not help me out with an unusual evacuation) through gentle purgatives. They did sometimes help, by accelerating an unusual movement. Most of the time, though, they produced a merely fluid evacuation, without dislodging the bulk of the impure stuff, and caused not only a feeling of weakness (which diuretic purgatives always do) but also an ensuing constipation. My doctor and good friend did not know what prescription would be exactly right for my condition.[2] I notice in Monro's book on dropsy a classification of purgatives that corresponds exactly to my idea.[3] He distinguishes *hydragogic* (diuretic) and *eccoprotic* (laxative) and notices correctly that the former cause weakness. He says that the strongest of diuretics is jalap resin [*resina Jalappae*] and that senna leaves and rhubarb are milder. On the other hand, he regards crystals of cream of tartar and tamarinds as laxatives, which is what I need. Mr. Mendelssohn says that he himself has found the latter useful and that it consists of the pulp of the tamarinds. I would be most grateful to you if you would write me a prescription for this, which I could use from time to time. The dosage must be small for me, for I have usually reacted more than I wanted to from a smaller dosage than the doctor prescribed. Please arrange it so that I can take more or less, as necessary.

I think your second gift robs you of an enjoyable and expensive collection, just to prove your friendship for me, a friendship that is all the more delightful because it springs from the pure sources of an excellent understanding. I have already entertained some of my

[2] Johann Gerhard Trummer.

[3] Donald Monro (1729–92), *An Essay on the Dropsy and its Different Species* (London, 1756). A German translation by K. C. Krause was published in Leipzig, 1777.

friends with this book, a stimulant to good taste and the knowledge of antiquity. I wish that this pleasure of which you have deprived yourself could be replaced in some way.

Since we parted company my philosophical investigations, gradually extended to all sorts of topics, have taken systematic form, leading me slowly to an idea of the whole system. Not until I have that will it be possible to judge the value and interrelationships of the parts. There is an obstacle to the completion of my "Critique of Pure Reason," and all my efforts are now devoted to removing it. I hope to be through this winter. The thing that detains me is the problem of presenting these ideas with total clarity. I know that something can seem clear enough to an author himself and yet be misunderstood even by knowledgeable readers, if it departs entirely from their accustomed way of thinking.

Every news of your growing success, honors, and domestic good fortune is received with the greatest interest by

Your always devoted friend and servant,
I. Kant

To Marcus Herz, August 28, 1778

- 140 - VOL. X, *pp. 240–42*

Most worthy friend,

I should be very pleased to gratify your wish, especially when the purpose is connected with my own interest.[1] However, it is impossible for me to do so as quickly as you ask. Whatever depends on the diligence and aptitude of my students is invariably difficult, because it is a matter of luck whether one has attentive and capable students during a certain period of time and also because those whom one has recently had disperse themselves and are not easily to be found again. It is seldom possible to persuade one of them to give away his own transcript. But I shall try to attend to it as soon as possible. I may yet find something here or there on the logic course. But metaphysics is a course that I have

[1] Herz had requested a set of lecture notes that he might use in Berlin for his own lectures on Kant's philosophy.

worked up in the last few years in such a way that I fear it must be difficult even for a discerning head to get *precisely* the right idea from somebody's lecture notes. Even though the idea seemed to me intelligible in the lecture, still, since it was taken down by a beginner and deviates greatly both from my formal statements and from ordinary concepts, it will call for someone with a head as good as your own to present it systematically and understandably.

When I have finished my handbook on that part of philosophy on which I am still working indefatigably, which I think will be soon, then every transcription of that sort will also become fully comprehensible, through the clarity of the over-all plan. In the meantime I shall make an effort to find a serviceable set of lecture notes for your purposes. Mr. Kraus has been in Elking for several weeks but will return shortly, and I shall speak to him about it. Why don't you start with the logic. While that is progressing, the materials for the remaining work will be gathered. Although this is supposed to be a task for the winter, it may be possible to gather the supplies before the summer is over, thus allowing you time for preparation. Mr. Joël says that he left me in good health, and that is so, for I have accustomed myself for many years to regard a very restricted degree of well-being as good health, a degree of which the majority of people would complain, and, to whatever extent I can, I take recreation, rest, and conserve my strength. Without this hindrance my little projects, in the pursuit of which I am otherwise content, would have been brought to completion long ago.

I am, in immutable friendship and dedication,

Your most devoted
I. KANT

P.S. Did you also receive my letter of about a half a year ago, with its enclosure for Breitkopf in Leipzig?

To Marcus Herz, October 20, 1778

- 141 - VOL. X, *pp. 242–43*

Dearest and worthiest friend,

To be of service to my upright and indefatigable capable friend, in a matter that will reflect back some approbation on myself as well, is always pleasant and important to me. However, there are many difficulties in carrying out the commission you gave me. Those of my students who are most capable of grasping everything are just the ones who bother least to take explicit and verbatim notes; rather, they write down only the main points, which they can think over afterward. Those who are most thorough in note-taking are seldom capable of distinguishing the important from the unimportant. They pile a mass of misunderstood stuff under that which they may possibly have grasped correctly. Besides, I have almost no private acquaintance with my listeners, and it is difficult for me even to find out which ones might have accomplished something useful. My empirical psychology is now briefer, since I lecture on anthropology. But since I make improvements or extensions of my lectures from year to year, especially in the systematic and, if I may say, architectonic form and ordering of what belongs within the scope of a science, my students cannot very easily help themselves by copying from each other.

However, I do not abandon the hope of gratifying your wish, especially if Mr. Kraus helps me. He will arrive in Berlin toward the end of November. He is one of my favorite and most capable students. Please have patience until then.

Especially I beg you to do me the favor of announcing to His Excellency, Mr. von Zedlitz,[1] through his secretary, Mr. Biester, that the aforementioned Mr. Kraus will deliver the requested transcript.

My letter to Breitkopf may actually have arrived there, but perhaps he had nothing to reply to the rather negative answer I had to give him; otherwise no reason.

I close hurriedly and am still

Your true friend and servant,
I. KANT

[1] Karl Abraham von Zedlitz (1731–93), minister of education in the Department of Spiritual Affairs, to whom Kant dedicated the *Critique*.

From Marcus Herz, November 24, 1778

- 143 - VOL. X, *pp. 243–45*

Honored professor, revered teacher,

Here I am again, dunning. Isn't it true, dearest sir, I'm an impetuous person? Forgive me, by assuming that I know the man to whom I dare to be impetuous; it can be no one else than he who dwells constantly in the center of my thoughts and my heart!

I am enjoying a degree of happiness this winter to which I never aspired even in my dreams. Today, for the twentieth time, I am lecturing on your philosophical teachings to approbation that exceeds all my expectations. The number of people in my audience grows daily; it is already over thirty, all of them people of high status or profession. Professors of medicine, preachers, lawyers, government administrators, and so on, of whom our worthy minister [Zedlitz] is the leading one; he is always the first to arrive and the last to leave, and until now he has not missed a single session, as neither have any of the others. It seems to me that this course is in many ways a remarkable thing, and not a day passes that I do not reflect on the impossibility of ever repaying you, through any act of mine, the tenth part of the happiness I enjoy in a single hour, which I owe to you and to you alone!

I have now completed half of the logic and hope to be finished with the other half by January. I have several very complete notebooks of your lectures on logic, and to these I owe my audience's applause; here and there your fruitful ideas led me to other views that appeal to my listeners. But the foundations of it all are yours.

It will all depend on you whether I can carry off the metaphysics course. I don't even have complete copies of your lectures, and certainly the whole business will be virtually impossible for me without them. To build up the course from scratch, all alone, is not within my powers, nor have I the time, since most of my time is taken up with my practical work.

I beg you again, therefore, to send me, with the earliest mail, at least some incomplete notebooks, if the complete ones are not to be had. Diversity, I think, will compensate for incompleteness, since each set of notes will have noticed something different. I beg you especially for an ontology and a cosmology.

I take the liberty of recommending to you a young nobleman, Mr. von Nolte, of Kurland, who is passing through here. He is a very clever and well-educated young man, who has been in the service of France for a year and now is going into that of Russia. He will bring you something that should go with your anthology.

From certain letters that Mr. Kraus wrote to his friends, I see how troubled the good man is about his stay here. Please be good enough to assure him that everything will be done to make his stay as pleasant as possible. He is always welcome to dine at Friedländer's, and free lodging has also been arranged.

I am and shall always be, with the greatest respect,

Your honored sir's most devoted servant,
M. Herz

To Marcus Herz, February 4, 1779

- 146 - vol. x, p. 248

. . . A certain misology that you, as I, detected and regretted in Mr. Kraus derives, as does much misanthropy, from this: that in the first instance one loves philosophy, in the second, people, but one finds both ungrateful, partly because one expected too much of them, partly because one is too impatient in awaiting the reward for one's efforts from the two. I know this sullen mood also; but a kind glance from either of them soon reconciles us with them again and serves to make our attachment to them even stronger. . . .

To Marcus Herz, May 1, 1781

- 164 - vol. x, pp. 266–67

In the current Easter book fair there will appear a book of mine, entitled *Critique of Pure Reason*. It is being published by Hartnoch's firm, printed in Halle by Grunert, under the direction of Mr. Spener's Berlin book company. This book contains the result of all the varied investigations, which start from the concepts we discussed under the heading "The sensible world and the intelligible." I am anxious to hand over the summation of my efforts to the same insightful man who deigned to cultivate my ideas, so discerning a man that he penetrated those ideas more deeply than anyone else.

With this in mind I beg you to deliver the enclosed letter in person to Mr. Carl Spener and to arrange the following matters with him; after you talk with him, please send me news with the earliest possible mail, if my demands are not too extravagant.

1. Find out how far along the printing is and on which day of the fair the book will appear in Leipzig.

2. Since I intended that four copies go to Berlin—a dedicatory copy to His Excellency, Minister von Zedlitz, one for you, one for Mr. Mendelssohn, and one for Dr. Sell, which last should please be delivered to the music master Mr. Reichard (who recently sent me a copy of Sell's *Philosophische Gespräche*)—I beg that you ask Mr. Spener to write to Halle immediately and see to it that these four copies be sent to Berlin, at my expense, as soon as the printing is done and that they be delivered to you. Please lay out the postage money for me, have the dedicatory copy elegantly bound, and present it in my name to His Excellency, Mr. von Zedlitz. It is of course taken for granted that this copy will reach Berlin so early that no other could possibly have reached the Minister before it. Please lay out the expenses for me or sign for them in my name. For the copies themselves, there is nothing to pay, for I arranged with Mr. Hartknoch to have ten or twelve of them at my disposal.

As soon as I hear from you about all this I shall take the time to write to you and Mr. Mendelssohn somewhat more fully about this work. Until then, with greatest respect and friendship,

Your devoted servant,
I. KANT

Honored sir, dearest friend,

Sincere thanks for your efforts in distributing the four copies of my book. I am even more thankful that you are determined to study this work thoroughly, despite the fact that you are busy with your own writings (for I hear that you are working on a medical encyclopedia). I can count on such effort only from a very few readers now, though I am most humbly convinced that in time this will become more general; for one cannot expect a way of thinking to be suddenly led off the beaten track into one that has heretofore been totally unused. That requires time, to stay that style of thinking little by little in its previous path and, finally, to turn it into the opposite direction by means of gradual impressions. But from a man who as a student delighted me by grasping my ideas and thoughts more quickly and exactly than any of the others—from this man I can hope that shortly he will grasp those concepts of my system that alone make possible a decisive evaluation of its worth. He, however, who becomes entirely clear about the condition in which metaphysics lies (not only at present, but always), that man will find it worthwhile, after only a cursory reading, at least to let everything lie fallow until the question here at issue is answered. And in this, my work, may it stand or fall, cannot help but bring about a complete change of thinking in this part of human knowledge, a part of knowledge that concerns us so earnestly. For my part I have nowhere sought to create mirages or to advance specious arguments in order to patch up my system; I have rather let years pass by, in order that I might get to a finished insight that would satisfy me completely and at which I have in fact arrived; so that I now find nothing I want to change in the main theory (something I could never say of any of my previous writings), though here and there little additions and clarifications would be desirable. This sort of investigation will always remain difficult, for it includes the *metaphysics of metaphysics*. Yet I have a plan in mind according to which even *popularity* might be gained for this study, a plan that could not be carried out initially, however, for the foundations needed cleaning up, particularly because the whole system of this sort of knowledge had to be exhibited in all its articulation. Otherwise I would have started with what I have entitled the "Antinomy of Pure Reason," which could have been done in colorful essays and would have given the reader a desire to get at the sources of this controversy. But the *school's* rights must first be served; afterward one can also see about appealing to the *world*.

I am very uncomfortable at Mr. Mendelssohn's putting my book aside; but I hope that it will not be forever.[1] He is the most important of all the people who could explain this theory to the world; it was on him, on Mr. *Tetens,* and on *you,* dearest man, that I counted most. Please give him, in addition to my highest regards, a diatetic observation that I made on myself, which, because of the similarity in our studies and our resultant weak health, might serve to restore this excellent man to the learned world, this man who for so long has withdrawn from it, finding that attention to it was incompatible with his health. . . . [Kant then recounts his own symptoms. His suggested remedy is not extant.].

To J. Bernoulli,[1] November 16, 1781

- 172 - VOL. X, *pp. 276–78*

Esteemed sir,

I received your letter of November 1st on the 10th. I have an obligation to satisfy your request in regard to Lambert's correspondence, an obligation that is based not only on my duty to the distinguished man's literary estate but on my own interests as well,

---

[1] Mendelssohn wrote, in a letter to Elise Reimarus, January 5, 1784: "Very nice to hear that your brother does not think much of the 'Critique of Pure Reason.' For my part, I must admit that I don't understand it. The summary that Mr. Garve put in the *Bibliotek* is clear to me, but other people say that Garve didn't understand him properly. It is therefore pleasant to know that I am not missing much if I go thence without understanding this work."

[1] Johann Bernoulli, mathematician and physicist (1744–1807). [A rule divides the footnotes for each letter when, as here, they fall on the same page.]

since the latter are bound up with your proposed publication.[2] It is, however, not entirely within my power to satisfy your expectations. I can tell you the exact date of his first letter: November 13, 1765. But I cannot seem to find his last letter,[3] written in 1770, though I am certain I kept it. However, since I received a letter from the late Mr. Sulzer on December 8, 1770, in answer to one that I wrote to him on the same occasion on which I wrote to Mr. Lambert, namely, when I sent him my dissertation, I suspect that Mr. Lambert's reply may have arrived at about the same time. The excellent man had made an objection to the ideas concerning space and time that I had expressed, an objection that I answered in the *Critique of Pure Reason,* pages 36–38.[4]

You are fully justified in expecting that I would keep a copy of my letters to such an important correspondent—but unfortunately I never wrote him anything worth copying—just because I attached so much importance to the proposal that this incomparable man made to me, that we collaborate on the reform of metaphysics. I saw at that time that this putative science lacked a touchstone with which to distinguish truth from deception, since different but equally persuasive metaphysical propositions lead inescapably to contradictory conclusions, with the result that one proposition inevitably casts doubt on the other. I had some ideas for a possible reform of this science then, but I wanted my ideas to mature first before submitting them to my friend's penetrating scrutiny and further development. For that reason the projected collaboration was postponed again and again, since the enlightment I sought seemed always to be near, yet always distanced itself on further investigation. In the year 1770 I was already able to distinguish clearly the *sensibility* in human knowledge from the *intellectual* part by means of precise limiting conditions [*Grenzzeichen*]. The main steps in this analysis, expressed in my dissertation (mixed with many theses that I should not accept today), I sent to the great man, hoping to have the remainder of my theory ready before long. But then the problem of the *source of the intellectual* elements in our knowledge created new and unforeseen difficulties, and my postponement became all the more necessary as it stretched on, until all the hopes I had set in anticipation of his

---

[2] Bernoulli was preparing an edition of Lambert's correspondence, which appeared between 1782 and 1785.

[3] October 13, 1770 [61].

[4] See Lambert's letter [61] and *Critique of Pure Reason* A 36–39 = B 53–55.

brilliant counsel were shattered by the untimely death of that extraordinary genius. I regret this loss all the more since, now that I think I have found what I was looking for, Lambert would be just the man whose bright and perceptive mind—all the more free of prejudice because of its very *inexperience* in metaphysical speculations and therefore all the more skillful—could have shown me the possible errors in my *Critique of Pure Reason* after examining its propositions in their total context. And with his concern for achieving something stable for human reason, the union of his efforts with mine might have brought about a truly finished piece of work. Even now I do not discount the possibility of such an achievement, but since the project is now deprived of that fine mind, it will be more difficult and more protracted.

These are my reasons for begging pardon of you and the public for not having used that fine opportunity better and the reasons why my answers to the departed man's kind letters are lacking. . . .

Your obedient servant,
I. KANT

To Christian Garve, August 7, 1783

- 205 - VOL. X, *pp. 336–43*

Honored sir,

I have long noticed in you an enlightened philosophical spirit, and I have appreciated your refined taste, the product of wide reading and worldly experience, so that I, along with Sultzer, have regretted the illness that has hampered you from rewarding the world with the total fecundity of your excellent talents. Now I experience the still greater pleasure of finding in your letter clear evidence of your fastidious and conscientious honesty and of your humane manner of thinking, which bestows genuine value upon those intellectual gifts. This last is something I think I cannot say of your friend in Göttingen, who, entirely without cause, has filled his review (which I can call "his" since it mutilates your essay) with the breath of pure animosity.[1] There were, after all, some things in my book that should have deserved mention, even if he did not immediately approve of the explanation of the difficulties I discovered; he should have mentioned them if only for the reason that I first showed those difficulties in their proper light and in their proper context, because I reduced the problem, so to speak, to its simplest terms, even if I did not solve it. Instead, he tramples

[1] J. G. H. Feder distorted Garve's review of the *Critique of Pure Reason*. The review appeared in the *Zugaben zu den Göttinger gelehrten Anzeigen*, January 19, 1782. Kant wrote his *Prolegomena to Any Future Metaphysics* partly in answer to the Garve-Feder review (see the appendix to that work). Feder attempted to justify his actions to Garve, in a letter of May 7, 1782, on the grounds that abbreviation was necessary and that "certain changes will be of help to some of the readers." Garve's review, as written, appeared in the *Allgemeine deutsche Bibliothek*, Suppl. to Vols. XXXVII–LII, Pt. II, pp. 838–62. But according to Hamann's letter to Herder, December 8, 1783, "Kant is not satisfied with it and complains of being treated like an imbecile. He won't answer it; but he will answer the Göttingen reviewer, if the latter dares to review the *Prolegomena*, too." To Johann Schultz, Kant wrote on August 22, 1783, "I have only been able to skim it, because of various distracting tasks; but leaving aside the many scarcely avoidable errors in getting my meaning, it seems to be something quite different and much more thought out than what was in the *Göttingen Anzeige* (which was supposed to be Garve's)."

Kant's only other extant letter to Garve, September 21, 1798, laments Garve's and his own ill health, complains of the "vegetative rather than scholarly condition (eating, walking, and sleeping)" to which he, Kant, is reduced, and makes one extremely interesting remark on the origins of the *Critique of Pure Reason:* "It was not from the investigation of the existence of God, of immortality, and so on, that I started but from the antinomy of pure reason, 'The world has a beginning——; it has no beginning——,' and so on, up to the fourth [*sic*] antinomy: 'Man has freedom'—against this: 'There is no freedom; everything belongs to natural necessity.' These were what first awoke me from the dogmatic slumbers and drove me to the critique of reason itself in order to end the scandal of reason's ostensible contradictions with itself."

Earlier in September, 1798, Garve had sent Kant a copy of his history of ethics, *Uebersicht der vornehmsten Principien der Sittenlehre, von dem Zeitalter des Aristoteles an bis auf unsre Zeiten* (Breslau, 1798). In it, Garve discusses Kant's ethics, and after commending Kant's illumination of the field, the edification of his teachings, and the "sensitivity of his heart," Garve raises the following objections: (1) that Kant starts from unproven presuppositions and develops his ideas according to postulated goals, (2) that his rational law lacks motivations, (3) that he ends by reuniting virtue and happiness after all, in contradiction to his own theory, and (4) that the moral law lacks content. Kant's *Opus Postumum* (Konv. 4, Bl. 3) contains a fragmentary answer to the first charge: "To Garve. My principles are not taken from a certain, previously extracted purpose, for example, what is best for everybody, but simply because that is the way it must be, without any conditions. It is in no way the assumption of a principle [*Grundsatz*]."

everything with a certain impetuosity, yes, I can even say with visible rage. I mention only one small example: he deliberately omits the word "Mr.," which customarily prefaces the word "author" in this newspaper to sweeten a criticism a little bit. I can guess very well who this man is, from his style, especially when he tells us his own ideas. As a contributor to a famous newspaper, he has, if not the honor, at least the reputation of an author in his power for a little while. But he is at the same time himself an author and thereby jeopardizes his own reputation in no small way. But I shall speak no more of this, since you are pleased to call him your friend. Actually he ought to be my friend as well, though in a broader sense, if common interest in the same science and dedicated if misdirected effort to secure its foundations can constitute literary friendship. It seems to me though that here as elsewhere it has failed; this man must have feared to forfeit something of his own pretentions at such innovations as mine, a fear that is entirely groundless. For the issue here does not concern the limitedness of authors but the limitedness of human reason. . . .

You can believe me, esteemed sir, and you can also make inquiries any time with my publisher, Hartknoch, at the Leipzig book fair, that I never believed any of his assurances that you were responsible for the review; and so I am highly pleased to obtain confirmation of my view, through your good letter. I am not so pampered and egotistic that criticism and reprimand—even assuming them to be directed against what I think are the most excellent merits of my work—would provoke me, if the deliberate intent to injure and to distort what is worthy of approval (which may still be found here and there) did not stare one in the face. And I await with pleasure your unmutilated review in the *Allgemeine deutsche Bibliothek*. You have presented your action to me in a most favorable light, with an uprightness and integrity of principles that characterize the true scholar and always fill me with respect, whatever your judgment may turn out to be. Furthermore, I must admit that I have not counted on an immediately favorable reception of my work. That could not be, since the expression of my ideas—ideas that I had been working out painstakingly for twelve years in succession—was not worked out sufficiently to be generally understandable. To achieve that I would have needed a few more years instead of the four or five months I took to complete the book out of fear that such an extensive project would finally become a burden, were I to linger any more, and that my advancing years (I am already sixty) would perhaps make it impossible for me to finish the whole system that I still have in my mind. And I am now actually satisfied with my decision, as the work stands, to such an extent that I should not wish it unwritten for any price, though neither would I want to take on again for any price the long labors that it took to produce it. People will get over the initial numbness caused unavoidably by a mass of unfamiliar concepts and an even more unfamiliar language (which new language is nonetheless indispensable). In time, a number of points will become clear (perhaps my *Prolegomena* will help this). These points will shed light on other passages, to which of course a clarifying essay from me may be requisite from time to time. And thus, finally, the whole work will be surveyed and understood, if one will only get started with the job, beginning with the main question on which everything depends (a question that I have stated clearly enough), gradually examining every part with concerted effort. In a word, the machine is there, complete, and all that needs to be done is to smooth its parts, or to oil them so as to eliminate friction, without which, I grant, the thing will stand still. Another peculiarity of this sort of science is that one must have an idea of the whole in order to rectify all the parts, so that one has to leave the thing for a time in a certain condition of rawness, in order to achieve this eventual rectification. Had I attempted both tasks simultaneously, either my capability or my life span would have proved insufficient.

You choose to mention, as a just criticism, the lack of popular appeal in my work, a criticism that can in fact be made of every philosophical writing, if it is not to conceal what is probably nonsense under a haze of apparent cleverness.* But such popularity cannot be attempted in studies of such high abstraction. If I could only succeed in getting people to go along with me for a stretch, in concepts that accord with those of the schools together

---

* [Kant's footnote] In order to clear myself of the charge that my innovations of language and my impenetrable obscurity cause my readers unnecessary difficulty in grasping my ideas, let me make the following proposal. It is of the highest importance to give a deduction of the pure concepts of the understanding, the categories, that is, to show the possibility of wholly a priori concepts of things in general; for, without this deduction, pure a priori knowledge can have no certainty. Well then, I should like someone to try to do this in an easier, more popular fashion; he will then experience the great difficulties that are to be found in this field of speculation. But he will never deduce the categories from any other source than that which I have indicated, of that I am certain.

with barbarisms of expression, I should like to undertake a popular yet thorough exposition myself (though others will be better at this), for which I already have a plan. For the time being, let us be called dunces [*doctores umbratici*], if only we can make progress with the insight, with whose development the sophisticated public will of course not sympathize, at least until the work emerges from its dark workshop and, seen with all its polish, need not be ashamed of being judged. Be so kind as to have another fleeting glance at the whole and to notice that it is not at all metaphysics that the *Critique* is doing but a whole new science, never before attempted, namely, the critique of *an a priori judging* reason. Other men have touched on this faculty, for instance, Locke and Leibnitz, but always with an admixture of other faculties of knowing. To no one has it even occurred that this faculty is the object of a formal and necessary, yes, an extremely broad, science, requiring such a manifold of divisions (without deviating from the limitation that it considers solely that uniquely pure faculty of knowing) and at the same time (something marvelous) deducing out of its own nature all the objects within its scope, enumerating them, and proving their completeness by means of their coherence in a single, complete cognitive faculty. Absolutely no other science attempts this, that is, to develop a priori out of the mere concept of a cognitive faculty (when that concept is precisely defined) all the objects, everything that can be known of them, yes, even what one is involuntarily but deceptively constrained to believe about them. Logic, which would be the science most similar to this one, is in this regard much inferior. For although it concerns the use of the understanding in general, it cannot in any way tell us to what objects it applies nor what the scope of our rational knowledge is; rather, it has to wait upon experience or something else (for example, mathematics) for the objects on which it is to be employed.

And so, my dearest sir, I beg you, if you should wish to apply yourself any further in this matter, to use your position and influence to encourage my enemies (not my personal enemies, since I am at peace with all the world), the enemies of my book, but not the *anonymous* ones, encourage them not to grab everything or anything at all at once, out of context, but to consider the work in its proper order: first, to examine or grant my theory concerning the distinction between analytic and synthetic knowledge; then, to proceed to the consideration of the general problem, how synthetic a priori knowledge is possible, as I have clearly stated it in the *Prolegomena;* then, to examine successively my attempts to solve this problem, and so on. For I believe I can demonstrate formally that not a single truly metaphysical proposition, torn out of the whole system, can be proved except by showing its relation to the sources of all our pure rational knowledge and, therefore, that it would have to be derived from the concept of the possible system of such cognitions. But regardless of how kind and eager you may be in carrying out my request, I am reconciled to the prevailing taste of our age, which imagines difficult speculative matters to be easy (but does not make them easy), and I believe your kind efforts in this regard will be fruitless. *Garve, Mendelssohn,* and *Tetens* are the only men I know through whose co-operation this subject could have been brought to a successful conclusion before too long, even though centuries before this one have not seen it done. But these men are leary of cultivating a wasteland that, with all the care that has been lavished on it, has always remained unrewarding. Meanwhile people's efforts continue in a constant circle, returning always to the point where they started; but it is possible that materials that now lie in the dust may yet be worked up into a splendid construction.

You are kind enough to praise my presentation of the dialectical contradictions of pure reason, though you are not satisfied with the solution of these antinomies.* If my critic from Göttingen had presented only a single judgment of this sort, I should at least have assumed him to be of good will and would have put the blame on the (not unexpected) failure of most of my sentences to express my meaning, that is, mainly on myself, instead of allowing a certain bitterness into my reply. Or perhaps I would have made no

* [Kant's footnote] The key is already provided, though its initial use is unfamiliar and therefore difficult. It consists in this: that all objects that are given to us can be interpreted in two ways [*nach zweyerley Begriffen nehmen kan*]: on the one hand, as appearances; on the other hand, as things in themselves. If one takes appearances to be things in themselves and demands of those appearances the *absolutely unconditioned* in the series of conditions, one gets into nothing but contradictions. These contradictions, however, fall away when one shows that there cannot be anything wholly unconditioned among appearances; such a thing could only be a thing in itself. On the other hand, if one takes a *thing in itself* (which can contain the condition of something in the world) to be an *appearance,* one creates contradictions where none are necessary, for example, in the matter of freedom; and this contradiction falls away as soon as attention is paid to the variable meaning that objects can have.

answer at all—in any case, only a few complaints at his absolutely condemning everything without having grasped the basic points. But such an insolent tone of contempt and arrogance ran through the review that I was necessarily moved to draw this great genius into the open, if I could, in order to decide, by comparison of his work to my own, however humble the latter may be, whether there really is such a great superiority on his side or whether, perhaps, a certain literary cunning may not lie behind it, an attempt to make people praise whatever agrees with him and condemn whatever opposes. Thus he achieves somewhat of a dominion over all the authors on a given subject (who, if they want to be well thought of, will be compelled to scatter incense and extol the writings of their presumed critic as their guide), and without extravagant effort, he manages to make a name for himself. Judge from this whether I have argued my "dissatisfaction" with the Göttingen critic, as you are pleased to call it, "somewhat harshly."

After your kind explanation of this matter, according to which the actual reviewer must remain incognito, my expectation concerning a challenge comes to nothing, for he would have to submit himself to it voluntarily, that is, reveal himself; but even in that case, I would be bound not to make the slightest public use of the information you have given me as to the true course of the affair. Besides, a bitter intellectual quarrel is so repugnant, and the frame of mind one has to assume in order to carry it on is so unnatural to me, that I would rather assume the most extensive labors in explaining and justifying what I have already written against the sharpest opponents (but against those who base their attacks only on reasons) than to activate and nourish a feeling in myself for which my soul would otherwise never have room. If the reviewer in Göttingen should feel it necessary to answer the statement I made in the newspaper—if he should do this without compromising his person—then I would feel called upon (though without prejudice to my obligation to you) to take appropriate measures to remove this burdensome inequity between an invisible assailant and one who defends himself before the eyes of all the world. A middle course is still open, namely, to reveal himself if not publicly then at least to me in writing (for the reasons I indicated in the *Prolegomena*) and to announce and settle publicly but peacefully the point of the controversy as he picks it out. But here one would like to exclaim: O cares of men! Weak men, you pretend that you are only concerned with truth and the spread of knowledge, whereas in fact it is only your vanity that occupies you!

And so, esteemed sir, let this occasion not be the only one for pursuing our acquaintance, which I so much desire. The sort of character you reveal in your letter (not to mention your excellent talents) is not so abundant in our literary world that a man who values purity of heart, gentleness, and compassion as greater than all science can help but feel a lively desire for closer ties with one who combines in himself these virtues. Any advice, any suggestion, from such an insightful, fine man, will always be treasured by me; and if there is ever any way in which I can reciprocate this favor, the pleasure will be doubled. I am, with true respect and devotion, esteemed sir,

Your most obedient servant,
I. KANT

To Moses Mendelssohn, August 16, 1783

- 206 - VOL. X, *pp. 344–46*

[Kant discusses a man whom Mendelssohn had recommended. He goes on to deny the rumor that he is planning a trip. He subscribes to the medical principle, "Every man has his own particular way of preserving his health, which he must not alter if he values his safety. . . . One lives longest if one does not strain or worry about lengthening one's life but also refrains from shortening it by disturbing the benevolent nature in us."]

. . . That you feel yourself dead to metaphysics does not offend me, since virtually the entire learned world seems to be dead to her, and of course, there is the matter of your nervous indisposition (of which, by the way, there is not the slightest sign in your book, *Jerusalem*). I do regret that your penetrating mind, alienated from metaphysics, cannot be drawn to the *Critique,* which is concerned with investigating the foundations of that structure. However, though I regret this, and regret that the *Critique* repels you, I am not offended by this. For although the book is the product of nearly twelve years of reflection, I completed it hastily, in perhaps four or five months, with the greatest attentiveness to its content but less care about its style and ease of comprehension. Even now I think my decision was correct, for otherwise, if I had delayed further in order to make the book more popular, it would probably have remained unfinished. As it is, the weaknesses can be remedied little by little, once the work is there in rough form. For I am now too old to devote uninterrupted effort both to completing a work and also to the rounding, smoothing, and lubricating of each of its parts. I certainly would have been able to clarify every difficult point; but I was constantly worried that a more detailed presentation would detract both from the clarity and continuity of the work. Therefore I abstained, intending to take care of this in a later discussion, after my statements, as I hoped, would gradually have become understood. For an author who has projected himself into a system and become comfortable with its concepts cannot always guess what might be obscure or indefinite or inadequately demonstrated to the reader. Few men are so fortunate as to be able to think for themselves and at the same time be able to put themselves into someone else's position and adjust their style exactly to his requirements. There is only one Mendelssohn.

But I wish I could persuade you, dear sir (granted that you do not want to bother yourself further with the book you have laid aside), to use your position and influence in whatever way you think best to encourage an examination of my theses, considering them in the following order: One would first inquire whether the distinction between analytic and synthetic judgments is correct; whether the difficulties concerning the possibility of synthetic judgments, when these are supposed to be made a priori, are as I describe them; and whether the completing of a deduction of synthetic a priori cognitions, without which all metaphysics is impossible, is as necessary as I maintain it to be. Second, one would investigate whether it is true, as I asserted, that we are incapable of making synthetic a priori judgments concerning anything but the formal condition of a possible (outer or inner) experience in general, that is, in regard to sensuous intuition and the concepts of the understanding, both of which are presupposed by experience and are what first of all make it possible. Third, one would inquire whether the conclusion I draw is also correct: that the a priori knowledge of which we are capable extends no farther than to objects of a possible experience, with the proviso that this field of possible experience does not encompass all things in themselves; consequently, there are other objects in addition to objects of possible experience—indeed, they are necessarily presupposed, though it is impossible for us to know the slightest thing about them. If we were to get this far in our investigations, the solution to the difficulties in which reason entangles itself when it strives to transcend entirely the bounds of possible experience would make itself clear, as would the even more important solution to the question why it is that reason is driven to transcend its proper sphere of activity. In short, the dialectic of pure reason would create few difficulties any more. From there on, the critical philosophy would gain acceptability and become a promenade through a labyrinth, but with a reliable guidebook to help us find our way out as often as we get lost. I would gladly help these investigations in whatever way I can, for I am certain that something substantial would emerge, if only the trial is made by competent minds. But I am not optimistic about this. Mendelssohn, Garve, and Tetens have apparently declined to occupy themselves with work of this sort, and where else can anyone of sufficient talent and good will be found? I must therefore content myself with the thought that a work like this is, as Swift says, a plant that only flowers when its stem is put into the soil. Meanwhile, I still hope to work out, eventually, a textbook for metaphysics, according to the critical principles I mentioned; it will have all the brevity of a handbook and be useful for academic lectures. I hope to finish it sometime, perhaps in the distant future. This winter I shall have the first part of my [book on] moral [philosophy] substantially completed.[1] This work is more adapted to popular tastes, though it seems to me far less of a stimulus to broadening people's minds than my other work is, since the latter tries to define the limits and the total content of the whole of human reason. But moral philosophy, especially when it tries to complete itself by stepping over into religion without adequate preparation and definition of the critical sort, entangles itself unavoidably either in objections and misgivings or in folly and fanaticism.

Mr. Friedländer [2] will tell you how much I admired the penetration, subtlety, and wisdom of your *Jerusalem*. I regard this book as

---

[1] Possibly the *Foundations of the Metaphysics of Morals*, which appeared in April, 1785.

[2] David Friedländer, friend of Herz and Mendelssohn (1750–1834), a merchant in Königsberg who later became a banker and *Stadrat* in Berlin.

the proclamation of a great reform that is gradually becoming imminent, a reform that is in store not only for your own people but for other nations as well. You have managed to unite with your religion a degree of freedom of thought that one would hardly have thought possible and of which no other religion can boast. You have at the same time thoroughly and clearly shown it necessary that every religion have unrestricted freedom of thought, so that finally even the Church will have to consider how to rid itself of everything that burdens and oppresses man's conscience, and mankind will finally be united with regard to the essential point of religion. For all religious propositions that burden our conscience are based on history, that is, on making blessedness contingent on belief in the truth of those historical propositions. But I am abusing your patience and your eyes, and shall add nothing further except to say that news of your welfare and contentment cannot be more welcome than to your

Most devoted servant,
I. KANT

To Johann Schultz,[1] August 26, 1783

- 210 - VOL. X, *pp. 350–51*

[Kant expresses his pleasure with Schultz's interpretation of him, praises Schultz's intelligence, and so on.]

I can see from your P.S. (as well as from other things you say) how deeply and correctly you have entered into the spirit of the case.[2] You suggest that each third category might well be derived from the preceding two concepts—an entirely correct opinion and one at which you arrived all by yourself, for my own statement of this property of the categories (*Prolegomena* § 39, Remark 1)

---

[1] Johann Schultz (1739–1805), court preacher, professor of mathematics in Königsberg, and Kant's favorite expositor.

[2] In his postcript to a letter of August 21, 1783 [208] Schultz asked "whether in each of the four groups of categories, the third category might not be derived from the first, as follows: totality is a plurality in which no unity is lacking or negated; limitation is a reality containing negation; community is that condition of a substance in which cause and effect are considered together; necessity is the impossibility of non-existence."

could easily be overlooked.[3] This and other properties of the table of categories that I mentioned seem to me to contain the material for a possibly significant invention, one that I am however unable to pursue and that will require a mathematical mind like yours. If an *ars characteristica combinatoria* is at all possible,[4] it would work most excellently with such basic concepts [*Elementarbegriffe*]. And since the conditions of a priori sensibility are entirely different from these concepts (sensation in general, empirically undetermined, must be added to supply the material for them), the former conditions would have an entirely different character. Rules would be possible that would make it perspicuous how objects of sensibility can have a category as predicate (in so far as they are considered as objects of experience), but also vice versa: that categories can in themselves contain no spatial or temporal determinations unless a condition is added to them that enables them to be related to sensible objects. I have touched on similar points already in my "Dissertation on the Sensible World," in the section entitled *De methodo circa sensibilia et intellectualia.* Perhaps your penetrating mind, supported by mathematics, will find a clearer prospect here where I have only been able to make out something hovering vaguely before me, obscured by fog, as it were. . . .

From Johann Schultz, August 28, 1783

- 211 - VOL. X, *pp. 352–53*

You will be kind enough to forgive me, dear sir, for failing to answer your two most excellent letters, but business and other

[3] Kant also added this remark to the second edition of the *Critique,* B 110 f.

[4] Leibniz, in his *Dissertation de arte combinatoria* (1666), proposed a sort of universal algebra that would exhibit the relations among simple ideas. The basic thought was that all complex ideas are compounded from a certain number of simple ideas and that, by constructing an ideal language, the properly selected name of a complex idea would show immediately what the constituent simple ideas were—in other words, that the analysis of the complex could be seen at a glance. The "Art of Combination" would be a method of invention whereby all the possible combinations of simple ideas would be shown, providing a table of all the possibilities in the world.

distractions kept me from it. Thank you for sending me the Garve review. I was very eager to see it and it was pleasant to have my desire satisfied sooner than I expected. The review is far better than that wretched Göttingen review [1] and shows in fact that Mr. Garve has thought his way through your *Critique* with considerable care. Nonetheless, it is so inadequate to that great book that, on the whole, it still casts an unfavorable shadow on it. It seems therefore that my modest essay [2] is not made superfluous by Garve's, all the more so since you are kind enough to assure me that I have been so fortunate as to grasp your meaning almost everywhere. I can therefore hope to realize my goal and make the public aware of the true purpose and meaning of your excellent work, so that people will not need to exert themselves too much— something that philosophers nowadays seem to fear. This has made me resolve to follow your suggestion and publish my discussion not as a review but as an independent book. In this way I need not worry so much about the length and can announce a more complete table of contents and not confine myself to the theory of the schematism, the concepts of reflection, and the necessary proofs of the principles of pure understanding, paralogisms, and antinomies. Now I can discuss the dialectic somewhat more explicitly and clearly. With regard to the latter, I look forward to your promised clarification of what needs to be added, which I know in advance will greatly facilitate my work. With equal pleasure I await your promised suggestions as to how the whole matter can be presented most conveniently and what general problems might be introduced at the outset before presenting your solutions. . . . I really did overlook the place in your *Prolegomena*,[3] which shows me once more how not even the smallest particular of your system has eluded your acute mind. Since I see from this that you actually do recognize every third category to be a concept derivable from the preceding two, it seems to me that the idea I had in mind when I raised this question is quite correct: the third category in each group should be eliminated, and the total number reduced by one third, since I take "category" to mean

---

[1] That is, the review of the *Critique* written by Garve but mutilated by Feder.

[2] *Erläuterungen über des Herrn Professor Kant Kritik der reinen Vernunft*, 1784.

[3] See the letter of August 26, 1783 [210].

simply a basic concept [*Stammbegriff*], that is, a concept that cannot be derived from any prior concept.

The ingenious idea of using the table of categories to invent an *ars characteristica combinatoria,* which you were kind enough to suggest to me, is most excellent and I agree completely that if such a thing were possible at all it would be particularly here. But except for you, I know of no man with sufficient creative genius to carry out such a project. . . .

J. SCHULTZ

To Johann Schultz, February 17, 1784

- 221 - VOL. X, *pp. 366–67*

It gives me special pleasure to learn from Mr. Dengel that your thorough and at the same time popular book on the *Critique* is ready for publication. I had intended to put at your disposal certain suggestions that might help to make my book easier to grasp; but external and internal distractions, among them my usual indisposition, have interrupted this plan several times. And now I am glad that none of those things had any influence on your work, which is so much the more consistent and original in the presentation of your ideas.

Allow me just one observation, dear sir, which I intended to communicate to you in answer to your note of August 22d last year but which only now occurred to me again as I read through your manuscript. I beg you to consider this question more closely in order that a possible major divergence in our views of one of the basic parts of the system may be avoided. This observation concerns the thought you expressed at that time, dear sir, *that there might be only two categories in each class,* since the third category arises out of the union of the first with the second [in each group]. You came to this insight by means of your own acute thinking. However, it does not, in my opinion, have the conse-quence that you draw from it; and thus your suggested change in the system is not required. (It would rob the system of an otherwise very uniform, systematic character.)

For although the third category does certainly arise out of a uniting of the first and second, it does not arise out of their mere conjunction but rather out of a *synthesis* [*Verknüpfung*] *whose possibility itself constitutes a concept,* and this concept is a particular category. Moreover, the third category is sometimes not applicable where the first two are valid. For example, *a year, many years* in future time—these are real [*reale*] concepts; but the totality of future years, the collective unity of a future eternity, which is to be thought as a whole (completed, as it were) cannot be conceived. And even when the third category is applicable, it always contains something more than the first and second alone or taken together, viz., the derivation of the second from the first. (And this is not always possible: for example, necessity is nothing else than existence *insofar as* it could be deduced from possibility; community is the reciprocal *causality* of *substances* with respect to their determinations. But the fact that determinations of one substance can be caused by another substance is an idea that one cannot absolutely presuppose; rather, the idea is one of the syntheses without which no reciprocal relation of objects in space, and consequently no outer experience, would be possible.) In short, I find that just as a syllogism shows in its conclusion something more than the activity of the understanding and judgment required by the premises, viz., *a further particular activity* belonging specifically to reason, so, too, the third category is a particular, to some extent original, concept. (In a syllogism a general rule is stated by the major premise, whereas the minor premise ascends from the particular to the general condition of the rule; the conclusion descends from the general to the particular, that is, it says that what was asserted to stand under a general condition in the major premise is also to be asserted of that which stands under the same condition in the minor premise.) For example, the concepts of *quantum, compositum,* and *totum* belong under the categories of unity, plurality, and totality; but a *quantum,* thought as a *compositum,* would not yet yield the concept of a *totality,* except insofar as the concept of the *quantum* is thought as *determinable* by the composition, which is not possible in the case of every *quantum*—for example, [the totality of] infinite space [cannot be thought as determined by the composition of particular regions or *quanta* of space.]

I hope, dear sir, that you will find these remarks correct and that you will think the issue of whether the system of categories needs to be changed an issue important enough to warrant your attention before your manuscript is printed. For nothing could please our opponents more than to detect dissension over fundamental principles.

But why do I dwell on these things when perhaps you have long ago abandoned these sketchy ideas on the basis of your own reflection and are besides completely free, here as elsewhere, to do as you wish. I have no doubts that your book, as also your ingenious theory of parallel lines,[1] will broaden and extend human knowledge and contribute to your deserved fame. With full respect I am

Your most obedient servant,
I. KANT

P.S. Since I now anticipate reading your work in print, I have the honor of returning with my most devoted thanks the pages you sent to me.

From F. V. L. Plessing,[1] March 15, 1784

- 226 - VOL. X, *pp. 371–72*

Since there is mail leaving for West Prussia I shall send along this note to you, to express my eternal esteem for you and to assure you that I think of you always with the deepest feelings of which my soul is capable. I have been very ill this winter and am still suffering from eye trouble that makes me utterly unfit for work. But now I hope to get better. Because my father happens to be sending letters to Graudenz today, I am writing these few words to thank you for your kindness in carrying out my request, as your letter of February 3 informed me.[2] Trusting in the very noble sentiments I know you to have, I am taking the liberty again of sending three thalers to that same woman, with my most humble

---

[1] *Entdekte Theorie der Parallelen nebst einer Untersuchung über den Ursprung ihrer bisherigen Schwierigkeit* (Königsberg, 1784).

[1] Friedrich Victor Leberecht Plessing (1749–1806). See Introduction, pp. 23–24, and the letter of April 3, 1784 [228].

[2] Kant acted as intermediary in transmitting money from Plessing to a woman whose child Plessing was accused of fathering. See also the letter of April 3, 1784 [228].

request that you deliver them to Mr. John [3] so as to take care of the quarterly compensation. This money is coming via Graundenz. I think that Mr. John can be trusted always to pay the money correctly, but I don't know whether he gets a receipt from that person or not. He has not written me for a year and a day. If I knew some other way to arrange it, I would not bother him with this chore.

As far as I am able and as far as the nature of the case permits, I shall answer your question as to what I meant in saying that fanaticism and superstition are now again threatening us with great restrictions on freedom of thought, indeed, something even worse, and all men of integrity who love humanity are trembling. You have guessed one of the directions from which danger threatens, only you do not picture the magnitude of it. Particularly Jesuits, those enemies of reason and human happiness, are now carrying on their work in every possible manner. Their organization is more powerful than ever, and they infiltrate M-r-n [Freemasons], Catholics, and Protestants. A certain Protestant king is himself supposed to be secretly a J-s-t. These hellish spirits have poisoned the hearts of princes and lords. They are responsible for the pretended toleration the Catholics are evincing, whereby they hope finally to convert the Protestants to Catholicism. Exorcism and similar fanatical nonsense, also alchemy and the like, are things in which the most distinguished people believe. I myself have heard sophisticated people in Berlin talking this way. Also, a former associate of Schröpfer's [4] is staying with an important person in Potsdam or Berlin. The Emperor's edict of toleration [5] is of little consequence, and Belial carries on his game even there.

Just as mankind has always raged against its own welfare, against reason and enlightenment, so, too, it is happening now. The Protestants are trying to combat the Enlightenment (they call it atheism and the work of the devil) by forming societies: one of them has spread its branches through Switzerland, Holland, Germany, and Prussia—even Königsberg. Here, in this locality where sound reason is completely contraband, where the inhabitants are

---

[3] George Friedrich John (1742–1800), author and financial officer.

[4] Johann Georg Schrepfer (1739–74), a leading apostle of Rosicrucianism, also a cafe proprietor in Leipzig. He was influential in the highest government circles, for example, on Bischoffswerder, a favorite of Friedrich Wilhelm II's.

[5] Joseph II of Austria (1741–90) issued his toleration edict in 1781.

nothing but Abderites,[6] there is also a lodge of this society (Urlsperger[7] of Augsburg is the founder, and in Berlin the members whom one may mention publicly include Silberschlag and Apitch.[8]) The Jesuits are behind these societies too, trying to nip reason in the bud as much as they can and to plant the seed of ignorance. How great our king seems to me! And how grateful to him must human reason be! If only he could live another 20 years.[9] It seems that despotism, fanaticism, and superstition are trying to conquer all of Europe. Catholicism and Jesuitism are reaching even England, Denmark, and Sweden. England will soon be overcome.

Forgive me for expressing all these thoughts so crudely. I cannot write more coherently at present. . . .

Plessing

From F. V. L. Plessing, April 3, 1784

- 228 - VOL. X, *pp. 374–78*

Dear sir,
Esteemed sir,

My heartfelt thanks for the trouble and the care that you have up till now always taken on my behalf. I shall never cease to acknowledge my indebtedness for it. The thought of you will be with me always.

I want to answer your letter immediately.[1] You are a just man and have an ardent feeling for the duties of humanity, and therefore your displeasure is aroused against a certain unnamed man, because you believe that he has not adequately done his duty

---

[6] The inhabitants of Abdera were considered proverbially stupid by the ancient Greeks, though Protagoras and Democritus also lived in this Thracian town.

[7] Johann August Urlsperger (1728–1806). The society was the Deutsche Christentums Gesellschaft zur Beforderung reiner Lehre und wahrer Gottseligkeit ("German Christian Society for the Advancement of Pure Doctrine and True Piety").

[8] Johann Esias Silberschlag; Apitch was a merchant.

[9] Frederick the Great died in 1786.

---

[1] Sometime in March, 1784; not extant.

toward a certain woman. Any vivid feeling tends, at some moments, to displace all our other feelings: let us now consider the conduct of that unnamed man more closely, so that perhaps those feelings for him that have been silenced in you for some time might be reawakened. For that man also deserves justice, and a man with your heart will not deny it to him.

First of all, I must assure you, *on my honor and conscience,* that the unnamed one used not the slightest artifice to seduce the person in question. He used neither persuasion nor protestations of love. The woman in question was subdued by the momentary feeling of a merely animal impulse; the unnamed one encountered no resistance. As little as I excuse the unnamed one for sinking into this weakness, he is nevertheless innocent of the offence of leading virtue astray, and he is innocent of this both in the present case and throughout his life. I can swear on the soul of the unnamed one that, had he found even the slightest sign of resistance, which might have betrayed a noble sense of virtue, he would have honored that sentiment. There is still another assurance I can give you in the name of the unnamed one: of the young people of today, he is one who least deserves the charge of leading a dissolute life devoted to the satisfaction of animal instincts in the love of the opposite sex. He could rather be blamed for having been excessive in his nobler metaphysical love, in the most unhappy way, thereby having lost virtually the total health of his body and soul. Only a few times did he give in to animal feelings with that person, and afterward he lived strictly removed from her and felt disgust and inner displeasure with himself.

The unnamed one is supposed to have behaved immorally in that, while engaging in this animal experience, he sought to guard against the unfortunate consequences of his action. Now I regard such illicit satisfactions of love as on the whole unpermissible, but if a man has once succumbed to this natural weakness, is it immoral of him to be moved by the fear of tragic consequences and thus not wholly to give himself up to his instincts in those moments? The confines of this letter do not permit any further discussion of this delicate matter, which can be viewed from so many sides. I only want to ask this one thing: Are married people immoral when, after conception, they continue to satisfy the drive of physical love nevertheless, even though the purpose of procreation cannot thereby be achieved any longer? I think this example is pertinent to the case of the unnamed one; for if it is a moral law, when satisfying this natural impulse, to do it only for the sake of procreation, then married people are immoral when they continue to practice the works of love after the goal of procreation can no longer be achieved. If, however, the unnamed one has really erred in this, I believe that one should not seek the source of this error in his heart—in his moral depravity. He must certainly not have believed at the time (in fact his mental state was highly unusual then, and it would be difficult to find examples of other people with whom to compare his mental state) that he had committed himself to a significantly immoral principle. This can be inferred from his whole behavior. However evil a man may be, he will yet try to have the appearance of a just man, assuming he has not yet been totally unmasked as a scoundrel. He will not freely reveal his innermost thoughts, admitting his evil intentions. The unnamed one, on the other hand, did reveal his thoughts to a distinguished man.[2] So there are only two possibilities: either the unnamed one must be the most simple-minded man in the world, not understanding that he exposes himself to the bitterest scorn by revealing his bad principles; or he must be the most shameless scoundrel, whose insensitivity and impudence have gone so far that disgrace and honor mean nothing to him. I doubt that the unnamed one has in any way given you cause to suspect that he is either entirely simple-minded or a thoroughgoing scoundrel. . . .

Furthermore, the unnamed one is supposed to have acted immorally in that he lied to the woman in question, since, in view of the resemblance between the child and the unnamed man, who has so many *distinguished* features, the truth of her testimony [that he is the father] is thereby confirmed. If the unnamed one has been unfair to that person, he sincerely begs her forgiveness. But having done that, I can assure you with the greatest certainty that the unnamed one had much evidence to support his suspicion. For in the first place, the unnamed one had an experience that is very common in Königsberg; there are so very many lewd females in Königsberg who misuse the names of people they don't know. I know a respected merchant in Königsberg who, within the space of a year, was accused by seven females of having got them pregnant; he swore to me on his honor and conscience that he had not even met all of them, especially the seventh one whom he had

[2] Theodor Gottlieb von Hippel (1741–96), privy war counselor and *Stadtpräsident* of Königsberg.

never seen in his life. He gave money to six of these lewd women, to avoid a spectacle. But he lost his patience with the seventh and threw her out the door, whereupon she sued him (for there are lots of those whore-lawyers in Königsberg; Mr. H[ippel] himself intervened in a praiseworthy manner, so that a few of these wicked men were suspended from practicing law). The woman testified as to the place, the hour, everything very precisely, and the man lost the case. He appealed to Berlin and finally won, but it cost him several hundred thalers. The unnamed one thus at least knew of many cases in which females of that sort practice deceit. True enough, this would not in itself justify his stating positively that her testimony was false. But there was another reason, which he explained to Mr. H., that persuaded him that what she said was false: if in fact her testimony should actually have some basis, he would have to admit his conviction that the male sex does not supply the cause but only the remote occasion of procreation.

Or can the alleged resemblance of the child constitute an adequate proof against the unnamed one? I don't think that this could be defended either on legal or on physical grounds. If it were [considered proof], then, for example, some mothers could be accused of sexual intercourse with animals—for I once saw in Leipzig a nine-year-old child whose body was almost wholly covered with deer hair and who also had other deerlike characteristics, especially the feet.[3] This phenomenon is also illustrated by the example of the late elector of Saxony.[4] Besides this, there are hundreds of cases where numerous resemblances between strangers have been noticed, without the suspicion being warranted that one of them owed his existence to the other. And then one would have to investigate to see whether this resemblance between the child and the unnamed one really exists; the power of the imagination often makes people see things. . . .

[Plessing agrees to double the payments in support of the child anyway, to one reichsthaler every month. He'll do better when his circumstances permit it. He regrets having been weak and causing trouble thereby. Plessing's whole life has been a chain of ills; the path of his life has always been over thorns. Evil always triumphs; goodness is defeated. The woman's present sad circumstances are not his fault. He gave her a great deal of money, which she

---

[3] Perhaps Anna Marie Herrig, b. 1771.

[4] Perhaps Friedrich Christian (1722–63), who suffered from congenital lameness.

mismanaged. There are ten more pages of this letter in the Prussian Academy edition.]

To C. G. Schütz,[1] September 13, 1785

- 243 - VOL. X, *pp. 406–7*

. . . I owe you a review that I promised to write. Dearest friend! You will forgive me for having been prevented from writing it by a feeling of obligation to work on something else, something on which I have felt obliged to work partly by its relationship to my whole project and partly because of the train of my thoughts. Before I can compose the "Metaphysics of Nature," which I have promised to do, I had to write something that is in fact a mere application of it but that presupposes an *empirical* concept. I refer to the metaphysical foundations of the theory of body [*Körperlehre*] and, as an appendix to it, the metaphysical foundations of the theory of soul [*Seelenlehre*]. For the metaphysics [of nature], if it is to be wholly homogeneous, must be a completely pure science. But I wanted to have some concrete examples available to which I could refer in order to make my discourse comprehensible; yet I did not want to bloat the system by including these examples in it. So I finished them this summer, under the title "Metaphysical Foundations of Natural Science" ["Metaphysische Anfangsgründe der Naturwissenschaft"], and I think the book will be welcomed even by mathematicians. It would have been published this Michaelmas, if I hadn't injured my hand and been prevented from writing the ending. The manuscript must now lie till Easter.

Now I am proceeding immediately with the full composition of the "Metaphysics of Morals."[2] Pardon me, therefore, dearest friend, if I cannot send anything to the *Allgemeine Literaturzeitung* for a long time. I am already rather old and find it more difficult now to adjust quickly to different kinds of work. I have to

---

[1] Christian Gottfried Schütz (1747–1832), professor of rhetoric and poetry in Jena. Founder, in 1785, with the aid of Wieland and Bertuch, of the *Allgemeine Literaturzeitung,* a journal devoted to the cause of Kant's philosophy.

[2] In fact it was not until 1797 that Kant published a work with this title.

hold my thoughts together without interruption, lest I lose the thread that unites the whole system. But I shall in any case undertake the review of the second part of Herder's *Ideen*.[3] . . .

From Marcus Herz, February 27, 1786

- 260 - VOL. X, *pp. 431–33*

Esteemed teacher,

You will receive, dearest teacher, via Mr. D. Joel, a copy of my *Essay on Vertigo* [*Versuch über den Schwindel*], which I mentioned in my letter of 25 November. I once expressed the main idea of the work in one of the conversations I was fortunate enough to have with you—I still recall all of them with delight. The idea lay in my mind awaiting adequate knowledge of physiology before it could have whatever weak influence it may have on practice. You see, dearest sir, that I am not entirely disloyal to you, that I am much more a deserter who still wears your uniform and who, while associating with other (not hostile) powers, is still in your service. Or, to express myself less Prussianly, I enjoy wandering around the border towns of both countries, philosophy and medicine, and it gives me joy when I can make suggestions and arrangements for their common government. I think it would be a good thing if similar border areas between philosophy and its neighboring territories were diligently visited by philosophers as well as by people in practical studies and artists of all sorts. The one would avoid thereby the frequently valid charge of useless meditation, the others that of empiricism.

What do you say to the uproar that has started up among our preachers and inspired heads, exorcists and droll poets, enthusiasts and musicians, since and concerning Moses' [Mendelssohn] death, an uproar for which the counselor of Pimplendorf [Pempelfort— the reference is to F. H. Jacobi] gave the signal?[1] If only a man

---

[3] See Kant's *Werke*, VIII, 58–66.

[1] For a general account of the Mendelssohn-Jacobi feud, see the Introduction to this volume of letters. The uproar to which Herz refers is enormously complicated. Mendelssohn had replied to Jacobi's book, *Concerning Spinoza's Theory*. The reply appeared after Mendelssohn's death, entitled *Moses Mendelssohn to the Friends of Lessing: An Appendix to Mr. Jacobi's Corre-*

like you would say "Shut up!" to this swarm of rascals, I bet they would scatter like chaff in the wind. Above all, I wish I had guessed the mischievousness of that foolish lyricist of Wansebeck; in his entire life and thought, the only things that rhyme are the endings of his childish verses. With what resolute malice he misinterprets our Moses, toward whom he had "*a certain tenderness*," just to destroy his fame and esteem. They have been saying here lately that you are going to publish a short essay against Jacobi's book, which seemed all the more probable to me since you did not answer Moses' last letter. If only you would take the opportunity to say something on behalf of your deceased friend against the contemporary and I suppose future irrational Jacobites!

We are now busy putting our Moses' papers in order. His

---

spondence concerning Spinoza's Theory (Berlin, 1786). The editor, a popular philosopher named J. J. Engel, wrote an introduction to the work, saying that the event which prompted Mendelssohn's writing of this work was also that which caused his death (p. iv). Mendelssohn's agitation over Jacobi's book had so stirred up his blood, according to Engel, that, with his nervous system already weakened, only the slightest external stress was needed to kill him. But Mendelssohn himself had told Herz that his illness was caused by a cold he had caught while on a walk to his publisher. A newspaper article claimed that Mendelssohn died nobly, a martyr to his defense of the suppressed rights of reason against fanaticism and superstition; Lavater had given him the first blow, and Jacobi had finished the job. In defense of Jacobi, the composer J. F. Reichardt wrote in the *Berliner Zeitung* that Mendelssohn had not in fact taken the controversy with Jacobi seriously. Engel replied that Reichardt had no right to consider himself one of Mendelssohn's confidants. Herz agreed and wrote as a physician, pointing out the difference between the immediate and dispositional causes of death. Herz and Friedländer contradicted Reichardt as to Mendelssohn's sensitivity to Jacobi's charges. The arguments continued, with the poet M. Claudius joining in on Jacobi's side; he is "that foolish lyricist of Wansebeck" to whom Herz alludes. An anonymous essay (actually by J. H. Schulz) maintained that Mendelssohn thought himself to have refuted atheism once and for all in his *Jerusalem*. But Mendelssohn was confronted with a work (also by Schulz) entitled *Philosophische Betrachtung über Theologie und Religion überhaupt, und über die jüdische insonderheit* (1784) and, seeing his defense of theism threatened, he became concerned about Jacobi's branding Lessing an atheist. Therefore he conspired against Jacobi, but without success, and his death was the result of the anger he felt at seeing his plans miscarry.

Hamann gives a number of impressions of Kant's reactions to the dispute. In a letter of October 25, 1786, Hamann wrote that Kant was not at one with the Berliners (that is, Herz *et al.*). In a letter to Herz, April 7, 1786 [267], Kant expressed his opinion of the feud. In October, 1786, Kant published his essay, *What Is Orientation in Thinking?* (*Was Heisst: Sich im Denken Orientiren?*), in which Kant opposed both Jacobi's philosophy of feeling as well as Mendelssohn's claim to establish theological knowledge on the basis of "sound common sense."

correspondence is perhaps the only important thing that might be given to the public, if his friends will give us their letters from him, since he himself copied only a very few. Will you be so good as to let us have yours, dearest sir? . . .

To be esteemed by you as you are by me is my warmest desire.

Your faithful student and servants,
M. HERZ

To J. Bering,[1] April 7, 1786

- 266 - VOL. X, p. 441

. . . You ask how soon my ["System of] Metaphysics" will appear. I now feel it will be another two years. In the mean time, if I remain healthy, I shall publish something to take its place temporarily, viz., a new, highly revised edition of my *Critique,* which will come out soon, perhaps within half a year; my publisher,

[1] Johann Bering (1748–1825), professor of philosophy in Marburg. Bering was a disciple of Kant, and it was he who informed Kant (September 21, 1786, letter 279) of the "Cabinets Order," dated Weissenstein, August 29, 1786, forbidding lectures on Kant's philosophy at Marburg during the coming winter semester—an interesting irony, in view of that university's later fame as a center of Kant scholarship. Bering did not know the source of the opposition to Kant—he suspected Professors Christoph Meiners and J. G. H. Feder in Göttingen. (Some scholars regard the theologian Samuel Endemann's denunciation as the probable source.) The philosophical faculty of Marburg was instructed to report to the government by the end of the year whether Kant's philosophy encouraged scepticism, and whether it sought "to undermine the certainty of human knowledge." The report sent on October 11, 1786, praised Kant's genius and depth of thinking but stated that his difficult terminology, obscurity, and unusual ideas insured his innocuousness, since he could never have any influence on the public even if his works did contain errors. The report then notes the distinction between doubt and scepticism and points out that the former is essential for scientific progress: Kant has in fact sought to refute the profound and dangerous doubts of the illustrious Hume; having rejected the traditional proofs of God and the immortality of the soul, he has nevertheless sought to establish these truths on a surer foundation. The report is signed by eight men, including Bering. They did not all agree on the correctness of Kant's views, but all of them favored freedom of inquiry for the university. For the full texts, see Kant's *Werke,* XIII, 182 f. An announcement in the *Allgemeine Literaturzeitung* in October, 1787, removed the injunction against lectures on Kant's philosophy, though the lectures were to be "privatissime," that is, restricted to advanced students.

hearing of my intention, quickly sold his entire stock of the book and is now spurring me on. In it I shall attend to all the misinterpretations and misunderstandings that have come to my attention since the book began circulating. A number of things will be condensed and many new things that will clarify the theory will be added. I shall not change any of its essentials, since I thought out these ideas long enough before I put them on paper and, since then, have repeatedly examined and tested every proposition belonging to the system and found that each one stood the test, both by itself and in relation to the whole. Since, if I am successful with this project, almost any insightful person would be able to construct a system of metaphysics in conformity with my theory, I am therefore putting off my own composition of such a system for a while longer, in order to gain time for my system of practical philosophy, which is the sister of the former system and requires a similar treatment, though the difficulties are fewer. . . .

To Marcus Herz, April 7, 1786

- 267 - VOL. X, *pp. 442–43*

I found the lovely work [1] with which you have once again made me a present worthy of you, my dearest friend, as far as I have read—for my current distractions (on account of which I beg you also to forgive the brevity of this letter) have not allowed me the time to read it through completely.

The Jacobi [-Mendelssohn] controversy is nothing serious; it is only an affectation of inspired fanatics trying to make a name for themselves and is hardly worthy of a serious refutation. It is possible that I shall publish something in the *Berliner Monatsschrift* to expose this fraud.[2] Reichardt, too, has been infected with the genius-disease and associates himself with the chosen ones. It is all the same to him how he does it, as long as he can make a big impression, as an author no less, and as to that too much has been granted him. I regret very much that no usable manuscripts can be

[1] *Versuch über den Schwindel.* Cf. letter from Herz, February 27, 1786 [260].

[2] See Kant's essay, *What Is Orientation in Thinking?*

obtained from the excellent Moses [Mendelssohn]. But I can contribute nothing to the publication of his correspondence, since his letters to me contain nothing really scholarly, and a few general remarks of that nature do not provide material for a scholarly *opus postumum*. I ask you also to leave out any letters of mine that might turn up among his papers. They were never intended to be read by the public. . . .

There are great difficulties here in collecting money for the monument in Berlin.[3] But I shall see what can be done.

Do maintain your love and habitual kind feeling for him who remains always, with warmth and respect,

Your loyal, devoted servant and friend,
I. KANT

To L. H. Jakob,[1] September 11 [?], 1787

- 303 - VOL. X, *pp. 493–95*

Esteemed sir,

I take this opportunity to thank you for sending me your very successful book and for the good news you mentioned in your last letter. My congratulations on your new professorship. Toellner's manual is quite good for a logic text.[2] In my humble opinion, it is necessary to present logic in its purity, as I said in the *Critique,* that is, as consisting merely of the formal rules of thinking, leaving aside all materials that belong to metaphysics (on account of the origin of the concepts, in regard to their content) or to psychology. In this way, those formal rules of logic are not only easier to grasp but also more coherent and comprehensive. Feder thinks this fastidiousness pedantic and useless. I have

---

[3] A monument to Leibniz, Lambert, and Sulzer. The fourth side was to have a portrait of Mendelssohn. Hamann wrote Jacobi, April 27, 1786, that Kant thought the Jewish community should bear all the costs alone for the honor given to a Jewish philosopher in putting him among such men. Since Hamann was himself an anti-Semite, his report of Kant's opinion may well be a lie.

[1] Ludwig Heinrich Jakob (1759–1827), professor of philosophy in Halle, later in Russia.

[2] Johann Gottlieb Toellner (1724–74), professor of theology in Frankfurt and elsewhere, editor of A. G. Baumgarten's *Acroasis logica* (1765).

never written a metaphysics; please tell Mr. Hemmerde [3] that I am opposed to the publication of my minor writings at present. I might revise them when I have the time for it and will then announce it, but don't expect this for another two years.

My *Critique of Practical Reason* is at Grunert's now.[4] It contains many things that will serve to correct the misunderstandings of the [critique of] theoretical [reason]. I shall now turn at once to the "Critique of Taste," with which I shall have finished my critical work, so that I can proceed to the dogmatic part. I think it will appear before Easter.[5]

I wish you would try to compose a short system of metaphysics for the time being; I don't have the time to propose a plan for it just now. The ontology part of it would begin (without the introduction of any critical ideas) with the concepts of space and time, only insofar as these (as pure intuitions) are the foundation of all experiences. After that, there are four main parts that would follow, containing the concepts of the understanding, divided according to the four classes of categories, each of which constitutes a section. All of them are to be treated *merely analytically,* in accordance with Baumgarten,[6] together with the predicables, their connection with time and space, and how they proceed, just as Baumgarten presents them. For every category, the corresponding synthetic principle (as presented in the second edition of the *Critique*) indicates how experience must conform to the category, and thus the whole of ontology is covered. Now after all this, the critical conception of space and time as form[s] of sensibility and the deduction of the categories are presented. For the latter, as well as the former, cannot be understood completely before this, and neither can the only possible way of proving the principles, as has been seen. Then come the transcendental ideas, which pertain either to cosmology, psychology, or theology, and so on. I must close now, and I am, with friendship,

Your devoted servant,
I. KANT

[3] Carl Hemmerde, printer in Halle.

[4] Friedrich August Grunert, printer in Halle.

[5] The *Critique of Judgment* appeared in 1790. On Kant's "dogmatic" plans, see the Introduction to this collection of letters, p. 29, n. 34.

[6] Alexander Gottlieb Baumgarten (1714–62), aesthetician and professor of philosophy in Frankfurt and elsewhere, whose works Kant used as textbooks.

From J. C. Berens,[1] December 5, 1787

- 310 - VOL. X, *pp. 507–8*

[Berens tells of his travels through West Prussia. Kant and his *Critique* are taking hold in Halle, Leipzig, and elsewhere. As yet there is no actual intrigue against Kant's philosophy, but teachers are reluctant to abandon their old ways and dislike seeing the foundations of their system undermined.]

. . . Plattner[2] refused to discuss your philosophy; he said only "We teach Kant" [*wir lesen Kanten*]. His elegant lectures are more on philosophizing than on philosophy as such. The year draws to a close; otherwise I would have liked to look up Wieland[3] and Reinhold,[4] both of whom are very enthusiastic about [the *Critique of*] *Pure Reason,* or so their countrymen tell me. Wieland maintains that if it is Kant who has defined the limits of the understanding we can all rest contented with that position. Reinhold, a former Capuchin monk or even Jesuit[5] but a thoroughly intelligent, unprejudiced man (he was in Berlin recently), weeps, or so Dr. Biester[6] told me, when he hears that your holy doctrine is not yet universally recognized. Prof. Eberhard[7] fears the moral consequences of your new philosophy and thinks you should have followed the old view. Your former admirer, Prof. Ulrich,[8] is becoming your enemy, since Reinhold has taken away his laurels. . . . So far we still have freedom of

---

[1] Johann Cristoph Berens (1729–92), merchant, friend of Kant's and Hamann's.

[2] Ernst Plattner (1744–1818), professor of medicine and physiology in Leipzig.

[3] Christoph Martin Wieland (1733–1813), the famous German author.

[4] Karl Leonhard Reinhold (1758–1823), son-in-law of Wieland, who became one of Kant's most famous disciples and popularizers. See the various letters to and from Kant in this collection.

[5] Jesuit.

[6] Johann Erich Biester (1749–1816). See his letter of October 5, 1793 [596], n. 1.

[7] Johann August Eberhard (1738–1809), professor of philosophy in Halle, opponent of Kant's. On Eberhard, see Kant's letters to Reinhold of May 12 and 19, 1789 [359 and 360].

[8] Johann August Heinrich Ulrich (1744–1807), professor of philosophy in Jena.

thought and freedom of the press. The secret personal letters of people in the current regime are circulated openly at court and in town. . . .

To K. L. Reinhold,[1] December 28 and 31, 1787

- 313 - VOL. X, pp. 513–15

. . . I was very pleased to learn at last that you are the author of those excellent *Letters*.[1] I had asked the printer Mr. Grunert in Halle to send you a copy of my *Critique of Practical Reason* as a small token of my respect, but till now I did not know your exact address and Grunert was therefore unable to carry out my request. If you would please show him the enclosed letter he will do it if he still has copies. This little book will sufficiently resolve the many contradictions that the followers of the old guard philosophy imagine they see in my *Critique,* and at the same time the contradictions in which they themselves are unavoidably involved if they refuse to abandon their botched job are made perspicuous. . . .

Without becoming guilty of self-conceit, I can assure you that the longer I continue on my path the less worried I become that any contradiction or alliance (of the sort that is common nowadays) will ever significantly damage my system. My inner conviction grows, as I discover in working on different topics that not only does my system remain self-consistent but also, when sometimes I cannot see the right way to investigate a certain subject, I find that I need only look back at the general picture of the elements of knowledge, and of the mental powers pertaining to them, in order to discover elucidations I had not expected. I am now at work on the critique of taste, and I have discovered a kind of a priori principle different from those heretofore observed. For there are three faculties of the mind: the faculty of cognition, the faculty of feeling pleasure and displeasure, and the faculty of desire. In the *Critique of Pure* (theoretical) *Reason,* I found a priori principles

[1] Karl Leonhard Reinhold (1758–1823), professor of philosophy in Jena, then Kiel, one of Kant's most important popularizers, disciples, and later, apostates. His *Letters on the Kantian Philosophy* (*Briefe über die Kantische Philosophie* [1786–88]) did much to bring Kant's ideas to the public.

for the first of these, and in the *Critique of Practical Reason,* a priori principles for the third. I tried to find them for the second as well, and though I thought it impossible to find such principles, the systematic nature of the analysis of the previously mentioned faculties of the human mind allowed me to discover them, giving me ample material for the rest of my life, material at which to marvel and if possible to explore. So now I recognize three parts of philosophy, each of which has its a priori principles, which can be enumerated and for which one can delimit precisely the knowledge that may be based on them: theoretical philosophy, teleology, and practical philosophy, of which the second is, to be sure, the least rich in a priori grounds of determination. I hope to have a manuscript on this completed though not in print by Easter; it will be entitled "Critique of Taste." [2]

Please convey to your esteemed father-in-law [3] not only my highest regard but also my sincerest thanks for the manifold pleasures that his inimitable writings have given me.

If you have time, I would appreciate any news of the learned world, from which we are here rather removed. The learned world has its wars, alliances, and secret intrigues just as much as the political world. I am neither willing nor able to play that game, but it is entertaining and it gives one a useful slant to know something of it. . . .

I. KANT

To Johann Schultz, November 25, 1788

- 340 - VOL. X, *pp. 554–57*

Venerable and esteemed sir,

When I consider writings that aim at the rectification of human knowledge, especially at the clear, unobscured presentation of our cognitive powers, I am entirely opposed to any factional or rhetorical concealment of whatever errors in my own system may be brought to my attention. My motto is rather, Honesty is the best policy. Therefore my motive in wanting to see your solid

---

[2] The *Critique of Judgment* did not appear until 1790, however.
[3] The famous German author, Christoph Martin Wieland (1733–1813).

book [1] before its publication was only to forestall the many future controversies that might be avoided by an easily resolved misunderstanding, especially since we live so close to each other and can exchange our views so easily.

Allow me therefore to state certain doubts I feel about your contention that, contrary to my own thesis, there are no synthetic a priori cognitions in arithmetic, only mere analytic ones.

Universal arithmetic (algebra) is an *ampliative* science to such an extent that one cannot name a single rational science equal to it in this respect. In fact the remaining parts of pure mathematics [*Mathesis*] make progress largely because of the development of that universal theory of quantities. If the latter consisted of merely analytic judgments, one would have to say at least that the definition of "analytic" as merely explicative was wrong. And besides that we face the difficult and important question, how is it possible to extend our knowledge by means of *analytic judgments alone?*

I can form a concept of one and the same quantity by means of many different additions and subtractions; (notice that both of these processes are syntheses, however.) Objectively, the concepts I form are identical (as in every equation). But subjectively, depending on the type of combination [*Zusammensetzung*] that I think, in order to arrive at that concept, they are very different. So that at any rate my judgment goes beyond the concept I get from the synthesis, in that the judgment substitutes another concept (simpler and more appropriate to the construction) in place of the first concept, though it determines the same object. Thus I can arrive at a single determination of a quantity by means of $3 + 5$, or $12 - 4$, or 2×4, or 2^3, namely 8. But my thought "$3 + 5$" did not include the thought "2×4." Just as little did it include the concept "8," which is equal in value to any of these.

Certainly arithmetic has no axioms, since its object is actually not any *quantum,* that is, any quantitative object of intuition, but rather *quantity as such,* that is, it considers the concept of a thing in general by means of quantitative determination.[2]

On the other hand, arithmetic has *postulates,* that is, immediately certain practical judgments. For if I regard $3 + 4$ as the setting of a problem, namely, to find a third number (7) such that

[1] J. Schulz [or Schultz], *Prüfung der Kantischen Kritik der reinen Vernunft* (Königsberg), Pt. I (1789) and Pt. II (1792).
[2] Cf. *Critique of Pure Reason* A 164 = B 204 f.; A 732 = B 760 ff.

the one number will be seen as the *complementum ad totum* of the other, the solution is found by means of the simplest operation, requiring no special prescription, namely, by the successive addition that the number 4 proposes simply as a continuation of the counting up to 3. The judgment "$3 + 4 = 7$" does seem to be a purely theoretical judgment, and objectively regarded, that is what it is; but subjectively, the sign "$+$" signifies the synthesis involved in getting a third number out of two other numbers, and it signifies a task to be done, requiring no instruction or proof. Consequently the judgment is a postulate. Now assuming it were an analytic judgment, I would have to think [*denken*] exactly the same thing by "$3 + 4$" as by "7," and the judgment would only make me more clearly conscious of what I thought. But since $12 - 5$ yields a number (7) that is actually the same number I thought when I was adding $3 + 4$, it follows, according to the principle "things equal to the same thing are equal to each other," that when I think "3 and 4" I must at the same time be thinking "12 and 5." And this does not jibe with my own awareness.

All analytic judgments by means of concepts have this characteristic: they can represent a predicate only as a constituent concept (*Theilbegrif*) contained in the subject concept. In the case of definitions, both concepts must be reciprocal. But in an arithmetic judgment, namely, an equation, both concepts must be absolutely reciprocal and objectively identical, for example, the concepts "$3 + 4$" and "7." In the problem, conjoin 3 and 4 in one number, the number 7 must arise not out of an analysis [*Zergliederung*] of the constituent concepts but rather by means of a construction, that is, synthetically. This construction, a single counting up in an a priori intuition, presents the concept of the conjunction of two numbers. Here we have the construction of the concept of quantity rather than that of a quantum. For the idea that the conjoining of 3 and 4, as distinct quantitative concepts, could yield the concept of *one* magnitude was only a thought. The number 7 is thus the presentation of this thought in an act of counting together.

Time, as you correctly notice, has no influence on the properties of numbers (considered as pure determinations of quantity), as it may have on the character of those changes (of quantity) that are possible only relative to a specific state of inner sense and its form (time). The science of numbers, notwithstanding the succession that every construction of quantity requires, is a pure intellectual synthesis, which we represent to ourselves in thought. But insofar as specific quantities (quanta) are to be determined in accordance with this science, they must be given to us in such a way that we can grasp their intuition successively; and thus this grasping is subjected to the time condition. So that when all is said and done, we cannot subject any object other than an object of a possible *sensible* intuition to quantitative, numerical assessment, and it thus remains a principle without exception that mathematics can be applied only to *sensibilia*. The magnitude of God's perfection, of duration, and so on, could only be expressed by means of the *totality* of reality; it could not possibly be represented by means of numbers, supposing someone wanted to measure even a merely intelligible unity.

I take this opportunity to note that, since the enemies of the *Critique* like to gnaw at every phrase, it would be advisable to change the passage on page 27 a little, where there is a reference to a "sensuous" understanding and the divine understanding appears to have a sort of *thinking* attributed to it. . . .

Your devoted servant,
I. KANT

To Heinrich Jung-Stilling [after March 1, 1789]

- 347 - VOL. XI, *p. 10, and* XXIII, *pp. 494–95*

Your interest in every investigation into the nature of man does honor to you, dear sir; it stands in contrast to the attitude of the majority of speculative minds, whose interests are motivated only by partisanship or vanity. And it is quite right of you to seek in the Gospels the final satisfaction of your striving for a secure foundation of wisdom and hope, since that book is an everlasting guide to true wisdom, one that not only agrees with the speculations of a perfected reason but sheds new light on the whole field surveyed by that reason, illuminating what still remains opaque to it.

That the *Critique of [Pure] Reason* has been useful to you in this quest must be owing not to me but to your own keen mind, which manages to draw something of value out of even an imperfect work. But I was quite surprised that the system of categories, which must indeed be the foundation for any classification of the principles of a science based on a priori concepts, would be the place you would look for help in setting up a system of civil law. I think that here, too, you are correct.

The principles that you suggest for your classification as the foundation of civil law cannot serve that purpose properly, since they are valid also as precepts for *Man in the state of nature,* even the third of your principles, "Be a member of civil society." One might raise the question how laws should be decreed if a civil society is already presupposed; and in that case, I think one might say following the order of the categories: (1) as regards *quantity,* the laws must be of such a nature that one [citizen] might have decreed them for all, and all for one; (2) as regards *quality,* it is not the citizen's *purpose* [*Zweck*] that the laws must decide, for everyone may be allowed to pursue his own happiness in conformity with his own inclination and power; but laws do concern everyone's freedom and the forcible limitation on that freedom imposed by the condition that each man's freedom must be compatible with every other man's;[1] (3) as regards the category of *relation,* it is not those of the citizen's activities that relate to himself or to God that are to be condemned but only those external activities that restrict the freedom of his fellow citizens; (4) as for *modality,* the laws (*qua* compulsive) must be given not as arbitrary and accidental commandments for some purposes that happen to be desired but only insofar as they are necessary for the achievement of universal freedom.

But the general problem of civil union is this: To combine freedom with a compulsion that is yet consistent with universal freedom and its preservation. In this manner there arises a state of external justice (*status iustitiae externae*) whereby that which was only an *Idea* in the state of nature (namely, the notion of law [*Recht*] as the mere *power* [*Befügnis*] to compel) is realized.

Around the end of this summer I shall begin to work on my "Metaphysics of Morals," and by next Easter I should be finished with it. In it the a priori principles for any civil constitution in general will also be discussed.

In view of the integrity of your thinking and the lively concern for all that is good that I perceive in your letters to me, I am sure

[1] Cf. *Critique of Pure Reason* A 316 = B 373. "A constitution allowing the greatest possible human freedom in accordance with laws by which the freedom of each is made to be consistent with that of all others. . . ."

that the peace of mind with which, not without justification, you are pleased to credit me, in the evening of my life, will brighten the days of your own life, and may there be many of them still to be lived through.

With respect and friendship, I am

Your most devoted servant,
I. KANT

From Salomon Maimon, April 7, 1789

- 352 - VOL. XI, *p. 15*

Esteemed sir,

Filled with the veneration owed to a man who has reformed philosophy and thereby reformed all other sciences as well, I am emboldened to approach you only by the love of truth.

Condemned at birth to live out the best years of my life in the woods of Lithuania, deprived of every assistance in acquiring knowledge, I finally had the good fortune to get to Berlin, late though it was. Here the support of certain noble-minded persons has put me in a position to study the sciences. It was natural, I think, that my eagerness to arrive at my main goal—*the truth*—should make me neglect to some extent those subordinate studies, language, method, and so on. Therefore, for a long time I dared not make any of my thoughts public, to expose them to a world whose taste is currently so sophisticated, even though I had read various systems of philosophy, had thought through them and, now and then, discovered something new. Finally I was lucky enough to see your immortal book, to study it, and to reconstruct the whole of my thinking in order to come into accord with it. I have tried as hard as I can to draw the final implications from this work, to impress them on my memory, and to seek out the track of the main argument, so that I might penetrate the author's mind. With this end in view, I have written down my results and have made a few comments, mainly concerning the following points:

1. The distinction you draw between analytic and synthetic propositions and the reality of the latter.

2. The question, *Quid Juris?* This question, because of its importance, deserves the attention of a Kant. If one spells it out the way you yourself do, it becomes: How can something a priori be applied with certainty to something a posteriori? The answer or deduction that you give in your book is, as the answer of only a Kant can be, totally satisfying. But if one wishes to amplify the question, one asks: How can an a priori concept be applied to an intuition, even an a priori intuition? This question must await the master's attention, if it is to be answered satisfactorily.

3. I define a new class of ideas which I call *ideas of the understanding* [*Verstandesideen*], which signify *material totality,* just as your ideas of reason signify *formal totality.* I believe I have opened the way to a new means of answering the aforementioned *Quid Juris* question.

4. The question, *Quid facti?* You seem to have touched on this, but it is, I think, important to answer it fully, on account of the Humean skepticism.

These comments summarize the content of the manuscript that I venture to submit to you. My good friends have urged me for a long time to publish this book, but I did not want to comply without having subjected it to your priceless judgment. If a Kant should find the book not utterly unworthy of his attention, he will certainly not scorn him who approaches so reverentially. He will answer, will instruct where errors are committed, or give his approval if the work is found to deserve it, and he will thereby make its author doubly happy.[1]

Your wholly devoted servant and admirer,

Salomon Maimon

Berlin

From J. B. Jachmann, April 15, 1789

- 354 - vol. xi, *pp. 21–25*

. . . Last Tuesday I presented my paper on the distinction between synthetic and analytic judgments to the Speculative Society. What I said was mainly what you said in the Introduction to your

[1] See the letter from Kant to Herz, May 26, 1789 [362] for Kant's reply.

Critique, and I also tried to acquaint the Society with the over-all intent and plan of your book. I especially tried to put the question, "How are synthetic a priori judgments possible?" in its most conspicuous light. My intention was to show the solution to this question and thus at the same time to discuss space and time. I had previously worked out my lecture in German with this end in mind, but I put off making an English translation so long that I was unable to finish it on time. I found it particularly difficult to find the right words for your ideas, and this was all the more difficult for me since I had never read any philosophical books in English. Besides this, I thought my essay too long for the occasion, and since the subject is so speculative, I feared it would fatigue the audience, since they would be unable to follow the arguments. As far as my reading of the essay went, it was highly successful. People marveled at the originality of the plan, the importance of the subject, the unusual precision in the definition of concepts, and so on. But they regretted that, after I had aroused their curiosity, I had not satisfied it, for I did not tell them the solution of this important question. They requested unanimously that I relate it to them as soon as possible. —Hume's views, and especially those of a certain Hardley [*sic*] [1] (I don't know whether this book has been translated into German), are strongly admired and defended in this Society and also among most of the philosophers in Scotland. A priori judgments are totally impossible, according to Hardley, whom I have, however, not read myself—I know him only from conversations. All our concepts rest on sensation, reflexion, and association, and so on. All necessary judgments, for example, are mere identities, as, for example, in mathematics, the proposition $7 + 5 = 12$. So that when I say "7 and 5," I am at the same time saying "12." Twelve is only another way of expressing "$7 + 5$," just as "Deus" is another word for God. They also talk a great deal about "common sense." The proposition that everything that happens has a cause is not a necessary proposition. It depends merely on the uniformity of experience, and so on. Dr. Reid of Glasgow [2] does not agree. . . . Hardley's theory of the passions [3]

---

[1] David Hartley (1705–57). The book referred to is his *Observations on Man, His Frame, His Duty, and His Expectations* (London, 1749). Part I, Ch. III, Sec. II, deals with mathematical judgments.

[2] Thomas Reid (1710–96).

[3] Joseph Priestley, *Hartley's Theory of the Human Mind: On the Principle of the Association of Ideas* (London, 1775), Ch. III, Sec. III, Prop. 41.

is especially popular here; I am convinced that the theory is without foundations. He maintains that all depressing [*niederschlagende*] passions are only abstractions or negations of the stimulating [*erregenden*] passions. For example, fear is only an abstraction derived from hope, as cold is the abstraction of heat, and therefore not truly a real thing. I have had some extraordinarily strong arguments over this, in the Medical Society as well as in the Speculative Society. . . .

Your most obedient friend and servant,
Joh. Benj. Jachmann

Edinburgh

To K. L. Reinhold, May 12, 1789

- 359 - VOL. XI, *pp. 33–40*

Sincerest thanks, my cherished and dearest friend, for the communication of your kind opinion of me, which arrived together with your lovely present on the day after my birthday! The portrait of me by Mr. Loewe, a Jewish painter, done without my consent, is supposed to resemble me to a degree, from what my friends say. But a man who knows painting said at first glance: a Jew always paints people to look like Jews. And the proof of this is found in the nose. But enough of this.

I couldn't send you my judgment of Eberhard's new attack, since our shop did not even have all three of the first issues of his magazine, and I could find them only in the public library. Whence the delay in my answer. *That Mr. Eberhard, along with a number of people, has not understood me* is the least you can say (for that might be partly my fault). But I shall show you in my following remarks that he sets out to misunderstand me, and even to make me incomprehensible.

In the first issue of the magazine he tries to appear as a man who is aware of his own importance in the eyes of the philosophical public. He speaks of "sensations" aroused by the *Critique,* of "sanguine hopes" that were "surpassed," of how many people were stunned and have not yet recovered (as if he were writing for the theater, or the boudoir, about some rival), and like a man who is fed up with watching the show, he determines to put a stop to it. —I wish that this insolent charlatanry might be shoved under his nose a bit.—The first three issues of the magazine more or less make up a unit, of which the third, from page 307 on,[1] attacks the main contention of my Introduction in the *Critique* and closes triumphantly with "We should therefore now. . . ." I cannot fail to make a few remarks about this, so that those readers who take the trouble to check up on it will not overlook the fraud with which this man, who is dishonest in every line he writes—on those matters where he is weak and on those where his opponent is strong—puts everything in an equivocal light. I shall only indicate the pages and the opening words of the places I discuss and beg you to look them up yourself. The refutation of the fourth part of the third issue will serve to reveal the whole nature of this man's "insight" as well as his character. My remarks concern mainly pages 314–19.

On pages 314 f. he writes, "According to this the distinction would be," and so on, to "insofar as anything definite can be made out of this."[2]

His explanation of an a priori synthetic judgment is pure deception, namely, a flat tautology. For in the expression "an a priori judgment" it is already implied that the predicate of the judgment is necessary; and the expression "synthetic" implies that the predicate is not the essence or any essential part of the concept that serves as subject of the judgment, for otherwise the predicate would be identical with the subject and the judgment would thus not be synthetic. Whatever is thought as necessarily connected with a concept, but is not thought through identity, is thought as something necessarily connected with, but *distinct* from, the essence of the concept, that is, connected with the essence through some ground. For it is one and the same thing to say that the predicate is not thought as part of the essence of the concept but yet as necessary through it, or to say that it is grounded in the

---

[1] "On the Distinction between Analytic and Synthetic Judgments."

[2] Eberhard wrote: "The distinction between analytic and synthetic judgments would seem to be this: analytic judgments are those whose predicates state the essence or some of the essential parts of the subject; those whose predicates assert no determination belonging to the essence or to the essential parts of the subject are synthetic. This is what Mr. Kant must say, if he presents the contrast so that the first are merely explicative and the latter are ampliative, insofar as we can make anything definite out of his explanation."

essence, that is, it must be thought as an attribute of the subject. Therefore his pretended great discovery is nothing but a shallow tautology in which by spuriously substituting other meanings for the technical terms of logic, one creates the illusion of having really offered *a basis of explanation.*

But this sham discovery has yet a second inexcusable flaw: as an alleged definition, it is not convertible. For I can say in any case: In every synthetic judgment the predicates are attributes of the subject. But I cannot say conversely: Every judgment that asserts an attribute of its subject is a *synthetic* a priori judgment—for there are also *analytic attributes.* Extension is an *essential part* of the concept of a body, for it is a *primitive* characteristic of the latter that cannot be derived from any other inner characteristic. Divisibility, however, is also a necessary predicate of the concept of body, and therefore an *attribute,* but only in the sense that it can be inferred (as subaltern) from another predicate (extension). Now divisibility can be derived from the concept of something extended (as composite), according to the law of identity; and the judgment "Every body is divisible" is an a priori judgment that has the attribute of a thing for its predicate (the thing for its subject) and thus is not a synthetic judgment. Consequently, the fact that a predicate in a judgment is an attribute does not at all serve to distinguish synthetic a priori judgments from analytic judgments.

All similar errors, which start out as confusions and end up as deliberate deceptions, are based on this point: the logical relation of ground and consequent is mistaken for a real relation. A ground is (in general) that whereby something else (distinct from it) is made determinate (*quo posito determinate* * *ponitur aliud*) ["where a determinate is posited, something else must be posited"]. A consequent (*rationum*) is *quod non ponitur nisi posito alio* ["that which is not posited unless something else has been posited"]. The ground must thus always be something distinct from the consequent, and he who can give no ground but the

---

* [Kant's footnote] This expression must never be left out of the definition of "ground." For a *consequent,* too, is something that, if I posit it, I must at the same time think something else as posited, that is, a consequent always belongs to something or other that is its ground. But when I think something as consequent, I merely posit *some* ground or other; *which* ground is undetermined. (Thus the hypothetical judgment is based on the rule, *a positione consequentis ad positionem antecedentis non valet consequentia.*) On the other hand, if the ground is posited, the consequent is determined.

given consequent itself shows that he does not know (or that the fact does not have) any ground! Now this distinction of ground and consequent is either merely *logical* (having to do with the manner of representation) or *real,* that is, in the object itself. The concept of extension is logically distinct from the concept of the divisible; for the former contains the latter, but it contains more besides. In the fact itself, however, the two are identical, for divisibility really does lie in the concept of extension. Now it is *real* distinctness that one requires for a synthetic judgment. When logic says that all (assertoric) judgments must have a ground, it does not concern itself with this real distinction at all. Logic abstracts from it, for the distinction depends on the content of cognition. If, however, one asserts that every *thing* has its ground, one always means by this the real ground.

Now when Eberhard names the principle of sufficient reason as the principle for synthetic propositions generally, he must mean none other than the logical axiom. This axiom, however, allows also for analytic grounds, and it can of course be derived from the law of contradiction; but then it is a clumsy absurdity on his part to justify his so-called *non-identical* judgments on the basis of the principle of sufficient reason, a principle that on his own view is merely a consequence of the law of contradiction (a law that is absolutely incapable of grounding any but identical judgments).

In passing I remark (so that in the future people may more easily take notice of Eberhard's wrong track) that the real ground is in fact twofold: either the *formal* ground (of the *intuition* of the object)—as, for example, the sides of a triangle contain the ground of the angle—or the *material* ground (of the existence of things). The latter determines that whatever contains it will be called the *cause.* It is quite customary that the conjurers of metaphysics, before one is taken in, make sleights of hand and leap from the logical principle of sufficient reason to the transcendental principle of causality, assuming the latter to be already contained in the former. The statement *nihil est sine ratione,* which as much as says "everything exists only as a consequence," is in itself absurd— either that, or these people give it some other meaning. Thus the whole discussion of *essence, attributes,* and so on, absolutely does not belong to metaphysics (where Baumgarten, along with several others, has put it) but only to logic. For I can easily find the logical essence, by the analysis of my concepts into all that I think under them, that is, I can find the primary *constitutiva* of a given concept, as well as the attributes, as *rationata logica* of this essence. But the *real* essence (the nature) of any object, that is, the primary *inner* ground of all that necessarily belongs to a given thing, this is impossible for man to discover. For example, extension and impenetrability are the whole logical essence of the concept of matter, that is, they are all that is necessarily and primitively contained in my, and every man's, concept of matter. But to recognize the real essence of matter, the primary, inner, sufficient ground of *all* that *necessarily belongs to* matter, this far exceeds the capacity of human powers. We cannot discover the essence of *water, of earth,* or the essence of any other empirical objects; even the real essence of space and time and the reason why the former has three dimensions, the latter only one, are unknowable. And the reason for this is precisely that since the logical essence is to be known analytically and the real essence must be known synthetically and a priori, there must be a ground of synthesis for the former, which bring *us* at least to a standstill.

The reason that mathematical judgments offer only synthetic attributes is not that all synthetic a priori judgments have to do exclusively with attributes; it is rather that mathematical judgments cannot but be synthetic and a priori. On page 314, where Eberhard introduces such judgments as examples, he writes, cautiously: "The question as to whether there are such judgments outside mathematics may for the present be put off." Why did he not at least offer one of the various examples from metaphysics for purposes of comparison? He must have found it difficult to find one that would stand such comparison. On page 319, however, he ventures to consider one, which he claims to be an obviously synthetic proposition. But it is obviously analytic, and the example fails. The proposition is: *Everything necessary is eternal; all necessary truths are eternal truths.* The latter judgment says no more than that necessary truths are not restricted by any accidental conditions (and therefore are also not restricted to any position in time); and this is exactly what the concept of necessity is, so that the proposition is analytic. But if what he wants to assert is that necessary truth *exists* at all times, this is an absurdity to which we cannot be expected to agree. He couldn't possibly intend the first proposition to mean the eternal existence of a *thing,* for then the second proposition would be totally unrelated to it. (At first I thought the expression *"eternal* truths" and its opposite, *"temporal*

truths," were merely affectations employing figurative terminology, rather improper for a transcendental critique. Now it
seems that Eberhard really takes them literally.)

On pages 318–19, we read: "Mr. K. seems to understand 'synthetic judgment' to mean judgments that are not absolutely necessary truths and, of absolutely necessary truths, just those whose
necessary predicates can only be discovered a posteriori by the
human understanding. For, except for mathematical judgments,
only experiential judgments are necessary." [3] This is such a crude
misunderstanding, or rather a deliberate misrepresentation of my
view, that one can predict how "genuine" the consequences are
going to be.

Of his opponents he says repeatedly that their distinction between synthetic and analytic judgments has already been known
for a long time. Maybe so! But the reason why the importance of
the distinction has not been recognized seems to be that all a priori
judgments were regarded as analytic, whereas only experiential
judgments [*Erfahrungsurteile*] were reckoned as synthetic, so that
the whole point of the distinction disappeared.

And finally, Mr. Eberhard says on page 316: "One seeks in vain
for Kant's *principle* for *synthetic judgments.*" But that principle is
unequivocally presented in the whole *Critique,* from the chapter
on the schematism on, though not in a specific formula. It is this:
*all synthetic judgments of theoretical cognition are possible only
by the relating of a given concept to an intuition.* If the synthetic
judgment is an experiential judgment, the intuition must be empirical; if the judgment is a priori synthetic, there must be a pure
intuition to ground it. It is impossible (for us human beings) to
have pure intuitions that do not consist merely of the form of the
subject and the form of his receptivity to representations, that is,
his capacity to be affected by objects (for otherwise no object is
given). For this reason, the reality of synthetic a priori propositions is itself sufficient to prove that these propositions concern
only sensible objects and cannot transcend appearances; this is
shown even without our having to know that space and time are
those forms of sensibility and that the a priori concepts to which
we relate our intuitions, in order to make synthetic a priori

[3] [Translator's note] I have inserted the whole passage in place of Kant's
brief reference. The last word, however, should be "synthetic" rather than
"necessary"—Kant misread Eberhard here.

judgments, are the categories. However, once we recognize these categories and their origin as the form of thinking, we shall be convinced that they do not by themselves provide genuine knowledge, and that, when supplied with intuitions, they do not give us any supersensible theoretical knowledge, though they can be used for *practical* ideas without stepping outside their proper sphere. This is so just because the limitation of our power of conferring objective reality upon our concepts is not a limitation on the possibility of things. Nor does this limitation restrict the use of the categories, as concepts of things in general, when considering the supersensible, which is grounded by the genuinely given practical ideas of reason. Thus the principle of synthetic a priori judgments has infinitely greater fruitfulness than the principle of sufficient reason, which determines nothing and which, regarded in its universality, is merely logical.

These then, dear friend, are my remarks on the third issue of Eberhard's magazine, which I put wholly at your disposal.[4] The delicacy to which you have committed yourself in your projected work, and the restraint of character that it requires, may be not only unearned by this man but actually disadvantageous, if you are driven too far. I shall have the honor of sending you the conclusion of my remarks on the second issue during the next week, which will serve to reveal his truly malicious character (leaving aside his ignorance). Since he is inclined to imagine every gentleness a weakness, he can only be stopped by a blunt confrontation with his absurdities and misrepresentations. Please use my remarks as you see fit, for they are only hints to help you recall what your own diligent study of this material must already have disclosed. I give you full permission even to use my name wherever and whenever you please.

For your lovely book, which I have not yet had time to read, my sincerest thanks. I am eager to hear of your theory of the faculty of representation [*Vorstellungsvermögen*], which should appear at the same book fair as my *Critique of Judgment* (a part of which is the "Critique of Taste") next Michaelmas. My compliments to

---

[4] Reinhold used Kant's replies to Eberhard in the *Jena Allgemeine Literaturzeitung*, 1789. Kant's polemical essay *On a Discovery according to Which Any New Critique of Pure Reason Has Been Made Superfluous by a Previous One* (*Ueber eine Entdeckung, nach der alle neue Kritik der reinen Vernunft durch eine ältere entbehrlich gemacht werden soll*) appeared in 1790; see *Werke*, VIII, pp. 185–251, and 492–97.

Messrs. Schütz, Hufeland, and your distinguished father-in-law [C. M. Wieland].

With the greatest respect and sincere friendship, I am

Your devoted
I. Kant

See enclosure

To K. L Reinhold, May 19, 1789

- 360 - VOL. XI, *pp. 40–48*

[Kant sends additional criticisms of Eberhard's magazine, "a disgusting piece of work," to expose the fraud of Eberhard's attack. . . .]

Page 12. "Plato and Aristotle denied the certainty of any sense-knowledge and restricted certainty to the area of non-sensible ideas or ideas of the understanding," says Eberhard.[1] Just the opposite is true of Aristotle. The principle *nihil est in intellectu, quod non antea fuerit in sensu* (a principle that agrees with Locke's) is the criterion for distinguishing the Aristotelian school. . . .

Pages 25–26. Eberhard writes: "If it is said that sensible concepts are intuitive [*anschauend*], this is quite true: they are *immediately* intuitive. But concepts of the understanding are also intuitive, only they are *mediately* intuitive. For they are derived from sensible concepts and can be intuited in the latter; and even if they are constructed out of abstract concepts, they bring with them the mediately intuitive signs [*Merkmale*] of the abstract concepts out of which they are constructed. . . ." Here there is a double absurdity. Pure concepts of reason [*reine Vernunftbegriffe*], which Eberhard identifies with pure concepts of the understanding, he interprets as concepts that have been drawn from sensuous concepts (like extension or color, which once resided in sense representations). This is just the opposite of the criterion I gave for pure concepts of reason. And then the notion of "mediate intuition" is self-contradictory. I say only that to a concept of pure reason a *corresponding* intuition could be given, in which, how-

[1] [Translator's note] I have inserted the full passages from Eberhard, in place of Kant's brief references.

ever, nothing of that concept is contained. It contains only the manifold upon which the concept of the understanding (the concept of an object in general) applies the synthetic unity of apperception, be the intuition what it may.

Page 156. [Eberhard speaks of necessary truths that have objects "lying entirely outside the sphere of sense-knowledge, which can neither be warranted nor refuted by experience." Later he says, "their logical truth follows necessarily from their metaphysical truth; the two are indivisibly united. That is, as soon as the power of representation has, in accordance with its necessary laws, thought something as possible and as independently actual, that thing must be possible and independently actual."] Here he talks of necessary laws, and so on, without noticing that in the *Critique* the task is just this: to show which laws are objectively necessary, and how we are authorized to assume them valid for the nature of things, that is, how they can possibly be synthetic and yet a priori. For otherwise we are in danger (like Crusius, whose language Eberhard uses here) of taking a merely subjective necessity (based on habit or on our inability to imagine an object any other way) for an objective necessity.

Pages 157–58. [Eberhard insists on the possibility of progress in metaphysics.] Here one might ask, as the foreign scholar did when they showed him the Sorbonne lecture hall, "They've argued here for three hundred years; what have they found out?"

Page 158. "We can always work to extend it, without committing ourselves. . . ." Here we mustn't let him get by. For his declaration concerns an important point, viz., whether a critique of pure reason must precede metaphysics or not. From page 157 to 159 he demonstrates his confusion as to what the *Critique* is trying to do, and he displays his ignorance just where he tries to parade as learned. This passage alone reveals the trickery he is up to. He sounds off about metaphysical truth and its demonstration (at the start of the section on transcendental truth), contrasting this with logical truth and its demonstration. But all judgmental truth, insofar as it rests on objective grounds, is logical, whether the judgment itself belongs to physics or to metaphysics. We are in the habit of contrasting logical truth with aesthetic truth (that of a poet), for example, heaven as a vault and the sunset dipping into the sea. For the latter sort we require only that the judgment have the appearance of truth for all men, that is, that it agree with subjective conditions of judgment. When we speak of objective determining grounds of a judgment, however, we make no distinction between geometric truth, physical or metaphysical truth, and logical truth.

. . . When he says, on page 158, "In this way the mathematicians have completed the design of whole sciences *without even discussing the reality of the objects of these sciences*," and so on, he shows himself to be supremely ignorant, not only in his make-believe mathematics, but in his utter lack of comprehension of what it is that the *Critique* demands with respect to the intuitions without which the objective reality of concepts cannot be secured. We must therefore pause a moment to discuss his examples.

Mr. Eberhard wants to free himself from the demand, so troublesome yet so unavoidable for all dogmatism, that no concept be admitted to the class of cognitions if its objective reality is not made evident by the possibility of the object's being presented in a corresponding intuition. He thus calls upon the mathematicians, who are supposed not to have made mention, with even a single word, of the reality of the objects of their concepts and who nevertheless have succeeded in designing entire sciences. He could hardly have hit upon a more unfortunate example for his purpose. For it is exactly the opposite: the mathematician cannot make the smallest assertion about any object whatsoever without exhibiting it (or, if we are considering only quantities without qualities, as in algebra, exhibiting the quantitative relationships for which the symbols stand) in intuition. As usual, he has, instead of investigating the subject himself, merely leafed through some books, which he has not understood, and has hunted up a place in Borelli (editor of Apollonius's *Conica*) that just accidentally seems to suit his business: "Subiectum enim . . . delineandi." Had he the slightest grasp of what Borelli was talking about, he would find that the definition that Apollonius gives, for example, of a parabola is itself the exhibition of a concept in intuition, viz., the intersection of a cone under certain conditions. In establishing the objective reality of the concept, here as always in geometry, the definition is at once a construction of the concept. If, however, in accordance with the characteristic of this conic section, drawn from this definition—viz., that the (semi-) ordinate is the mean proportional between one parameter and the abscissa—the problem is set as follows: given the parameter, how do you draw the parabola? (that is, how are the ordinates to be applied upon the given diameter), the solution, as Borelli correctly says, belongs to art, which follows science as a practical corollary. For science has to do with the properties of an object, not with the manner in which the object may be produced under given conditions. If a circle is defined as a curve all of whose points are equidistant from a mid-point, is not this concept given in intuition? And this even though the practical proposition that follows, viz., *to describe a circle* (as a straight line is rotated uniformly about a point), is not at all considered. Mathematics is the most excellent paradigm for the synthetic use of reason, just because the intuitions with which mathematics confers objective reality upon its concepts are never lacking. This demand for intuitions is one we cannot always sufficiently comply with in philosophy (insofar as philosophy is supposed to be theoretical knowledge). When intuitions are lacking, we must be resigned to forego the claim that our concepts have the status of cognitions (of objects). We must admit that they are only ideas, mere regulative principles for the use of reason directed toward objects given in intuition, objects that, however, can never be known completely, since they are conditioned.

Page 163. "Now this principle of sufficient reason. . . ." Here he makes a confession that will not appeal to many of the empiricists who are his allies in attacking the *Critique,* viz., *that the principle of sufficient reason is only possible a priori.* He explains, though, that the principle could only be demonstrated by means of the principle of contradiction, which makes it *ipso facto* an analytic judgment and thus demolishes right at the outset his projected attempt to account for the possibility of synthetic a priori judgments by means of that principle. The demonstration thus turns out pathetically. First he treats the principle of sufficient reason as a logical principle (which it must be if he wants to derive it from the principle of contradiction), so that the principle says in effect, "Every *assertoric* judgment has a ground"; but then he proceeds to use the principle as if it had a metaphysical meaning, that is, in the sense of "Every event has a cause," which is an entirely different sense of "ground." In the latter proposition, it is the "real ground," the relation of causality, and this relation cannot in any way be represented by the principle of contradiction, as the relation of logical ground can. On page 164 the argument begins, "Two propositions that contradict each other cannot both be true," and the example, page 163, is "An amount of air moves eastward." If this example is related to the proposition just cited, the application of the logical principle of sufficient reason would read: The proposition, "An amount of air moves eastward," must have a ground. For without a ground, that is, a representation other than that of the concept of air and that of an eastward movement, the representation of the predicate (that is, the ground) is wholly undetermined. But this proposition is an experiential one, and consequently it is not merely thought problematically but assertorically, as *grounded,* and grounded in experience, a cognition by means of the perceptions that have been combined [*verknüpft*]. But this ground is identical to that stated in the proposition (I refer to what is present perceptually, not to what is merely possible conceptually); it is consequently an analytic ground of *judgment,* in accordance with the principle of contradiction, and has nothing in common with the real ground, which concerns the synthetic relationship between cause and effect in the objects themselves. So Eberhard starts with the analytic principle of sufficient reason (as a logical principle) and leaps to the metaphysical principle of causality, which is always synthetic and which is never mentioned in logic. His argument is thus a crude fallacy of *ignoratio elenchi;* it does not prove what he wants it to but only shows something that was never in fact disputed. But this is not the reader's only problem: the paralogism on pages 163–64 is too awful to be mentioned.[2] Put in syllogistic form it would read: If there were no sufficient reason why the wind moves eastward, it could just as well (*instead of that*—Eberhard has to add this, otherwise the conclusion of the hypothetical proposition is false) move toward the west; now there is no sufficient reason why, and so on. Therefore the wind could just as well move *both* eastward and westward, which is self-contradictory. This syllogism walks on all fours.

The principle of sufficient reason, so far as Mr. Eberhard has shown, is thus still only a logical principle and analytic. Viewed from this perspective, there are not two but three principles of knowledge: (1) the principle of contradiction, for categorical

---

[2] "Either everything has a ground or not everything has a ground. If the latter, something could be possible and thinkable though its ground is nothing. But if, of two opposing things, it were possible for one of them to be without a sufficient reason, then the other one could also be without a sufficient reason. If, for example, an amount of air could move eastward, so that the wind is eastward, even though the air was not warmer and thinner in the east, this amount of air could just as well move westward as eastward; the same air would thus simultaneously be able to move in two opposing directions, east and west, and thus both east and not-east, that is, something could simultaneously be and not be, which is contradictory and impossible."

judgments, (2) the principle of (logical) ground, for hypothetical judgments, and (3) the principle of division [*Eintheilung*] (excluded middle between two mutually contradictory propositions), for disjunctive judgments. All judgments must first, as *problematic* (as mere judgments) insofar as they express *possibility*, conform to the first principle; second, as *assertoric* (*qua* propositions) insofar as they express logical *actuality*, that is, *truth*, they must conform to the principle of sufficient reason; third, as *apodictic* (as items of knowledge), they must conform to the principle of excluded middle. The reason for the last point is that an apodictic truth can only be thought possible by negating its contrary, that is, by dividing the representation of a predicate into two contradictory opposites and excluding one of them.

On page 169 the attempt to prove that the simple, *qua* intelligible, can be made intuitive, comes out more pitifully than all the other arguments. For he talks of "concrete" time as something synthesized [*Zusammengesetzten*], whose simple elements are supposed to be representations, and he does not remark that in order to conceive the succession of that concrete time one would already have had to presuppose the *pure* intuition *of time* wherein those representations are supposed to succeed one another. But since there is nothing simple in the pure intuition, which the author calls non-pictorial [*unbildlich*] (or non-sensible), it follows without question that the understanding does not in any way elevate itself above the sphere of sensibility when it is conceiving time. With his would-be primary elements for the composition of space, his "simples," he opposes not only Leibniz' correct opinion but also the whole of mathematics. From my remarks concerning page 163 you can determine the value of pages 244–56 and the claimed *objective* validity of his logical principle of sufficient reason.[3] He wants to infer, from a consideration of the ideas and connections of ideas that make up the principle (which he really takes for the principle of causality), and from its objective necessity, that the ground of the principle must lie not merely in the subject but in objects; however, I am not sure I understand this

---

[3] Eberhard attacks the question, "Can we attribute external reality—a possibility or actuality—beyond our cognitive power" to objects that we judge to be external? His proof that external objects are actual is then derived from "healthy reason" [*gesunden Vernuft*], which requires "true objects external to it," corresponding to those representations that are not grounded in the subject himself.

confused discussion. But why does he need such circumlocutions, when he thinks he can deduce it from the principle of contradiction?

I don't remember whether in my previous letter I mentioned this man's strange and thoroughly provocative misinterpretation or misrepresentation of my account of *ideas of reason* (ideas for which no corresponding intuition can be given) and of my discussion of the supersensible in general. He maintains that the concept of a chiliagon is such an idea and that nevertheless we can have a good deal of mathematical knowledge of it. Now this is so absurd a misunderstanding of the concept of "supersensible" that a child would see through it. For the question is just whether there can be an exhibition of the idea in a possible intuition, in accordance with our *kind* of sensibility; the *degree*—the power of the imagination to grasp the manifold—may be as great or small as it will. Even if something were presented to us as a million-sided figure and we were able to spot the lack of a single side at first glance, this representation would still be a sensible one; and only the possibility of exhibiting the concept of a chiliagon in intuition can ground the possibility of this object itself in mathematics. For then the construction of the object can be completely prescribed, without our worrying about the size of the measuring stick that would be required in order to make this figure, with all its parts, observable to the eye. You can tell what sort of a man Eberhard is from this example of his misrepresentation.

He is good at giving false citations, particularly, for example, on page 301. But on pages 290 and 298 ff. he surpasses himself, for there he becomes a veritable *Falsarius*. He cites A 44 of the *Critique,* where I said, "The philosophy of Leibniz and Wolff, in thus treating the difference between the sensible and the intelligible as merely logical, has given a completely wrong direction to all investigations into the nature and origin of our knowledge," and expounds it thus: "Mr. Kant accuses the philosophy of Leibniz and Wolff of counterfeiting the concept of sensibility and appearance by making the distinction between the sensible and the intellectual a merely logical one." Just as some people are inclined to believe lies that they themselves have often repeated, so Eberhard becomes zealous to the point that he attributes the word "counterfeit" (*verfälscht*) to me, when the word in fact exists only in his brain. He does this three times on one page (page 298) in discussing my supposedly unrestrained attack on Leibniz. What do you call someone who deliberately falsifies a document in a legal trial?

I content myself with these few remarks and beg you to use them as you see fit but, where possible, in a vigorous fashion. You must not expect restraint of this man who has made braggadocio his maxim in order to trick people into granting him recognition. I would fight him myself, but for the time it would take, which I must rather use to complete my project; for already I feel the infirmities of age and must therefore leave the struggle to my friends, if they deem it worth the effort to defend my cause. Basically I cannot help but be pleased by the general movement that the *Critique* has inspired and still stimulates, even with all the alliances that are formed against it (though the opponents of the *Critique* are split and will remain so); for all this calls attention to the book. Besides, the unending misunderstandings and misinterpretations provide a stimulus to the further clarification of expression that occasions the misunderstanding. So I really do not fear these attacks, as long as we remain calm under fire. Still, it is a good deed to the community to unmask at the outset a man composed entirely of deceit, who uses nimbly, from long experience, every device that can seduce a casual reader into blind faith in him, for example, the appeal to misinterpreted passages in the writings of distinguished men. Feder is with all his limitations at least honest, a property totally absent from Eberhard's thinking. . . .

With warmth and friendship, and with the greatest respect for the integrity of your character, I am, faithfully,

Your entirely devoted servant,
I. KANT

Königsberg

To Marcus Herz, May 26, 1789

- 362 - VOL. XI, *pp. 48–55*

Every letter that I receive from you, dearest friend, gives me genuine pleasure. Your noble feeling of gratitude for the small contribution I made to the development of your excellent native talents sets you apart from the majority of my students. What can be more consoling, when one is close to leaving this world, than to see that one has not lived in vain, since one has brought up *some,* even if only a few, to be good human beings.

But what are you thinking of, dearest friend, in sending me a large package of the most subtle investigations, not only to read through but to think through, I who in my 66th year am still burdened with the extensive work of completing my plan (partly in producing the last part of the critique, namely, that of *judgment,* which should appear soon, and partly in working out a *system of metaphysics,* of nature as well as of morals, in conformity with those critical demands). Besides, I am continuously kept on the move by many letters, demanding special explanations of certain points, and my health grows progressively worse. I had half decided to send the manuscript back immediately, with the aforementioned, totally adequate apology. But one glance at the work made me realize its excellence and that not only had none of my critics understood me and the main questions as well as Mr. Maimon does but also very few men possess so much acumen for such deep investigations as he; and this moved me to lay his book aside till I might have a few moments of leisure, which I have found only now and then only enough to get through the *first two parts,* of which I can write only briefly.

Please convey this to Mr. Maimon. I assume it is taken for granted that this is not meant for publication.

If I have correctly grasped the sense of his work, the intention is to prove that if the understanding is to have a law-giving relationship to sensible intuition (not only to the empirical but also to the a priori sort), then the understanding must itself be the originator not only of sensible forms but even of the material of intuition, that is, of objects. Otherwise the *quid juris* could not be answered adequately; which question could, however, be answered according to Leibnizian-Wolfian [*sic*] principles, if one grants them the view that sensibility is not specifically different from the understanding but differs from it only in degree of consciousness, belonging to the understanding *qua* knowledge of the world. The degree is infinitely small, in the first kind of representation; it is of a given (finite) magnitude in the second. An a priori synthesis can have objective validity only because the divine understanding, of which ours is only a part (or as he expresses it, "though only in a limited way"), is one with our own understanding; that is, it is itself the originator of forms and of the possibility of the things (in themselves) in the world.

However, I doubt very much that this was Leibnitz' or Wolf's opinion, or that this could really be deduced from their explanations of the distinction between sensibility and the understanding; and those who are familiar with the teachings of these men will find it difficult to agree that they assume a Spinozism; for, in fact, Mr. Maimon's way of representing *is* Spinozism and could be used most excellently to refute the Leibnizians *ex concessis*.

Mr. Maimon's theory consists basically in the contention that an understanding (indeed, the human understanding) not only is a faculty of thinking, as our understanding and perhaps that of all creatures essentially is, but is actually a faculty of intuition, where thinking is only a way of bringing the manifold of intuition (which is obscure because of our limitations) into clear consciousness. I, on the other hand, conceive of the understanding as a *special* faculty and ascribe to it the concept of an object in general (a concept that even the clearest consciousness of our intuition would not at all disclose). In other words I ascribe to the understanding the synthetic unity of apperception, through which alone the manifold of intuition (of whose *every feature* I may nevertheless be *particularly* conscious), in a unified consciousness, is brought to the representation of an object in general (whose concept is then determined by means of that manifold).

Now Mr. Maimon asks: How do I explain the possibility of agreement between a priori intuitions and my a priori concepts, if each has its specifically different origin, since this agreement is given as a fact but the legitimacy or the necessity of the agreement of two such heterogeneous manners of representation is incomprehensible. And vice versa, how can I prescribe, for example, the law of causality to nature, that is, to objects themselves, by means of my category (whose possibility in itself is only problematic). Finally, how can I even prove the necessity of these functions of the understanding whose existence is again merely a fact, since that necessity has to be presupposed if we are to subject things, however conceived, to those functions.

To this I answer: All of this takes place in relation to an experiential knowledge that is only possible under these conditions, a "subjective" consideration, to be sure. It must, however, be objectively valid as well, because the objects here are not things in themselves but mere appearances. Therefore, the form in which they are given depends on our understanding, on the one hand, on the subjective, that is, specific, manner of our intuition; on the other hand, it depends on the uniting of the manifold in a consciousness, that is, according to the thinking both of the object and of the cognition. Only under these conditions, therefore, can we have experiences of objects; and consequently, if intuition (of objects of appearance) did not agree with these conditions, objects would be nothing for us, that is, not objects of *knowledge* at all; we should have knowledge neither of ourselves nor of other things.

In this way it can be shown that if we are able to make synthetic judgments a priori, these judgments are concerned only with objects of intuition as mere appearances. Even if we were capable of an intellectual intuition (for example, in such a way that the infinitely small elements of intuition were noumena), it would be impossible to show the necessity of such judgments in conformity with the nature of our understanding in which concepts such as "necessity" exist. For such intuitions would still be mere perceptions; for example, the perception that in a triangle two sides taken together are larger than the third side—not the recognition that this property would have to belong to a triangle *necessarily*. But we are absolutely unable to explain further how it is that a sensible intuition (such as space and time), the form of our sensibility, or such functions of the understanding as those out of which logic develops are possible; nor can we explain why it is that one form agrees with another in forming a possible cognition. For we should have to have still another manner of intuition than the one we have and another understanding with which to compare our own and with which everyone could perceive things in themselves. But we can only judge an understanding by means of our own understanding, and so it is, too, with all intuition. It is, however, entirely unnecessary to answer this question. For if we can demonstrate that *our knowledge* of things, even experience itself, is only possible under those conditions, it follows that all other concepts of things (which are not thus conditioned) are for us empty and utterly useless for knowledge. But not only that; all sense data for a possible cognition would never, without those conditions, represent objects. They would not even reach that unity of consciousness that is necessary for knowledge of myself (as object of inner sense). I would not even be able to know that I have sense data; consequently for me, as a knowing being, they would be absolutely nothing. They could still (I imagine myself to be an animal) carry on their play in an orderly fashion, as representations connected according to empirical laws of association, and thus even have an influence on my feeling and desire, without my being aware of them (assuming that I am even conscious of each individual representation, but not of their relation to the unity of representation of their object, by means of the synthetic unity of their apperception). This might be so without my knowing the slightest thing thereby, not even what my own condition is.

It is difficult to guess the thoughts that may have hovered in the mind of a deep thinker and that he himself could not make entirely clear. Nevertheless I am quite convinced that Leibniz, in his pre-established harmony (which he, like Baumgarten after him, made very general), had in mind not the harmony of two different natures, namely, sense and understanding, but that of two faculties belonging to the same nature, in which sensibility and understanding harmonize to form experiential knowledge. If we wanted to make judgments about their origin—an investigation that of course lies wholly beyond the limits of human reason —we could name nothing beyond our divine creator; once they are given, however, we are fully able to explain their power of making a priori judgments (that is, the *quid juris*).

I must content myself with these remarks and cannot, because of my limited time, go into details. I remark only that it is not necessary to assume, with Mr. Maimon, *"ideas of the understanding"* [*Verstandesideen*].[1] Nothing is thought in the concept of a circle other than that *all* straight lines drawn between it and a

---

[1] Maimon wrote: "The material completeness of a concept, insofar as this completeness cannot be given in intuition, is an idea of the understanding [*Verstandsidee*]. For example, the understanding dictates a rule or condition to itself: that from a given point, an infinite number of equal lines can be drawn. Out of this (by the uniting of their end points), the concept of a circle is produced. The possibility of this rule, and thus the possibility of the concept itself, can be shown in intuition (by the movement of a line around a given point). Consequently, the formal completeness (the unity in the manifold) can also be shown. However, its material completeness (in the manifold) cannot be given in intuition, for one can always draw only a finite number of lines equal to one another. It is therefore not a concept of the understanding [*Verstandsbegriff*] to which an object corresponds but only an idea of the understanding [*Verstandsidee*], which one can approach asymptotically in intuition by means of the successive production of such lines. It is thus a limiting concept [*Gränzbegriff*]." *Versuch über die Transcendentalphilosophie* (Berlin, 1790), pp. 75 f. Cf. Maimon's letter to Kant of April 7, 1789 [352], p. 133.

single point (the center) are equal. This is a merely logical function of the universality of judgment, in which the concept of a line constitutes the subject and signifies only as much as *"any line,"* not the *totality* of lines, that could be inscribed on a plane from a given point. Otherwise every line would, with equal justice, be an idea of the understanding; for the idea includes all lines as parts that can be thought between two points (thinkable only in it) and whose number is also infinite. That this line can be infinitely divided is also not an idea, for it signifies only a continuation of the division unlimited by the size of the line. But to see this infinite division in its totality, and consequently as completed, is an idea of reason, the idea of an absolute totality of conditions (of synthesis) demanded of an object of sense, which is impossible since the unconditioned is not at all to be found among appearances.

Furthermore, the possibility of a circle is not merely *problematic,* dependent, as it were, on the practical proposition "to inscribe a circle by the movement of a straight line around a fixed point"; rather, the possibility is *given* in the definition of the circle, since the circle is actually constructed by means of the definition, that is, it is exhibited in intuition, not actually on paper (empirically) but in the imagination (a priori). For I may always draw a circle free hand on the board and put a point in it, and I can demonstrate all properties of the circle just as well on it, presupposing the (so-called) nominal definition, which is in fact a real definition, even if this circle is not at all like one drawn by rotating a straight line attached to a point. I assume that the points of the circumference are equidistant from the center point. The proposition "to inscribe a circle" is a practical corollary of the definition (or so-called postulate), which could not be demanded at all if the possibility— yes, the very sort of possibility of the figure—were not already given in the definition.

As for defining a straight line, it cannot be done by referring to the identity of direction of all the line's parts, for the concept of direction (as a *straight line,* by means of which the movement is distinguished, *without reference to its size*) already presupposes this concept. But these are incidentals.

Mr. Maimon's book contains besides this so many acute observations that he could have published it at any time, with no small advantage to his reputation and without offending me thereby, though he takes a very different path than I do. Still, he agrees with me that a reform must be undertaken, if the principles of metaphysics are to be made firm, and few men are willing to be convinced that this is necessary. But, dearest friend, your request for a recommendation from me, to accompany the publication of this work, would not be feasible, since it is after all largely directed *against me.* That is my judgment, in case the work were published. But if you want my advice about publishing the work as it is, it seems best to me, since Mr. Maimon is presumably not indifferent to being fully understood, that he use the time required for the publication to work up a complete theory. There he should indicate clearly not merely the manner in which he thinks of the principles of a priori knowledge but also what his system implies concerning the solution of the tasks of pure reason, which constitute the essential part of the goals of metaphysics. The antinomies of pure reason could provide a good test stone for that, which might convince him that one cannot assume human reason to be of one kind with the divine reason, distinct from it only by limitation, that is, in degree—that human reason, unlike the divine reason, must be regarded as a faculty only of *thinking,* not of *intuiting;* that it is thoroughly dependent on an entirely different faculty (or receptivity) for its intuitions, or better, for the material out of which it fashions knowledge; and that, since intuition gives us mere appearances whereas the fact itself is a mere concept of reason, the antinomies (which arise entirely because of the confusion of the two) can never be resolved except by deducing the possibility of synthetic a priori propositions according to my principles.

I remain as ever your loyal servant and friend,

I. KANT

To F. H. Jacobi, August 30, 1789

- 375 - VOL. XI, pp. 75–77

Esteemed sir:

The gift from Count von Windisch-Graetz,[1] containing his philosophical essays, has arrived (thanks to you and to Privy Commercial Counselor R. Fischer), and I have also received the first edition of *Histoire métaphysique* . . . from the book dealer Sixt.

Please thank the Count for me and assure him of my respect for his philosophical talent, a talent that he combines with the noblest attitudes of a cosmopolite. In the last mentioned work, I observed with pleasure that the Count discusses, with the clarity and modesty of one who is at home in the great world, the same matters with which I in my scholastic fashion have also been concerned, viz., the definition and encouragement of human nature's noblest incentives [*Triebfedern*], incentives that have so often been confused with (and even taken for) physical urges and that have failed to produce the results that one rightfully expects of them. I long passionately to see him complete this work, for it obviously is systematically related to his other two books (the one on secret societies and the one on voluntary changes of the constitution in monarchies). This system would certainly have great influence, partly as a wonderfully realized prophecy, partly as sage counsel to despots, in the current European crisis. No statesman has heretofore inquired so deeply into the principles of the art of governing men or has even known how to go about such an inquiry. But that

---

[1] Joseph Nicolaus v. Windisch-Graetz (1744–1802), a writer on political philosophy, whom Kant mentions also in *Perpetual Peace*. His position resembled Kant's on several points; for example, he insisted that human activity could not be understood in terms of merely passive sensations, he rejected eudaemonism, and he argued that the idea of immortality must be based on virtue, not vice versa. The writings to which Kant alludes are: *Solution provisoire d'un Probleme, ou Histoire métaphysique de l'organiza-tion animale* (1789), *Objections aux sociétés sécrètes* (1788), and a discourse on the question whether a monarch has the right to change a constitution (1789).

is why none of the proposals of such people have succeeded in convincing anyone, much less in producing results.

For the newest edition of your handsome book on Spinoza's theory, my warmest thanks. You have earned distinction, first of all for having clearly presented the difficulties of the teleological road to theology, the road that Spinoza seems to have chosen. To dash with hasty, enterprising steps toward a far away goal has always been injurious to a thorough insight. He who shows us the cliffs has not necessarily set them up, and even if someone maintains that it is impossible to pass through them *with full sails* (of dogmatism), he has not on that account denied *every* possibility of getting through. I think that you will not find the compass of reason to be unnecessary or misleading in this venture. The indispensible supplement to reason is something that, though not part of speculative knowledge, lies only in reason itself, something that we can name (viz., freedom, a supersensible power of causality within us) but that we cannot grasp. The question whether reason could only be *awakened* to this concept of theism by being instructed with historical events or whether it would require an incomprehensible supernatural inspiration [*Einwirkung*], this is an incidental question, a question of the origin and introduction of this idea. For one can just as well admit that if the gospel had not previously instructed us in the universal moral laws, in their total purity, our reason would not yet have discovered them so completely; still, *once we are in possession of them,* we can convince anyone of their correctness and validity using reason alone.

You have thoroughly refuted the syncretism of Spinozism and the deism of Herder's God. All syncretistic talk is commonly based on insincerity, a property of mind that is especially characteristic of this great artist in delusions (which, like magic lanterns, make marvelous images appear for a moment but which soon vanish forever, though they leave behind in the minds of the uninformed a conviction that something unusual must be behind it all, something, however, that they cannot catch hold of.)

I have always thought it my duty to show respect for men of talent, science, and justice, no matter how far our opinions may differ. You will, I hope, appraise my essay on orientation, in the *Berlinische Monatsschrift,* from this perspective. I was requested by various people to cleanse myself of the suspicion of Spinozism, and therefore, contrary to my inclination, I wrote this essay.[2] I

[2] *What Is Orientation in Thinking? (Was heisst: Sich im Denken Orientieren?* [1786]). The essay is included in L. W. Beck's edition of

hope you will find in it no trace of deviation from the principle I have just affirmed. With inner pain I have read some other attacks upon your views and those of some of your worthy friends, and I have even spoken out against such attacks. I do not understand how it is that otherwise good and reasonable men are often inclined to regard as meritorious an attack that they would take to be highly unfair were it directed against themselves. Yet true merit cannot be diminished by such shadows cast on its gleaming brilliance; it will not be mistaken.

Our Hamann [3] has accepted the position of private tutor at Count von Keyserling's in Curland, principally with the intention of systematizing his many-sided knowledge by presenting it to others, and he likes it there. He is a decent, honest soul. He is thinking of devoting himself to schoolteaching since he recently lost his father and mother and needs to help his orphaned sisters at home.

I wish you many years of good health, good cheer, and good fortune to pursue the work you so love, the noblest task of all, viz., reflection on the serious principles on which the general welfare of mankind depends, and I am, most respectfully,

Your most devoted servant,
I. KANT

To L. E. Borowski [1] [between March 6 and 22, 1790]

- 411 - VOL. XI, *pp. 141–43*

You ask me what might be the source of the fanaticism [*Schwärmerei*] that is so rapidly gaining ground and how this disease might be cured. Both of these questions are as difficult for physicians of the soul as was the influenza epidemic that spread all around the world a few years ago (what the Viennese call "Russian catarrh") for physicians of the body. The influenza infected people one right after the other, but it soon cleared up by itself. I

Kant's *Critique of Practical Reason and Other Writings in Moral Philosophy* (Chicago: University of Chicago Press, 1949). It is Kant's answer to the famous pantheism controversy between Jacobi and Mendelssohn.

[3] Johann Michael Hamann, son of J. G. Hamann, (1769–1813).

[1] Ludwig Ernst Borowski (1740–1832), one of Kant's first students and, later, biographer. Borowski's profession was the ministry.

think the two sorts of doctors have much in common, being better able to describe the illnesses than to discover their origin or cure. How fortunate are the sick when the doctor's only prescription is dietary, a recommendation of pure cold water as an antidote to the disease, trusting kind nature to do the rest.

It seems to me that the universally prevailing mania for reading [*Lesesucht*] is not only the carrier that spreads this illness but also the poison (miasma) that produces it. The more well-to-do and fashionable people, claiming their insights at least equal if not superior to the insights of those who have troubled to pursue the thorny path of thorough investigation, are content with indices and summaries, skimming the cream off the sciences. These people would like to obscure the obvious difference between loquacious ignorance and thorough science, and this is easiest to do by snatching up incomprehensible things that are no more than airy possibilities and presenting them as facts that the serious natural scientist is supposed to explain. They ask him how he can account for the fulfilment of this or that dream,[2] presentiment, astrological prophecy, transmutation of lead into gold, and so on. For in matters of this kind, when once the fact is conceded (and these people will not let it be questioned), one man is as ignorant of the explanation as another. They find it hard to learn everything the natural scientist knows, so they take the easier road, attempting to dissolve the inequality between them and him by showing that there are matters about which neither of them knows what to say, matters of which the unscientific man is therefore free to judge in any way whatsoever, since the scientist cannot correct him. This is where the mania begins, and from there it spreads to ordinary people as well.

I see only one antidote for this disease: thoroughness must be substituted for dilettantism in education, and the desire to read must not be eradicated but redirected so as to become purposeful. When this happens, the well-instructed man will enjoy reading only what will genuinely profit his understanding, and everything else will disgust him. In his *Observations of a Traveller,* a German doctor, Mr. Grimm,[3] finds fault with what he calls "the French omniscience," but that is not nearly as tasteless as what the German does, usually constructing a ponderous system that he

[2] The reference is to Swedenborg.
[3] J. F. C. Grimm (1737–1821), of Weimar, *Bemerkungen eines Reisenden durch Deutschland, Frankreich, England und Holland* (Altenburg, 1775).

becomes fanatically unwilling to abandon. The Mesmer-show [4] in France is only a fad and will soon disappear completely.

The customary trick the fanatic uses to give his ignorance the appearance of science is to ask, "Do you understand the real cause of magnetic force, or do you know the material stuff that exercises such marvelous effects in electrical phenomena?" Thus he thinks he is justified in expressing his opinions on a subject that, in his view, the greatest natural scientist understands as little as he does, and he ventures to hold forth even on the most likely effects of this force. But the scientist considers only those effects to be genuine that are susceptible of experimental testing, so that the object of investigation is wholly under his control. The fanatic, on the other hand, snatches up effects that could have originated in the imagination of either the observer or the subject being observed, so that there is no possibility of experimental control.

There is nothing to be done about this mischief except to let the animal magnetist magnetize and disorganize, as long as he and his credulous fellows desire. We can only advise them to keep away from moral issues and recommend that they pursue the single road of natural science, using experiment and observation to discover the properties of objects of outer sense. Elaborate refutation here is beneath the dignity of reason and, furthermore, accomplishes nothing. Disdainful silence is more appropriate toward such madness. Movements of this kind, in the moral realm, have but a short duration before they make way for new follies.

To J. G. C. C. Kiesewetter, April 20, 1790

- 419 -   VOL. XI, *pp. 154–55*

. . . The criterion of a genuine moral principle is its unconditional practical necessity; thereby it differs entirely from all other sorts of practical principles. The possibility of freedom, if this be considered (as in the *Critique of Pure Reason*) prior to any discussion of the moral law, signifies only the transcendental concept of the causality of an earthly creature in general insofar as that causality is *not* determined by any ground in the sensible

[4] Mesmer's theory of "animal magnetism" was taken up throughout France.

world; and all that is shown there is that there is nothing self-contradictory about this concept (it is not specifically the concept of the causality of a will). This transcendental idea [of freedom] acquires content by means of the moral law, and it is given *to the will* (the will being a property of a rational being—man) because the moral law allows no ground of determination from nature (the aggregate of objects of sense). The concept of freedom, as causality, is apprehended in an affirmation, and this concept of a free causality is without circularity interchangeable with the concept of a moral ground of determination.[1]

From J. G. C. C. Kiesewetter, April 20, 1790

- 420 - VOL. XI, *pp. 155–60*

Dearest, best professor,

[Kiesewetter apologizes for not writing sooner and gives a somewhat lengthy account of his circumstances, his success as a private tutor and lecturer, and news of various mutual acquaintances. He tells of a Professor Selle,[1] a physician in Berlin, who was about to publish an essay that, Selle hoped, would give the death blow to Kant's system.]

. . . As far as I have learned, his main argument is that even assuming that you had proved space and time to be forms of our sensibility, you could not show that they were *only* forms of

---

[1] This passage is one of the places where Kant tries to answer the charge that his arguments for freedom and the moral law are circular, each assuming the reality of the other. The circularity is only apparent, he explains, since "freedom" is used in two senses: first, to signify the negative, "transcendental" idea of independence from the determinism of nature (a concept whose non-contradictoriness Kant thinks he has shown in the antinomy of the first *Critique*), and second, to signify the positive concept of freedom as autonomy, a unique sort of causality possessed by rational beings. Cf. *Grundlegung zur Metaphysik der Sitten,* in *Werke,* IV, 450, in which Kant offers a somewhat different solution: the activity of thinking, he maintains there, is itself a manifestation of freedom. The charge of circularity came from a critic named J. F. Flatt. The two concepts of freedom have been discussed by L. W. Beck in his *Commentary on Kant's Critique of Practical Reason* (Chicago: University of Chicago Press, 1960), p. 59.

[1] Christian Gottlieb Selle (originally Sell) (1748–1800), an empiricist and one of the men to whom Kant sent complimentary copies of the *Critique.*

sensibility, since it is still *possible* to imagine them to belong to things in themselves, a possibility that you are in no position to deny, in view of your claim that we can know nothing of things in themselves. Besides, one might also try to show why we intuit in just these and no other forms. In his opinion, space and time are subjectively necessary conditions of our intuitions, but there are properties of things in themselves that correspond to them.—If it turns out that his whole attack contains nothing more significant than that, I shall not find it so frightening. How is Mr. S. going to prove that space and time belong to things in themselves? And if he admits that space and time are forms of sensibility, how can he claim that they are nevertheless dependent on things in themselves? For if they were given by means of objects, they would be part of the matter of intuition, not its form. I shall gladly send you a copy as soon as the book appears.

Strange things are happening here nowadays. A week ago last Sunday the King got married to the Countess of Dehnhof,[2] in one of the rooms of the castle here. The probability is—virtually a certainty, to my mind—that Zöllner[3] performed the wedding. Minister Wöllner[4] and Mr. von Geysau[5] attended the King; the

---

[2] Sophie Juliane Friederike Wilhelmine, Countess of Dönhoff (1768–1834) married Friedrich Wilhelm II on April 11, 1790. She is mentioned again in the letter from Kiesewetter of June 14, 1791 [474].

[3] Johann Friedrich Zöllner, preacher and *Oberkonsistorialrat* (prior in charge of the principal church in the district) in Berlin (1753–1804). Zöllner argued warmly against the King's new catechism.

[4] Johann Christoph Wöllner, favorite of Friedrich Wilhelm II (1732–1800). Wöllner, an orthodox theologian, was once characterized by Frederick the Great as "a deceitful, scheming priest and nothing more." (K. Vorländer, *Immanuel Kant's Leben* [Leipzig: Felix Meiner, 1921], p. 157.)

Friedrich Wilhelm II put special trust in Wöllner, elevating him on July 3, 1788, to the position of minister of justice (replacing Minister Zedlitz, to whom Kant dedicated the *Critique of Pure Reason*) and head of the departments concerned with spiritual matters. Six days later his *Religionsedict* appeared, asserting that even Lutheran and Calvinistic teachers were trying to destroy the basic truths of Holy Scripture and were disseminating countless errors under the pretense of enlightenment. The edict paid lip service to the Prussian tradition of toleration and freedom of conscience but insisted that everyone should keep his opinions to himself and take care not to undermine other people's faith. On December 19, 1788, a new censorship edict followed, designed to limit "the impetuosity of today's so-called enlighteners" and the "freedom of the press, which has degenerated into insolence of the press." All writings published domestically or to be exported beyond Prussia were put under censorship. The King anticipated that the censorship would "put a check on those works that oppose the universal principles of religion, the state, and civil order." (See Vorländer, *op. cit.*, p. 158.)

At first, the edict had no effect. Liberal theologians preached more freely

mother and sister of the Countess and her stepbrother (or cousin, I forget which) attended the bride. The King arrived Saturday evening from Potsdam and the marriage took place Sunday evening at 6. The Countess was dressed in white (like the heroine of a novel), with hair unfurled. She resides in Potsdam now. It is presumed that the Elector of Saxony [6] will have to promote her to imperial princess. Formerly she was lady-in-waiting to the reigning queen. For almost a year the king has been carrying on negotiations with her, but her public behavior was such that one couldn't tell whether she gave him a hearing or not.

About two weeks ago her mother came, or so the Countess has let it be circulated, to take her to Prussia, at her request. The Countess then publicly makes her farewells at court. The reigning queen makes her a present of a pair of brilliant earrings and tells her she will know best of what they may remind her. Everybody thinks she has left, just as the marriage is taking place. The Queen has received the news rather calmly. What I have told you up to now is, apart from precise details, known to almost everyone, and it is causing a mighty sensation among the public. The crowd at Zöllner's sermons has diminished and even at an introduction that he recently held, where people used to come in droves, the church was empty.—The following facts are known only to a few persons. The King and Queen are divorced, a decree to which she agreed at the time of the "negotiations" with the late Lugenheim.[7] The King gave up all marital rights, and the Queen retained only the honorary title. Dr. Brown [8] declared her unbalanced, and this is very probably true, since insanity ran in the family. She often dances around on chairs and tables and sees ghosts. What a

than ever, Kant's friend Berens wrote to him. One man wanted to print Luther's essay on freedom of thought, especially the sentence, "Knights, Bishops, and Nobles are fools if they meddle in matters of faith." Berens thought that similar passages written by the late Frederick the Great should be published as an appendix. He asked Kant (as had others before him) to express his views on the problem in Biester's journal, the *Berliner Monatsschrift*.

For a time, Wöllner pretended to be friendly to Kant, allowing Kiesewetter to lecture on Kant's philosophy (though with his own spy sometimes in attendance). See Kiesewetter's letter of June 14, 1791 [474].

[5] Levin von Geysau, a Prussian army officer.

[6] Friedrich August III (1763–1817); after 1806, as king, Friedrich August I.

[7] Julie von Voss, Countess Lugenheim, another mistress of Friedrich Wilhelm II (1767–89).

[8] Dr. Carl Brown, royal physician.

misfortune it would be for our state if this defect had been transmitted to her children.

War preparations are still continuing here.[9] The most remarkable thing, though, is that the King and not the ministry wants war. The official plan is as follows: our army will be divided into four corps, the first, led by the King, with Möllendorf[10] commanding under him, will fight the Austrians; the second, led by the Duke of Braunschweig,[11] will oppose the Russians; Prince Friedrich[12] commands the reconnaissance corps against the Saxons; and besides these there is supposed to be a so-called flying corps. As far as Saxony is concerned, they say that at the time that the late Emperor was still alive a special envoy of the Emperor's who had come for a private audience with the Elector at the Saxon court was arrested. The audience was, however, granted, and the envoy inquired of the Elector how he would act if Prussia should go to war. The Elector replied that he would remain neutral. The envoy received this answer with pleasure and asked the Elector to make an official proclamation. But happily the Marquis Lucchesini[13] prevented this, though the Elector had given his answer orally. So now an army will compel the Elector to join our side. . . .

[Kiesewetter wishes Kant a happy 67th birthday tomorrow.]

Your devoted servant,
J. G. C. KIESEWETTER

Berlin

P.S. My last letter[14] told you the story of the catechism rejected by the Ober Consistorium. Now Mr. Silberschlag and Preacher Hecker[15] are reworking an old catechism, composed by the late Inspector Hecker,[16] containing a compilation of theological twaddle.

[9] Against Austria.

[10] W. J. H. v. Möllendorf, general field marshall, governor of Berlin (1724–1816).

[11] Carl Wm. Ferdinand, Prussian field marshall (1735–1806).

[12] Duke of York (1763–1827).

[13] Girolamo Lucchesini (1752–1825), Italian by birth, at that time sent to Warsaw by Friedrich Wilhelm II as envoy extraordinary and minister plenipotentiary.

[14] March 3, 1790 [409], in Werke, XI, 137.

[15] Andreas Jakob Hecker (1746–1819), chaplain at the Dreifaltigkeitskirche and, from 1785, director of the united institutes of the royal Realschule.

[16] Johann Julius Hecker (1707–68), founder of the Realschule in Berlin.

To A. W. Rehberg[1] [before September 25, 1790]

- 448 - VOL. XI, pp. 207–10

The question is: Since the understanding has the power to create numbers at will, why is it incapable of thinking $\sqrt{2}$ in numbers? For if the understanding could *think* it, it ought to be able to *produce* it, too, since numbers are pure acts of its spontaneity, and the synthetic propositions of arithmetic and algebra cannot limit this spontaneity by the condition of intuition in space and time. It seems, therefore, that we must assume a transcendental faculty of imagination, one that, in representing the object independently even of space and time, connects synthetic representations solely in pursuance of understanding. From this faculty, a special system of algebra could be constructed, a knowledge of which (were it possible) would advance the method of solving equations to its highest generality.

This is how I understand the question put to me.

An Attempt to Answer This Question

(1) I can regard every number as the product of two factors, even if these factors are not immediately given to me or even if they could not be given in numbers. For, if the given number is 15, I can take one of the factors as 3, so that the other is 5, and $3 \times 5 = 15$. Or let the given factor be 2; then the second factor sought is $15\frac{1}{2}$. Or let the first factor be the fraction $\frac{1}{7}$; the other factor is $105\frac{5}{7}$, and so on. It is thus possible, given any number as product and given one of its factors, to find the other factor.

(2) If neither of the factors is given but only a relationship between them—for example, it is given that they are equal—so that we have a and the factor sought is x, where $1 : x = x : a$ (that is, x is the mean proportional between 1 and a), then, since $a = x^2$, x must $= \sqrt{a}$. That is, the square root of a given quantity, for example, $\sqrt{2}$, is expressed by the mean proportional between 1 and the given number (in this case, 2). It is thus also possible to think numbers such as that one.

---

[1] On August Wilhelm Rehberg, see the letter to J. E. Biester of April 10, 1794 [621], n. 2.

Geometry shows us, by the example of the diagonal of a square, that the mean *proportional quantity* between the quantities 1 and 2 can be found and that $\sqrt{2}$ is consequently not an empty, objectless concept. So the question is only, why cannot a *number* be found for this quantity, a number whose *concept* would represent the quantity (its relation to unity) clearly and completely.

From the fact that every number could be represented as the square of some other number, *it does not follow* that the square root must be rational (that is, have a denumerable relation to unity). This can be seen by means of the principle of identity, if we consider the concepts basic to the question: the idea of two equal (but undetermined) factors of a given product. For there is no determinate relation to unity given in these concepts, only an interrelationship. It follows from paragraph 1 above, however, that this root, located in the series of numbers between two members of that series (let them be divided into decades, for instance), will always encounter still another intermediate number and thus another relation to unity. This must be so when one part of the root is found in this series. But the reason why the understanding, which has arbitrarily created the concept of $\sqrt{2}$, must content itself with an asymptotic approach to the number $\sqrt{2}$ and cannot also produce the complete numerical concept (the rational relationship of $\sqrt{2}$ to unity)—the reason for this has to do with time, the successive progression as form of all counting and of all numerical quantities; for time is the basic condition of all this producing of quantities.

It is true that the mere concept of the square root of a positive quantity, that is, $\sqrt{a}$, as represented in algebra, requires no synthesis in time. Similarly, one can see the impossibility of the square root of a negative quantity, $\sqrt{-a}$ (where the same relation would have to hold between the *positive* quantity, unity, and another quantity, x, as holds between x and a *negative* quantity *), if the condition of time did not enter into this insight. This can be seen from the mere concepts of quantities. But as soon as, instead of a, the number for which a stands is given, so that the square root is not simply to be *named* (as in algebra) but *calculated* (as in arithmetic), the condition of all producing of numbers, viz., time,

---

* [Kant's footnote] Since this is self-contradictory, the expression $\sqrt{-a}$ stands for an impossible quantity.

becomes the inescapable foundation of the process. Indeed, we then require a pure intuition, in which we discover not only the given quantity but also the root, and we learn whether it can possibly be a whole number or can only be found as an irrational number by means of an infinite series of diminishing fractions.

The following consideration shows that what is needed for the concept of the square root *of a definite number,* for example, 15, is not the mere concept of a number, provided by the understanding, but rather a synthesis in time (as pure intuition): from the mere concept of a number, we cannot tell whether the root of that number will be rational or irrational. We have to *try it out,* either by comparing the products of all smaller whole numbers up to 100 with the given square, according to the multiplication table, or, in the case of larger numbers, by dividing them up, in accordance with demonstrated theorems, trying to find the components of the square or the parts of a twofold or *n*-fold root; and wherever the test of multiplying a whole number by itself does not yield the square, we increase the divisors of unity in order to obtain an infinite series of diminishing fractions, a series that expresses the root, though only in an irrational way (since the series can never be completed, though we can carry it out as far as we like).

Now if it were assumed to be impossible to explain or to prove a priori that *if the root of a given quantity cannot be expressed in whole numbers it also cannot be expressed determinately in fractions* (though it could be given as accurately as one wants), this would be a phenomenon concerning the relation of our power of imagination to our understanding, a phenomenon that we perceive by means of experiments with numbers but that we are totally unable to explain by means of the concepts of the understanding. But since we *can* explain it and demonstrate it, there is no need to assume this conclusion.

It seems to me that the puzzle about the mean proportional, which the penetrating author who questions the adequacy of our imaginative powers to execute the concepts of the understanding has discovered in arithmetic, is really based on the possibility of a *geometric construction* of such quantities, quantities that can never be completely expressed in numbers.

For the puzzlement one feels about $\sqrt{2}$ seems to me not to be produced by the proposition that, for every number, one can find a square root that, if not itself a number, is a rule for approximating the answer as closely as one wishes. What perplexes the understanding is rather the fact that this concept $\sqrt{2}$ can be constructed geometrically, so that it is not merely thinkable but also adequately visualizable, and the understanding is unable to see the basis of this. The understanding is not even in a position to assume the possibility of an object $\sqrt{2}$, since it cannot adequately present the concept of such a quantity in an intuition of number, and would even less anticipate that such a quantity could be given a priori.

The necessity of the synthesis [*Verknüpfung*] of the two forms of sensibility, space and time, in determining the objects of our intuition—so that time, when the subject makes himself the object of his representation, must be imagined as a line, if it is to be quantified, just as, on the other hand, a line can be quantified only by being constructed in time—this insight of the necessary synthesis of inner sense with outer sense, even in the determination of the time of our existence, seems to me of aid in proving the objective reality of our representations of outer things (as against psychological idealism) though I am not able to pursue this idea farther at the moment.

To C. F. Hellwag, January 3, 1791

- 461 - VOL. XI, *pp.* 245–47

. . . I shall think over your remarks on the distinction between synthetic and analytic propositions,[1] insofar as this concerns *logic*

---

[1] In his letter of December 13, 1790 [460], Hellwag suggested that convertible synthetic propositions would have analytic propositions as their converses, whereas the converse of an analytic proposition would in some instances be synthetic. For example, " 'All physical bodies are heavy' is synthetic; the synthesis of 'physical' and 'bodies' is the condition for the predicate 'heavy,' since it is not true that all physical things are heavy (a rainbow is physical but not heavy) or that all bodies, in a broad sense, are heavy (geometrical bodies are in a way bodies but are not heavy). Conversion yields two mutually independent analytic propositions: 'Everything heavy is a physical body' and 'Everything heavy is a body.' If we convert these [analytic] propositions, the subject of the converse synthetic propositions needs to be supplemented by the word 'certain': 'Certain physical things are heavy' and 'Certain bodies are heavy.' Another example: 'All bodies are extended' is analytic. Add to this 'All bodies are three-dimensional'—conversion yields the fully synthetic proposition 'All extended, three-dimensional things are bodies.' The connection of the two concepts in the subject of this proposition is the

rather than metaphysics. In metaphysics, where we are not so much concerned with the place of concepts in a judgment (the question of form) as with the question whether or not the concepts of certain judgments have any material content, your suggestions about convertibility are not relevant.

But as for the question, What is the ground of the law that matter, in all its changes, is dependent on *outer* causes and also requires the equality of action and reaction in these changes occasioned by outer causes?—I could easily have given a priori the universal transcendental ground of the possibility of these laws as well, in my *Metaphysical Foundations of Natural Science*. It might be summarized as follows.

All our concepts of matter contain nothing but the mere representation of outer relationships (for that is all that can be represented in space). But that which we posit as existing in space signifies no more than a *something* in general to which our imagination can attribute no characteristics but those of an outer thing, insofar as we regard the thing as mere matter, consequently as devoid of any *genuinely inner* properties such as the power of conception, feeling, or desire. From this it follows that, since every change presupposes a cause, and we cannot conceive of an absolutely inner cause producing change in outer, lifeless things (things that are merely material), the cause of all change (from a state of rest to a state of motion and, conversely, along with the specification of such changes) must lie in external matter, and without such a cause no change can take place. It follows that no special, *positive* principle of the conservation of motion in a moving body is required but only a negative one, viz., the absence of any cause of change.

As for the second law, it is based on the relationship of *active forces* in space in general, a relationship that must necessarily be one of reciprocal opposition and must always be equal (*actio est aequalis reactioni*), for space makes possible only relationships such as these, precluding any unilateral relationships. Thus the changes in spatial relationships, that is, motion and the action of bodies in producing motion in other bodies, requires that there be nothing but reciprocal and equal motions. I cannot conceive of a line drawn from body *A* to every point of body *B* without drawing equally as many lines in the opposite direction, so that I conceive

---

condition for the predicate, for not every extended thing is a body (a plane is extended) and not all three dimensional things are bodies. . . ."

the change of relationship in which body B is moved by the thrust of body A as a reciprocal and equal change. Here, too, there is no need for a special positive cause of opposition of the moved body, just as there was no such need in the case of the law of inertia, which I mentioned above. The general and sufficient ground of this law lies in the character of space, viz., that spatial relationships are reciprocal and *equal* (which is not true of the relations between successive positions in time). I shall look over Lambert's opinion on this matter in his *Beyträgen*.[2] . . .

To J. F. Gensichen,[1] April 19, 1791

- 466 -   VOL. XI, *pp. 252–53*

Dear tutor Gensichen,

In order to give proper credit to everyone who has contributed to the history of astronomy, I wish you would add an appendix to your dissertation and explain how my own modest conjectures differ from those of subsequent theorists.

1. The conception of the Milky Way as a system of moving suns analogous to our planetary system was formulated by me six years before Lambert published a similar theory in his *Cosmological Letters*.[2]

2. The idea that nebulae are comparable to remote milky ways was not an idea ventured by Lambert (as Erxleben maintains in his *Foundations of Natural Philosophy*[3] on p. 540, even in the new edition), for Lambert supposed them (at least one of them) to be dark bodies, illuminated by neighboring suns.

---

[2] *Beyträgen zum Gebrauche Mathematik und deren Anwendung* (Berlin, 1770). See Kant's *Werke*, XIII, 292.

[1] The original German version of this letter is not extant. A virtually incomprehensible English translation appeared in *Kantstudien*, II (1897), 104 f., under the title "A New Letter of Kant, by Walter B. Waterman, Boston, Mass." My translation is a reworking of this, with several obvious mistranslations corrected. It may nevertheless be false to the original here and there. On Gensichen, see notes to the letter to J. H. Tieftrunk of October 13, 1797 [784].

[2] J. H. Lambert, *Kosmologische Briefe* (1761). Cf. the letter from Lambert of November 13, 1765 [33].

[3] Johann Christian Polykarp Erxleben (professor of physics in Göttingen [1744–77]), *Anfangsgründe der Naturlehre* (1772).

3. A long time ago I defended a view that has been supported by recent observations, namely, that the production and conservation of the ring of Saturn could be accounted for by the laws of centripetal force alone. This view now appears to be well confirmed. There is, it seems, a revolving mist whose center is that of Saturn, and this mist is composed of particles whose revolution is not constant but varies with their distance from the center. This also confirms the rate of Saturn's revolution on its axis, which I inferred from it, and its flatness.

4. The agreement of recent findings with my theory as to the production of the ring of Saturn from a vaporous matter moving according to the laws of centripetal force seems also to support the theory that the planets [great globes] were produced according to the same laws, except that their property of rotation must have been produced originally by the fall of this dispersed substance as a result of gravity. Mr. Lichtenberg's approval of this theory gives it added force.[4] The theory is that prime matter, dispersed throughout the universe in vaporous form, contained the materials for an innumerable variety of substances. In its elastic state, it took the form of spheres simply as a result of the chemical affinity of particles that met according to the laws of gravitation, mutually destroying their elasticity and thus producing bodies. The heat within these bodies was sufficient to produce the illumination that is a property of the larger spheres, the suns, whereas it took the form of internal heat in the smaller spheres, the planets. . . .

Please do not be offended at my request, and do me the honor also of favoring me with your company at dinner tomorrow if you possibly can.

I. Kant

From J. G. C. C. Kiesewetter, June 14, 1791

- 474 - vol. xi, pp. 264–66

Dearest professor,

[Kiesewetter apologizes for not writing. He sends Kant a copy of his new logic book, which he has dedicated to Kant.] . . .

[4] Georg Christoph Lichtenberg (1742–99). In 1791 Lichtenberg published an edition of Erxleben's book.

The fact that your [book on] moral [philosophy] has not appeared at the current book fair has created quite a stir, since everyone was expecting it. People around here are saying (though it must be their imagination) that Woltersdorf, the new *Oberconsistorialrath*,[1] has managed to get the King to forbid you to write anymore. I myself was asked about this story at court. I talked with Wöllner[2] recently and his flattery made me blush. He tried to appear very favorably disposed toward me, but I don't trust him at all. People are now virtually convinced that he is being used by others who are forcing him to do things he otherwise would not do.

The King has already had several visions of Jesus; they say he is going to build Jesus a church in Potsdam for his very own. He is weak in body and soul now, and he sits for hours, weeping. Dehnhof[3] has fallen from grace and has gone to her sister-in-law, but the King has written to her again and in all probability she will come back soon. Rietz[4] is still an influential woman. The people who tyrannize over the King are Bischofswerder,[5] Wöllner, and Rietz. A new edict on religion is expected, and the populace grumbles at the prospect of being forced to go to church and Holy Communion. For the first time they have the feeling that there are some things that no prince can command them to do. Caution is necessary, lest the spark ignite. The soldiers are also very discontented. They have received no new uniforms this past year, on account of Rietz, who took the money to go to Pyrmont. Besides that, the late King used to give them 3 gulden after every review, as a bonus, and now they get only 8 groschen.

Models for floating batteries are being built here, everything is being made battle-ready, and this time we are going to war even with our treasury. The Turkish ambassador,[6] one of the most insignificant men I have ever seen, is still here, boring himself and everybody else. There is much talk of a marriage of the Duke of

[1] Theodor Carl Georg Woltersdorf (1727–1806) held this position from 1791.

[2] Johann Cristoph Wöllner. See Kiesewetter's letter of April 20, 1790 [420] and notes.

[3] Countess Dönhoff, mistress and then wife of Friedrich Wilhelm II. Cf. Kiesewetter's letter of April 20, 1790 [420].

[4] Wilhelmine Enke (1752 [or '54]–1820), another mistress of Friedrich Wilhelm II, who was engaged to the court official Rietz; she later became Countess Lichtenau.

[5] Johann Rudolf von Bischofswerder (1741–1803), a favorite of the King's.

[6] Ahmed Axmi Effendi.

York [7] and Princess Friederike, but the minor details of the story make it improbable. They say, namely, that the King wants to give two million toward effacing his debts and, in addition, to give her 100,000 thalers annually, even though the law allows only a total of 100,000 thalers for every princess's dowry.

But what all have I been chattering about to you—things that you either know already or have no desire to hear. Only the suspicion that these matters might interest you has induced me to write of them.

Literary news I have none, at least none that you have not got from the scholarly papers. Snell [8] has published an explanation of your critique of aesthetic judgment. It seems to me admirable. Spatzier [9] has published an abridgement of your critique of teleological judgment, but it is not nearly as good. . . .

Your devoted friend and servant,
J. G. C. KIESEWETTER

From Maria von Herbert, [August] 1791

- 478 - VOL. XI, *pp. 273–74*

Great Kant,

As a believer calls to his God, I call upon you for help, for solace, or for counsel to prepare me for death. The reasons you gave in your books were sufficient to convince me of a future existence—that is why I have recourse to you—only I found nothing, nothing at all for this life, nothing that could replace the good I have lost. For I loved an object that seemed to me to encompass everything within itself, so that I lived only for him. He was the opposite of everything else for me, and everything else seemed to me a bauble, and I really felt as if human beings were

---

[7] Prince Friedrich, Duke of York (1763–1827) married Princess Friederike Charlotte Ulrike Katharine, daughter of Friedrich Wilhelm's first marriage.

[8] Friedrich Wilhelm Snell (1761–1827), *Darstellung and Erläuterung der Kantischen Kritik der ästhetischen Urtheilskraft* (Mannheim, 1791 and 1792).

[9] Karl Spatzier (1761–1805), *Versuch einer kurzen und fasslichen Darstellung der teleologischen Principien, ein Auszug aus Kants Kritik der teleologische Urtheilskraft* (Neuwied, 1791).

all nonsense, all empty. Well, I have offended this person, because of a protracted lie, which I have now disclosed to him though there was nothing unfavorable to my character in it—I had no viciousness in my life that needed hiding. The lie was enough, though, and his love has vanished. He is an honorable man, and so he doesn't refuse me friendship and loyalty. But that inner feeling that once unbidden led us to each other, it is no more. O my heart splits into a thousand pieces. If I hadn't read so much of your work I would certainly have taken my own life by now. But the conclusion I had to draw from your theory stops me—it is wrong for me to die because my life is tormented, and I am instead supposed to live because of my being. Now put yourself in my place and either damn me or give me solace. I read the metaphysic of morals and the categorical imperative, and it doesn't help a bit. My reason abandons me just where I need it most. Answer me, I implore you, or you yourself will not be acting according to your own imperative.

My address is Maria Herbert in Klagenfurt, Carinthia, care of the white lead factory, or perhaps you would rather send it via Reinhold because the mail is more reliable there.

From Salomon Maimon, September 20, 1791

- 486 -   VOL. XI, *pp. 285–87*

Dear sir,
Esteemed professor,

I know how unjust is any man who robs you of the least bit of your time, so precious to the world. I know that nothing could be more important to you than to complete your work. Yet I cannot refrain from bothering you, with just this one letter.

I vowed some time ago that I would henceforth read nothing but your books. I am totally convinced by the skeptical part of your *Critique*. As for the dogmatic part, it can be assumed hypothetically and, even though I have constructed a psychological deduction of the categories and ideas (which I attribute not to the understanding and to reason but to the power of imagination), I can nevertheless grant what you propound as at least problematical. Thus I have made my peace with the *Critique* very nicely.

Mr. Reinhold, however (a man whose sagacity I value second only to your own), claims in his writings that he has given your system *formal completeness* and also that he has found the *only universally valid* principle (*si diis placet*) on which the system can be founded. This claim attracted my total attention. After more careful investigation, however, I found my expectation deceived. I *value* every system that has formal completeness, but I can praise its *validity* only insofar as it has *objective reality* and according to its degree of *fruitfulness*.

Now as regards its systematic form, I find Mr. Reinhold's theory of the faculty of representation unimprovable. But I cannot subscribe to this highly lauded universally valid principle (the proposition of consciousness), and still less can I bring myself to have great expectations of its fruitfulness.

I question specifically whether in every consciousness (even in an intuition or sensation, as Mr. Reinhold maintains) the representation is distinguished from both the subject and the object and is at the same time related to both of these by the subject. An intuition, in my opinion, is not related to anything other than itself. It becomes a *representation* only by being united with other intuitions in a synthetic unity, and it is as an element of the synthesis that the intuition relates itself to the representation (that is, to its object). The determined synthesis to which the representation is related is the *represented object;* and any undetermined synthesis to which the representation could be related is the concept of an *object in general*. How, then, can Mr. Reinhold claim that the proposition of consciousness is a universally valid principle? It can be valid, as I have shown, only in the consciousness of a representation, that is, an intuition related to a synthesis as part to whole. But, says Mr. Reinhold, we are of course not always conscious of this relating of the intuition to the subject and object, though it always takes place. Just how does he know that? Whatever is not represented [thought] in a representation does not belong to the representation. How can he then claim that this principle is a fact of consciousness that obtains universally? Anyone can easily deny this, on the basis of his own consciousness. It is a *delusion of the transcendent imagination* that every intuition is referred to some substratum or other; we have the habit of referring every intuition, as representation, to a real object (a synthesis) and, finally, to no real object at all but to a mere *idea* that has been foisted in place of a real object.

The word "representation" (*Vorstellung*) has made much mischief in philosophy, since it has encouraged people to invent an objective substratum for each mental event (*Seelenmodifikation*). Leibniz made matters worse with his theory of *obscure* [unconscious] *representations*. I admit the supreme importance of his theory for anthropology. But in a critique of the cognitive faculty, it is certainly worthless. "Obscure" representations are not states of mind (which can only be conscious) but rather of the body. Leibniz makes use of them only in order to fill in the gaps in the substantiality of the soul. But I do not believe that any independent thinker will seriously think he can manage it that way. "Obscure" representations are merely bridges with which to cross from soul to body and back again (though Leibniz had good reason to prohibit this passage).

I cannot be satisfied even with Mr. Reinhold's definition of philosophy. He means by "philosophy" what you rightly placed under the special title of "transcendental philosophy" (the theory of the conditions of knowledge of a real object in general).

I wish you would comment on this, and on my dictionary (which from all appearances will either be badly reviewed or not at all). Awaiting this, I remain, most respectfully,

Your wholly devoted servant,
SALOMON MAIMON

Berlin

To K. L. Reinhold, September 21, 1791

- 487 - VOL. XI, *pp. 287–89*

. . . Since about two years ago my health has undergone a drastic change. Without any actual illness (other than a cold that lasted 3 weeks) or any visible cause, I have lost my accustomed appetite, and although my physical strength and sensations have not diminished, my disposition for mental exertion and even for lecturing have suffered greatly. I can only devote 2 or 3 uninterrupted hours in the morning to intellectual work, for I am then overcome with drowsiness (regardless of how much sleep I have had the night before), and I am forced to work at intervals, which slows up my work. I have to look forward impatiently to a good mood without getting into one, being unable to exercise any control over my own mind. I think it is nothing but old age, which brings everyone to a standstill sooner or later, but it is all the more unwelcome to me just now when I foresee the completion of my plan. I am sure you will therefore understand, my kind friend, how this need to utilize every favorable moment, in such circumstances, leads one to a fatal postponement of many resolutions whose execution does not seem pressing, and every postponement tends to prolong itself.

I shall be happy to acknowledge that the further analysis of the foundations of knowledge in [your] investigations of the faculty of representation in general [1] (insofar as that faculty is the foundation of knowledge) constitutes a great contribution to the critique of reason. I plan to acknowledge this publicly one of these days, as soon as I can get clear about those parts that are still obscure to me. But I cannot conceal from you, at least not in a private communication, that I think it would be possible to develop the consequences of the principles [that I have] already laid down as basic, so as to show their correctness, perhaps using your excellent literary talents to make comments that would disclose just as much of your profounder investigations as would be needed to clarify the subject fully, without requiring the friends of the *Critique* to struggle through such an abstract work and thereby risk having many of them frightened off.

This is what I have been hoping for, but I am not now telling you what to do, nor, still less, am I issuing a public verdict that would put your meritorious efforts in an unfavorable light.

I shall have to postpone any public pronouncement a while longer, for, leaving aside my university business, I am presently working on a small but taxing job [2] and also on a revision of the *Critique of Judgment* for the second edition, which is being published next Easter, and what little strength I have is more than consumed by these projects.

Do remain well disposed toward me, in friendship and candid trust. I have never shown myself unworthy of it, nor ever shall. May I be included in the company of you and your true, merry,

---

[1] The reference is to Reinhold's *Versuch einer neuen Theorie des menschlichen Vorstellungsvermögens* (1789).

[2] Probably the first part of *Religion innerhalb der Grenzen der blossen Vernunft* ("Religion within the Limits of Reason Alone").

and clever friend, Erhard,[3] a company whose minds, I flatter myself, will forever be in accord.

With fondest devotion and respect, I am. . . .

To J. S. Beck, September 27, 1791

- 488 - VOL. XI, p. 289

[Kant has recommended Beck to his publisher, Hartknoch, as a likely person to compose an original summary of Kant's works. He thinks Beck will find the project stimulating and entertaining for the hours when Beck is relaxing from his mathematical studies.] . . . For, partly from my experience, partly from the example of the greatest mathematicians, I have become convinced that mere mathematics cannot fulfil the soul of a thinking man, that something more must be added (even if it is only poetry, as in Kästner's case [1]) to refresh the mind by exercizing its other talents and also by providing it with a change of diet. Now what can serve better for this and for a lifetime than investigating something that concerns the whole nature of man, especially if one has the hope of making some progress from time to time by a systematic effort of thought. Besides, the history of the world and of philosophy are tied up with this enterprise, and I am hopeful that, even if this investigation does not shed new light on mathematics, the latter may, inversely, by considering its methods and heuristic principles together with the entailed requirements and desiderata, come upon new discoveries for the critique and survey of pure reason. And the *Critique's* new way of presenting abstract concepts may itself yield something analogous to Leibniz's *universalis*

[3] J. B. Erhard (1766–1827). See the letters of December 21, 1792 [552] and January 17, 1793 [557].

[1] Abraham Gotthelf Kästner (1719–1800), professor of mathematics and physics in Göttingen, also wrote epigrams. Kant corresponded with him twice. Kant addressed him as "the Nestor of all philosophical mathematicians in Germany." Cf. letter 439, in Kant's *Werke*, XIII, 278. There Kant makes the interesting remark that the critical philosophy does not aim to attack the "long neglected" Leibniz-Wolffian philosophy but to reach the same objective by a different path, "an intention that will become clearer when, if I live long enough, the coherent system of metaphysics that I propose is completed."

characteristica combinatoria.[2] For the table of categories and the table of ideas (under which the cosmological ideas disclose something similar to impossible roots [in mathematics] *) are after all enumerated and as well defined in regard to all possible uses that reason can make of them as mathematics could ask, so that we can see to what extent they at least clarify if not extend our knowledge.

[In the remainder of this letter, Kant advises Beck to check for inaccuracies in the criticisms made of Kant and tells Beck how much money to require of his publisher. He also advises gentleness in the treatment of Reinhold, "an otherwise nice man who has attached himself too passionately to his theory." Kant says that Reinhold's theory is incomprehensible to him.]

From J. S. Beck, November 11, 1791

- 499 - VOL. XI, *pp. 310–11*

. . . Allow me to ask where I have understood you correctly. . . .

The *Critique* calls "intuition" a representation that relates immediately to an object.[1] But in fact, a representation does not become objective until it is subsumed under the categories. Since intuition similarly acquires its objective character only by means of the application of categories to it, I am in favor of leaving out that definition of "intuition" that refers to it as a representation relating to objects. I find in intuition nothing more than a manifold accompanied by consciousness (or by the *unique "I think"*), a manifold determined by the latter, in which there is as such no relation to an object. I would also like to reject the definition of "concept" as a representation mediately related to an object.[2] Rather, I distinguish concepts from intuitions by the fact that they are thoroughly determinate whereas intuitions are not thoroughly determinate. For both intuitions and concepts acquire objectivity

---

[2] See notes to the letter to Johann Schultz of August 26, 1783 [210].

* [Kant's footnote] When, in accordance with the principle "In the series of appearances, everything is conditioned," I seek the unconditioned and the highest ground of the totality of the series, it is as if I were looking for $\sqrt{-2}$.

[1] *Critique of Pure Reason* A 19 = B 33.
[2] *Critique of Pure Reason* A 50 = B 74.

only after the activity of judgment subsumes them under the pure concepts of the understanding.

[Kant's marginal comment: To make [*Bestimmung*] a concept, by means of intuition, into a cognition of an object, is indeed the work of judgment; but the reference of intuition to an object in general is not. For the latter is merely the logical use of representation insofar as a representation is thought as being a cognition.[3] When, on the other hand, a single representation is referred only to the subject, the use is aesthetic (feeling), in which case the representation cannot become a piece of knowledge.]

I understand the words "to combine" [*verbinden*] in the *Critique* to mean nothing more or less than to accompany the manifold with the identical "I think" whereby a *unitary* representation comes to exist. I believe that the *Critique* calls the original apperception the *unity* of apperception just because this apperception is what makes such a *unitary* representation possible. But am I right in regarding original apperception and the unity of apperception as the same thing or, rather, in finding the only difference between them to be that the *pure "I think,"* though it can only be discovered in the synthesis of the manifold, is nevertheless thought as something independent of the manifold (since in itself it contains nothing manifold) whereas the unity of consciousness in its self-identity, on the other hand, is thought to be connected with the parts of the manifold? This unity seems to me to acquire the character of objective unity when the representation itself is subsumed under the category. Mr. Reinhold speaks of a combination [*Verbindung*] and a unity in the concept, a second combination and a second unity (a unity "to the second power," as he expresses it) in the judgment. Besides these, he has a third combination, in inferences. I don't understand a word of this, since I take "combination" to mean nothing more than the being conscious of the manifold. Still, his discussion makes me doubt myself.

[Beck then asks for Kant's advice.] . . . .
Halle

---

[3] That is, relation to an object in general is part of the meaning of "representation" if we intend that word to stand for an item of knowledge.

To J. S. Beck, January 20, 1792[1]

- 500 - VOL. XI, *pp. 313–16*

You have presented me with your thorough investigation of what is just the hardest thing in the *Critique,* viz., the analysis of an experience in general and the principles of its possibility. I have already planned a "System of Metaphysics" to overcome these difficulties. I should begin with the categories, in their proper order (after first expounding, without investigating their possibility, just the pure intuitions of space and time, in which alone objects can be given to them). Then I should prove, at the conclusion of the exposition of each category (for example, quantity, and all predicables included under it, together with examples of their use), that no experience of objects of sense is possible except insofar as I presuppose a priori that every such object must be *thought* as a magnitude; similarly with all the other categories, and here it will always be remarked that such objects can be represented by us only as *given* in space and time. From this there emerges a whole science of ontology as *immanent* thinking, that is, a science of that thinking in which the objective reality of the concepts employed can be established with certainty. Only after it has been shown, in the second part, that in this same science all *conditions* of the possibility of objects are always again conditioned and that reason nevertheless strives unavoidably after the unconditioned—where our thinking becomes transcendent, that is, involves concepts whose objective reality (since they are "ideas") cannot be assured at all and by means of which, therefore, no knowledge of objects can take place—I wanted to show in the dialectic of pure reason (setting up its antinomies) that those objects of possible experience must be viewed as objects of sense, appearances only, not things-in-themselves. I want first of all to present the deduction of the categories in relation to the sensuous forms of space and time, as conditions of the uniting of these into

[1] This letter is an answer to Beck's letter (not extant) of December 9, 1791.

a possible experience; I want to think of the categories themselves, however, as concepts of objects in general (be the intuition of whatever form it will) and then to determine their scope beyond the boundaries of sense, where, however, no knowledge can be had. Well, enough of this.

You put the matter quite precisely when you say, "The content of a representation is itself the object; and the activity of the mind whereby the content of a representation is presented is what is meant by 'relating it to the object.'" But one may ask: How can a *complex* content of representations be presented? Not simply through the awareness that it is given to us; for a content requires *synthesis* [*Zusammensetzen*] of the manifold. The content must thus (as content) *be created* [*gemacht werden*] by an inner activity, which is valid for a given manifold in general and which precedes a priori the manner in which the manifold is given; that is, the content can only be thought by means of the synthetic unity of consciousness—thought in a concept (of objects in general) that is undetermined as regards the manner in which anything may be given in intuition. And this concept, applied to the object in general, is the category.

The merely subjective state of the representing subject, insofar as the manifold is given in a special manner (for its uniting and its synthetic unity), is called "sensibility"; and this manner of intuition, given a priori, is the sensible form of intuition. By means of these forms and the categories, objects are known, but only as things in the realm of appearance and not as they are in themselves; without any intuition they would not be known at all, though they would nevertheless be thought; and if one not only abstracts from all intuition, but actually excludes it, the objective reality of the categories (that they in fact represent anything and are not empty concepts) cannot be assured.

Perhaps right at the outset you can avoid defining "sensibility" in terms of "receptivity," that is, the manner of representations in the subject insofar as he is affected by objects; perhaps you can locate it in that which, in a cognition, concerns merely the relation of the representation to the subject, so that the form of sensibility, in this relation to the object of intuition, makes knowable no more than the appearance of this object. That this subjective thing constitutes only the manner in which the subject is affected by representations, and consequently nothing more than the receptivity of the subject, is already implied by its being merely the determination of the subject.

In short, since this whole analysis is only intended to show that experience is impossible without certain synthetic a priori principles, and this thesis cannot be made truly comprehensible until those principles are actually exhibited, I therefore think it prudent to keep the work as brief as possible before they are presented. Perhaps the way I proceed in my lectures, in which I have to be brief, can be of some help to you.

I begin by defining "experience" in terms of empirical knowledge. But knowledge is the representation through *concepts* of a *given* object as such; it is empirical if the object is given in a sensuous representation (which at the same time includes sensation and what connects this with consciousness, that is, perception); it is a priori knowledge if the object is given but not given in a sensuous representation (which of course can never be anything but sensible). For knowledge, two sorts of representations are required: (1) intuition, by means of which an object is given, and (2) conception, by means of which an object is thought. To make a single cognition out of these two pieces, a further activity is required: the combining [*zusammensetzen*] of the manifold given in intuition in conformity with the synthetic unity of consciousness that the concept expresses. Since combination cannot be given either through the object or its representation in intuition but has to be made, it must rest on the pure spontaneity of the understanding in concepts of objects in general (of the combination of the given manifold). But since concepts to which no corresponding objects could be given, being objectless, would not even be concepts (thoughts through which I think nothing at all), just for that reason a manifold must be given a priori for those a priori concepts. And because it is given a priori, it must be given in an intuition without any thing as object, that is, given in the mere form of intuition, which is merely subjective (space and time). It is therefore in conformity with the merely sensuous intuition, whose synthesis through the imagination, under the rules of the synthetic unity of consciousness, the concept expresses; for the rule of the schematism of concepts of the understanding is then applied to perceptions (in which objects are given to the senses by means of sensation).

I close herewith my hurriedly composed sketch and beg you not to let my delay, caused by accidental hindrances, keep you from revealing your thoughts and any suggestion of difficulties to me.

Your
I. KANT

Königsberg
P.S. Please mail the enclosed letters right away.

To J. H. Kant,[1] January 26, 1792

- 503 - VOL. XI, *p. 320*

Dear brother,

Mr. Reimer, the bearer of this letter, a relative [nephew] of your wife's, my dear sister-in-law,[2] visited me, and I could not refrain from putting aside my tremendous chores (which I seldom do) in order to send you greetings. Despite my apparent indifference, I have thought of you often and fraternally—not only for the time we are both still living but also for after my death,[3] which, since I am 68, cannot be far off. Our two surviving sisters,[4] both widowed, the older of whom has 5 grown and (some of them) married children, are provided for by me, either wholly or, in the case of the younger sister, by my contribution to St. George Hospital, where provision has been made for her. So the duty of gratitude for our blessings that is demanded of us, as our parents taught us, will not be neglected. I would be pleased to receive news of your own family and its situation.

Please greet my dear sister-in-law. I am, ever affectionately,

Your loyal brother,
I. KANT

[1] Johann Heinrich Kant (1735–1800), studied in Königsberg, served as private tutor in Courland, then as rector of the municipal school in Mitau, and later as pastor in Altrahden. Judging from this letter, Kant's feelings for his siblings were not exceptionally warm.

[2] Kant and his sister-in-law were unacquainted with one another, according to J. H. Kant's letter of February 8, 1792.

[3] Kant had made his will, August 29, 1791; but his brother did not survive him.

[4] Marie Elizabeth Kröhnert (1727–96) and Katharina Barbara Theyer (1731–1807). Another sister, Anna Luise (b. 1730), died in 1774.

To J. G. Fichte, February 2, 1792

- 504 - VOL. XI, pp. 321-22

You ask my advice on how your manuscript, rejected by the current strict censor, might be salvaged. My answer is, it can't be done! Although I have not read your book myself, I gather from your letter that its main thesis is "that faith in a given revelation cannot be rationally justified on the basis of a belief in miracles." [1] It follows necessarily that a religion may contain no article of faith other than one that exists for pure reason as well. I think that this proposition is completely innocent and denies neither the subjective necessity of a revelation nor the fact of miracles (since one can assume that, if it is possible at all, the actual occurrence of such a thing could be rationally understood as well, without revelation, even though reason would not have introduced these articles of faith by itself. It is not necessary to base the belief in those articles on miracles, once they are established, even if a miracle was needed originally.) But by today's assumed maxims, it seems that the censor would not allow you to say this. For according to those maxims, certain texts in the confession of faith are supposed to be taken so literally that the human understanding can barely grasp their sense, much less see their rational truth, with the result that they need perpetually to be supported by a

[1] In his letter of January 23, 1792 [501], Fichte explains his position on faith and miracles. No miracle as such can be proved. There might be other good grounds for believing a revelation, however; viz., the miracles it reports may inspire awe in the mind of someone who needs this. But a revelation can extend neither our dogmatic nor our moral knowledge, since it concerns transcendent objects of which we may believe the "that" but cannot know the "how." It might be "subjectively true" for someone who wants to believe it; but it is not knowledge. (Kant's *Werke*, XI, 317.)

Fichte's manuscript, "A Critique of Revelation" ("Versuch einer Kritik aller Offenbarung"), had been denied the *Imprimatur* by J. L. Schulze, dean of the theological faculty in the University of Halle. Schulze's successor, G. C. Knapp, however, allowed the book to be published without any changes. Since the work appeared anonymously, and was published by the Königsberg publisher Hartung (at Kant's suggestion), many people believed it to be by Kant himself. This was the start of Fichte's career. As Kant indicates in the present letter, he had not actually read the book before recommending it to Hartung. See also a letter to Borowski [485], not included in this book.

miracle and could never become articles of faith prescribed by reason alone. That the revelation of such propositions was only intended, as an accommodation to our weakness, to provide a visible cloak for them, and that this revelation can have merely subjective truth, is not acknowledged by the censor. He demands that they be taken as objective truths.

There is one way still open to bring your book into accord with the (as yet not widely known) opinions of the censor: If you could manage to make him understand and find *attractive* the distinction between a *dogmatic* faith, elevated above all doubt, and a purely *moral* assumption that freely bases itself on moral grounds (the imperfection of reason in its inability to satisfy its own demands). For then the religious faith that the morally good conscience has grafted onto the faith in miracles says in effect: "Lord, I believe!" (that is, I gladly assume it, whether or not I or anyone else can adequately prove it); "Help Thou mine unbelief!" (that is, I have moral faith in relation to everything that I can extract from the historical miracle story for my inner improvement, and I wish, too, that I might possess faith in those historical events insofar as that would also contribute to my inner improvement). My unintentional *non-belief* is not an intentional *un-belief*. But you will have a hard time making this compromise attractive to a censor who, it would seem, has made the historical credo into an essential religious duty.

You may do whatever you think best with these hurriedly written but not unconsidered ideas of mine, as long as you do not explicitly, or covertly indicate their author; I assume of course that you would first have persuaded yourself sincerely of their truth.

I wish you contentment in your present position,[2] and should you wish to move, I hope I shall have some means of helping you to improve your situation.

Respectfully and with friendship,
Your devoted servant,
I. KANT

[2] Kant, after refusing to lend Fichte some money for which he had asked, had secured him a position as private tutor in the household of Count Reinhold of Crackow.

To Maria von Herbert, Spring, 1792
(Kant's rough draft)

- 510 - VOL. XI, *pp. 331–34*

Your deeply felt letter is the product of a heart that must have been created for the sake of virtue and honesty, since it is so receptive to instruction in those qualities, instruction that will not stoop to flattery. I am thus compelled to do as you asked, namely, to put myself in your place and to reflect on the prescription for a pure moral sedative (the only thorough kind) for you. The object of your love must be just as sincere and respectful of virtue and uprightness, the spirit of virtue, as you are, though I do not know whether your relationship to him is one of marriage or merely friendship. I take it as probable from what you say that it is the latter, but it makes no significant difference for the problem that disturbs you. For love, be it for one's spouse or for a friend, presupposes the same mutual esteem for the other's character, without which it is no more than a very perishable, sensual delusion.

A love like that, the only virtuous love (for the other sort is only a blind inclination), wants to communicate itself completely, and it expects of its respondent a similar sharing of heart, unweakened by any distrustful reticence. That is how it should be and that is what the ideal of friendship demands. But there is in man an element of improbity, which puts a limit on such candor, in some men more than in others. Even the sages of old complained of this obstacle to the mutual outpouring of the heart, this secret distrust and reticence, which makes a man keep some part of his thoughts locked within himself, even when he is most intimate with his confidant: "My dear friends, there is no such thing as a friend!" And yet the superior soul passionately desires friendship, regarding it as the sweetest thing a human life may contain. Only with candor can it prevail.

This reticence, however, this want of candor—a candor that, taking mankind en masse, we cannot expect of people, since everyone fears that to reveal himself completely would make him despised by others—is still very different from that lack of sincerity that consists in dishonesty in the actual expression of our thoughts.

The former flaw is one of the limitations of our nature and does not actually *spoil* our character. It is only a wrong that hinders the expression of all the possible good that is in us. The other flaw, however, is a corruption of our thinking and a positive evil. What the honest but reticent man says is true but not the whole truth. What the dishonest man says is, in contrast, something he knows to be false. Such an assertion is called a *lie,* in the theory of virtue. It may be entirely *harmless,* but it is not on that account innocent. It is, rather, a serious violation of duty to oneself and one for which there can be no remission, since the transgression subverts the dignity of man in our own person and attacks the roots of our thinking. For deception casts doubt and suspicion on everything and even removes all confidence from virtue, if one judges virtue by its external character.

As you see, you have sought counsel from a physician who is no flatterer and who does not seek to ingratiate himself. Were you wanting a mediator between yourself and your beloved, you see that my way of defining good conduct is not at all partial to the fair sex, since I speak for your beloved and present him with arguments that, as a man who honors virtue, are on his side and that justify his having wavered in his affection for you.

As for your earlier expectation, I must advise you first to ask yourself whether in your bitter self-reproach over a lie that as a matter of fact was not intended to cloak any wicked act you are reproaching yourself for a mere imprudence or are making an inner accusation on account of the immorality that is intrinsic to the lie. If the former, you are only rebuking yourself for the candor of your disclosure of the lie, that is, you regret having done your duty on this occasion (for that is doubtless what it is when one has deceived someone, even harmlessly, and has after a time set him straight again). And why do you regret this disclosure? Because it has resulted in the loss, certainly a serious one, of your friend's confidence. This regret is thus not motivated by anything moral, since it is produced by an awareness not of the act itself but of its consequences. But if the rebuke that pains you is one that is really grounded in a purely moral judgment of your behavior, it would be a poor moral physician who would advise you to cast this rebuke out of your mind, just because what is done cannot be undone, and tell you merely to behave henceforth with whole-hearted, conscientious sincerity. For conscience must focus on every transgression, like a judge who does not dispose of the documents, when a crime has been sentenced, but records them in the archives in order to sharpen the judgment of justice in new cases of a similar or even dissimilar offense that may appear before him. But to brood over one's remorse and then, when one has already caught on to a different set of attitudes, to make one's whole life useless by continuous self-reproach on account of something that happened once upon a time and cannot be anymore— that would be a fantastic notion of deserved self-torture (assuming that one is sure of having reformed). It would be like many so-called religious remedies that are supposed to consist in seeking the favor of higher powers without one's even having to become a better human being. That sort of thing cannot be credited in any way to one's moral account.

When your change in attitude has been revealed to your beloved friend—and the sincerity of your words makes it impossible to mistake this—only time will be needed to quench little by little the traces of his indignation (a justified feeling and one that is even based on the concepts of virtue) and to transform his indifference into a more firmly grounded love. If this should fail to happen, the earlier warmth of his affection was more physical than moral and, in view of the transient nature of such a love, would have vanished in time all by itself. That sort of misfortune we encounter often in life, and when we do, we must meet it with composure, since the value of life, insofar as it consists of the enjoyment we can get out of people, is generally overestimated, whereas life, insofar as it is cherished for the good that we can do, deserves the highest respect and the greatest solicitude in preserving it and cheerfully using it for good ends.

Here then, my friend, you find the customary divisions of a sermon: instruction, penalty, and solace, of which I beg you to devote yourself somewhat more to the first two, since the last, and your lost contentment with life, will surely be found by themselves when once these others have had their effect.

From J. S. Beck, May 31, 1792

- 515 - VOL. XI, *pp. 338–40*

I should like to know whether you agree with the following remarks. It seems to me that one ought not to define "intuition," in the Transcendental Aesthetic, as "a representation immediately related to an object" or as a representation that arises when the mind is affected by the object. For not until the Transcendental Logic can it be shown how we arrive at objective representations. The fact that there are pure intuitions also rules out such a definition. I really do not see where I err when I say: intuition is a thoroughly determinate representation in relation to a given manifold. In this way it also becomes clear to me that mathematics is a science dependent on the construction of concepts. For even in algebra we cannot prove theorems except by means of thoroughly determinate representations. I think we must also take care to distinguish the subjective and objective aspects of sensibility, in order that we may afterward see all the more clearly the unique function of the categories, which confer objectivity on our representations.

Second, I understand quite well that the objects of the sense world must be subjected to the principles of our transcendental faculty of judgment. To see this clearly, let someone try to subsume empirical intuitions under the schemata of the categories; he will see immediately that they only obtain objectivity because the question "How does it happen that objects must conform to those synthetic a priori propositions?" is terminated. For objects are objects only to the extent that their intuition is thought as subjected to the synthetic synthesis [*Verknüpfung*] of the schema. For example, I see the validity of the analogy that something permanent must underlie all appearances, just because the intuition becomes objective when I relate the schema of substantiality to that empirical intuition. Consequently the object itself must be subjected to this synthetic synthesis of substance and accident. But when I ascend to the principle of this whole matter, I find one place where I would gladly have more clarification. I say that the combination of representations in a concept differs from combination in a judgment in that the latter presupposes, in addition to the first synthesis, the further *activity* of objective relation, that is, the very activity through which one thinks an object. It is in fact quite different if I say "the black man" or "the man is black," and I think one is not incorrect if one says that the representations in a concept are united into a subjective unity of consciousness, whereas those in a judgment are united into an objective unity of consciousness. But I would give a great deal to be able to penetrate more deeply into this matter of the *activity of objective relation* and to form a clearer idea of it. In my last letter I mentioned this point as one that seems to me obscure. Your silence, dearest sir, made me fear that I had uttered some nonsense in connection with this. Yet the more I turn the matter over in my mind, the more I fail to find any error in asking you for instruction, and I beg you for it once more. [Kant's marginal remark: The expression "the black man" means "the man insofar as the concept of him is given as determined in respect to the concept of blackness." But "the man is black" indicates my activity of determining.]

Third, the procedure of the *Critique of Practical Reason* seems extraordinarily illuminating and excellent. It takes its start from the objective practical principle that pure reason, independently of all the material of the will, must acknowledge as binding. This originally problematical concept obtains irrefutable objective reality by means of the fact of the moral law. But I confess that, although the transition from synthetic principles of the transcendental faculty of judgment to objects of the sense world (by means of the schemata) is quite clear to me, the transition from the moral law by means of its *typus* is not clear. I would feel myself freed from a burden if you would kindly show me the answer to this question: Can't one imagine the moral law commanding something that might contradict its *typus?* In other words, can't there be activities that would be inconsistent with a natural order but that nevertheless are prescribed by the moral law? It is a merely problematical thought, but it has this truth as its basis: the strict necessity of the categorical imperative is in no way dependent on the possibility of the existence of a natural order. Yet it would be a mistake to account for the agreement of the two as accidental.

BECK

To J. S. Beck, July 3, 1792

- 520 - VOL. XI, *pp. 347–48*

The difference between a connection of representations in a concept and one in a judgment, for example, "the black man" and "the man *is* black" (in other words, "the man *who* is black" and "the man *is* black"), lies, I think, in this: in the first, one thinks of a concept as *determined;* in the second, one thinks of the *determining activity* of this concept. But you are quite right to say that in the *synthesized* concept, the unity of consciousness should be *subjectively* given, whereas in the *synthesizing* of concepts the unity of consciousness should be *objectively* made; that is, in the first, the man is merely *thought* as black (problematically represented), and in the second, he is recognized as black. Therefore the question arises whether I can say without contradiction: the black man (who is black at a certain time) is white (that is, he is white, has paled, at another time). I answer no; for in this judgment I carry over the concept of black along with the concept of non-black, since the subject is thought as determined through the first. Consequently, since the subject would be both black and non-black at once, we would have an unavoidable contradiction. On the other hand, I can say of the same man, *"He is black,"* and also, *"Just this man is not black"* (namely, at some other time, when he is bleached), since in both judgments only the *activity of determination,* which here depends on experiential and temporal conditions, is indicated. You will find more of this in the discussion of the principle of contradiction, in my *Critique of Pure Reason.*[1]

As for your definition of intuition as a thoroughly determinate representation in respect to a given manifold, I would have nothing further to add except this: the thorough determination here must be understood as objective, not merely as existing in the subject (since it is impossible for us to know all determinations of the object of an empirical intuition). For then the definition would only say that an intuition is the representation of a given unit. Now nothing composite can *as such* be given to us—we always have to *perform* the synthesis of a given manifold ourselves—and the synthesis, in order to be in accord with the object, cannot be arbitrary. Consequently, if the composite must have the only form according to which the given manifold can be synthesized, it follows that this form is the merely subjective (sensuous) aspect of the intuition. The form must be a priori, but it is not *thought* (for only the synthesizing as activity is a product of thought); it must rather be *given* in us (space and time) and must therefore be a *single* representation and not a concept (*repraesentatio*

---

[1] "The Highest Principle of All Analytic Judgments" and "The Transcendental Ideal," *Critique of Pure Reason,* B 189 ff. and B 599 ff.

communis).—It seems to me sound not to spend too much time on the most subtle dissecting of elementary representations, for they become sufficiently clear in the following discussion.

As for the question, Can't there be actions that are incompatible with the existence of a natural order and that yet are prescribed by the moral law? I answer, Certainly! If you mean, a *definite order of nature,* for example, that of the present world. A courtier, for instance, must recognize it as a duty always to be truthful, though he would not remain a courtier for long if he were. But there is in that *typus* only the form of a *natural order in general,* that is, the compatibility of actions as events in accord with *moral laws,* and as [events] in accord with *natural laws,* too, but merely in terms of *their generality,* for this in no way concerns the special laws of any particular nature.

To *J. S. Beck, October 16 [or 17], 1792*

- 537 - VOL. XI, *p. 376*

[Kant returns Beck's manuscript.]

. . . In my judgment everything depends on the following: Since in the empirical concept of a *composite* the synthesis cannot be given or represented in intuition by means of the mere intuition and its apprehension but only through the spontaneous connection of the manifold—that is, it can be presented in a consciousness in general (which is not empirical)—this connection, and its functioning, must stand a priori in the mind, under rules that constitute the pure thought of an object in general (the pure concept of the understanding). The apprehension of the manifold must be subject to this pure concept of the understanding, insofar as the apprehension constitutes an intuition and also insofar as it [the pure concept] constitutes the condition of all possible experiential knowledge of the composite or of what belongs to that knowledge —that is, there is a synthesis contained in it—and this experiential knowledge is expressed by these principles. The representation of the composite as such proceeds according to the general concepts under the representations of the manifold that is apprehended as given, and consequently it does not entirely belong, as must be the case, to spontaneity, and so on. . . .

From J. S. Beck, November 10, 1792

- 545 -   VOL. XI, *pp. 384–85*

[. . . Beck sends back the part of his manuscript dealing with the deduction of the categories. He reports on conversations between Garve and Eberhard. As much as Garve defended the *Critique of Pure Reason,* he was forced to admit that critical idealism was identical to Berkeleian idealism. Beck cannot agree.]

Even if we assume that the *Critique* should not even have mentioned the distinction between things-in-themselves and appearances, we would still have to recall that one must pay attention to the conditions under which something is an object. If we ignore these, we fall into error. Appearances are the objects of intuition, and they are what everybody means when he speaks of objects that surround us. But it is the reality of just these objects that Berkeley denies and that the *Critique,* on the other hand, defends. If one once sees that space and time are the conditions of the intuiting of objects and then considers what the conditions of the thinking of objects are, one sees easily that the dignity that representations achieve in referring to objects consists in the fact that the synthesis of the manifold is thus thought as necessary. This determination of thought is, however, the same as the function in a judgment. In this way the contribution of the categories to our knowledge has become clear to me, in that the investigation has made me see that they are the concepts through which the manifold of a sensuous intuition is presented as necessarily (valid for everyone) grasped together. Certain summarizers, as I see it, have expressed themselves incorrectly on this matter. They say, To judge means to grasp objective representations together. It is quite another thing when the *Critique* tells us: To judge is to bring representations to an objective unity of consciousness, through which the activity of synthesis, represented as necessary, is expressed. . . .

. . . You maintain that the representations of space and time are forms of sensibility, that is, necessary conditions of the manner in which objects of sense are represented *in us.*

I maintain on the contrary (on psychological grounds) that this is not universally true. Homogeneous objects of sense are represented by us neither in space nor in time. We can represent them in space and time only mediately, by means of a comparison with heterogeneous objects with which those homogeneous objects are bound up spatio-temporally. Time and space are thus forms of the *diversity* of [things represented by] sensibility, not forms of *sensibility as such.* The appearance of red or green is not represented in time or space any more than a concept of the understanding as such is thus represented. But we can represent a comparison of red with green and we can imagine the coexistence or succession of red and green only in space and time.

Time and space are therefore not representations of the properties and relations of things-in-themselves—as the critical philosophy has already demonstrated against the dogmatic philosophy. But neither are they conditions of the way in which objects-of-sense-in-themselves, prior to their comparison with each other, are represented in us. What are they then? They are *conditions of the possibility of a comparison between objects of sense,* that is, of the possibility of a judgment as to their relation to each other. Let me explain:

1. Different representations cannot coexist in the same subject at the same time (at exactly the same instant).

2. Every judgment concerning the relation of objects to each other presupposes the existence of a representation of each of them in the mind. The question therefore arises, How is a judgment regarding the relation of objects to each other possible—for example, the highly evident judgment that red differs from green? The representations of red and green would have to precede this judgment in the mind. But since they cannot be in the mind of a

subject simultaneously, and the judgment nevertheless relates to both of them, uniting them in consciousness, there is only one possible explanation. Certain psychologists appeal to "traces" at this point, but to no avail. For the "traces" of different representations can no more occur simultaneously in the mind than the representations themselves, if they are to retain their distinctness.

Only by means of the idea of a temporal succession [*Zeitfolge*] is this judgment possible. Even if we ignore what objects are represented in it, a temporal succession is a *unity in diversity* [*Einheit im Mannigfaltigen*]. The earlier point of time is *as such distinguished* from the succeeding one. They are therefore not *analytically* unified, and yet neither one can be represented without the other. Thus they constitute a *synthetic unity*. The idea of a temporal succession is thus a necessary condition not of the possibility of objects in themselves (even of sensible objects) but rather of the possibility of judgments concerning their *diversity*. Without [the idea of] temporal succession, such diversity could not be an object of our knowledge.

On the other hand, objective diversity is a condition of the possibility of temporal succession, not only as object of our knowledge, but also as object of intuition as such (since temporal order is imaginable only if this [1] becomes an object of our knowledge). The *form of diversity* (also objective diversity itself) and the idea of temporal order are thus mutually related. If red were not, as an appearance in itself, *different* from green, we could not place them in a temporal order. But had we no idea of such an order, we could never *recognize* them [as diverse] even though they were objectively distinct objects of intuition.

This same relationship exists also between the form of *diversity* and the representation of spatial *separation* [*Aussereinanderseyns im Raum*]. The latter cannot be without the former. The former cannot be *recognized by us* without the latter.

The diversity of outer appearances is represented in time only if it is not represented in space, and vice versa. One and the same sensible substance (for example, this tree) is represented as *different from itself* (changed) in time, not in space. Distinct sensible substances are represented *as distinct* in space, not in time (in that the judgment of their distinctness embraces them in one and the same moment of time).

[1] The reference of "this" [*sie*] is not clear; it could refer to either objective diversity or temporal order.

The form of time thus does not belong to all objects of outer intuition without distinction but only to those that are not represented in space; and vice versa, the form of space belongs only to those outer objects that are not represented in time (in a *temporal succession*, for the property of being simultaneous is not, I maintain, a positive determination but merely the negation of the idea of temporal succession). . . . [Maimon then pleads for a reply from Kant. Kant did not answer either this letter or Maimon's earlier ones.]

To J. S. Beck, December 4, 1792

- 549 - VOL. XI, *p. 395*

. . . Messrs. Eberhard's and Garve's opinion that Berkeley's idealism is the same as that of the critical philosophy (which I could better call "the principle of the ideality of space and time") does not deserve the slightest attention. For I speak of ideality in reference to the *form of representations;* but they interpret this to mean ideality with respect to the *matter,* that is, the ideality of the *object* and its very existence. Under the assumed name "Aenesidemus," however, an even wider skepticism has been advanced, viz., that we cannot know at all whether our representations correspond to anything else (as object), which is as much as to say: whether a representation *is* a representation (stands for anything). For "representation" means a determination in us that we relate to something else (whose place the representation takes in us). . . .

[1] Gottlob Ernst Schulze (1761–1833), known as "Aenesidemus-Schulze" because of his book *Aenesidemus,* which appeared anonymously in 1792. The full title of the work is *Aenesidemus; or, On the Foundations of Professor Reinhold of Jena's* Elementarphilosophie, *together with a Defense of Skepticism against the Presumptions of the Critique of Reason.* Schulze, who was later Schopenhauer's teacher, was one of the sharpest critics of Kant and Reinhold. Like Jacobi, he argued that it was inconsistent to make an unknowable thing in itself the cause of the "material" of experience, since causality is supposed to be a mere form of the subject's thinking. Schulze maintained further that Kant had refuted neither the skepticism of Hume nor the idealism of Berkeley and that Kant's position was in fact "dogmatic."

To J. B. Erhard,[1] December 21, 1792

- 552 - VOL. XI, *pp. 398-99*

. . . Allow me to make a few remarks about Mr. Klein's discussion of criminal right [*Criminalrecht*].[2] Most of what he says is excellent and quite in accord with my own views. I assume that you have a numbered copy of the points on your letter.

Concerning No. 5:[3] The scholastic theologians used to talk of the actual punishment (*poena vindicatiua*) ["avenging penalty"] as being imposed not *ne peccetur* [so that there be no offense] but *quia peccatum est* ["because there is an offense"]. Therefore they defined punishment as *malum physicum* ob *malum morale illatum* ["physical evil inflicted *because of* moral evil"]. In a world of moral principles governed by God, punishments would be categorically necessary (insofar as transgressions occur). But in a world governed by men, the necessity of punishments is only hypothetical, and that direct union of the concept of transgression with the idea of deserving punishment serves the ruler only as a prescription for what to do. So you are right in saying that the *poena meremoralis* ["ethical penalty"] (which perhaps came to be called *vindicativa* ["avenging punishment"] for the reason that it preserves the divine justice), even if its goal is merely medicinal for the criminal and the setting of an example for others, is indeed a *symbol* of something deserving punishment, as far as the condition of its authorization is concerned.

No. 9 and No. 10:[4] Both propositions are true, though entirely

[1] Johann Benjamin Erhard (1766-1827), physician, traveler, and friend of Kant, Reinhold, Schiller, and the von Herberts. Erhard was one of Kant's main disciples in southern Germany (Nürnberg).

[2] Ernst Ferdinand Klein, a friend of Erhard's, whose views Erhard summarized in a letter to Kant [497].

[3] "Since the aim of punishment is not compensation for damages, or improvement, or example, we cannot say that it is the suffering of a physical evil as such on account of a moral transgression. Rather, punishment is the symbol of an action's deserving punishment, by means of a mortification of the criminal that corresponds to the crime committed."

[4] "9. The moral law prescribes to me not only how I should treat others but also how I should allow myself to be treated by others; it forbids not only that I misuse others but also that I allow them to misuse me, that is, destroy

misunderstood in ordinary moral treatises. They belong under the heading of "Duties to Oneself," which I shall discuss in my "Metaphysics of Morals" in an unusual way.

No. 12: [5] Well said. It is often claimed that, according to natural right, civil society is based on the *desirability* of *pactum sociale* ["social contract"]. But we can prove that the *status naturalis* is a state of injustice and, consequently, that it is a duty of right to change over to the condition of civil society. . . .

I would like to hear from you, especially as to whether Miss Herbert [6] was encouraged by my letter. I am ever your respectful and devoted

I. KANT

From Maria von Herbert, [January] 1793

- 554 - VOL. XI, *pp. 400–402*

Dear and revered sir,

The reason I delayed so long in telling you of the pleasure your letter gave me was that I value your time too highly, so that I allow myself to pilfer some of it only when it will serve to relieve my heart and not merely to satisfy an impulse. And this you have already done for me once, when my spirit was most turbulent and I appealed to you for help. You understood me so perfectly that I am encouraged, both by your kindness and by your precise comprehension of the human heart, to describe to you without embarrassment the further progress of my soul. The lie on account of which I appealed to you was no cloaking of a vice but

myself. 10. Therefore I am just as much commanded not to suffer an injustice as not to commit injustice, but this is only possible for me (unaided) as far as the intention goes, not in its realization. Therefore I and all men have the task of finding a means of making my physical powers equal to my moral obligations. From this there derives the moral drive [*Trieb*] and the need for society."

[5] "No. 12. Insofar as society's main purpose is to protect the right and to punish crime, it is called civil society. As such, it is not only useful but holy."

[6] Maria von Herbert. See letters of August, 1791 [478], Spring, 1792 [510], January, 1793 [554], January 17, 1793 [557], and February 11, 1793 [559].

only a sin of keeping something back out of consideration for the friendship (still veiled by love) that existed then. The conflict I felt, foreseeing the terribly painful consequences and knowing the honesty one owes to a friend, was what made me disclose the lie to my friend after all, but so late. Finally I had the strength, and with the disclosure I got rid of the stone in my heart at the price of the tearing away of his love. I enjoyed as little peace before, when I begrudged myself the pleasure I possessed, as afterward, when my heart was torn apart by the suffering and anguish that plagued me and that I wouldn't wish on anyone, even someone who would want to prove his wickedness in a court of law. Meanwhile my friend hardened in his coldness, just as you said in your letter, but later he changed, babbled like a brook, and offered me his sincerest friendship. It pleases me for his sake, but I am still dissatisfied, because it is only pleasant and pointless. My vision is clear and I have the sense of constantly reproaching myself and I get an empty feeling that extends inside me and all around me, so that I am almost superfluous to myself. Nothing attracts me, and even getting every possible wish I might have would not give me any pleasure, nor is there a single thing that seems worth the trouble of doing. I feel this way not out of malcontentment but from weighing the amount of sordidness that accompanies everything good. I wish I were able to increase the amount of purposeful activity and diminish the purposeless; the latter seems to be all that the world is concerned with. I feel as if the urge to really do something only arises in me in order to be smothered. Even when I am not frustrated by any external circumstances and have nothing to do all day, I'm tormented by a boredom that makes my life unbearable, though I should want to live a thousand years if I could believe that God might be pleased with me in such a useless existence. Don't think me arrogant for saying this, but the commandments of morality are too trifling for me; for I should gladly do twice as much as they command, since they get their authority only because of a temptation to sin and it costs me hardly any effort to resist that. It makes me think that if someone has become really clear about the commandments of duty he is not at all free to transgress them any more. For I would have to insult my sinful feeling itself if I had to act contrary to duty. It seems so instinctive to me that my being moral could not possibly have the slightest merit.

Just as little I think, can one hold those people responsible who in all their lives do not reach a real self-awareness. Always surprised by their own sensuality, they can never account to themselves for their action or inaction; and if morality were not the most advantageous thing for nature, these people would probably challenge her to further duels.

I console myself often with the thought that since the practice of morality is so bound up with sensuality, it can only count for this world, and with that thought I could still hope not to have to live another life of empty vegetating and of so few and easy moral demands after this life. Experience wants to take me to task for this bad temper I have against life by showing me that almost everyone finds his life ending too soon and everyone is so glad to be alive. So as not to be a queer exception to the rule, I shall tell you a remote cause of my deviation, namely, my chronic poor health. I have not been well at all since the time I first wrote you. This sometimes causes a frenzy of mind that reason alone cannot cure. So I forego being healthy. What I could otherwise still enjoy doesn't interest me. I can't study any of the natural sciences or the arts of the world, for I feel I have no talent for extending them. And for myself alone I have no need to know them. Whatever bears no relation to the categorical imperative and to my transcendental consciousness is indifferent to me, though I am all finished with thoughts on those topics, too. Taking all these things together, you can perhaps see why I want only one thing, namely, to shorten this so useless life of mine, a life in which I am convinced I shall become neither better nor worse. If you consider that I am still young and that each day interests me only to the extent that it brings me closer to death, you can then estimate what a benefactor you would be to me and how much it would cheer you if you would examine this question in detail. I can ask it of you because my concept of morality is silent on this point, whereas it speaks very decisively on all other issues. But if you are unable to give me the negative good I seek, I appeal to your feeling of benevolence and ask you to give me something with which to end this unbearable emptiness of soul. If I become a useful part of nature and if my health will permit, I hope to take a trip to Königsberg in a few years, for which I beg permission in advance to visit you. You will have to tell me your life's story then, and whether it never seemed worth the trouble to you to take a wife or to give yourself to someone with all your heart or to reproduce your likeness. I have an engraved portrait of you by

Bause from Leibpzig [*sic*], in which I see a calm moral depth although I cannot discover there the penetration of which the *Critique of Pure Reason* above all else is proof and I am also dissatisfied not to be able to look you right in the face.

Will you guess what my sole sensuous wish is, and fulfil it, if it is not too inconvenient. Please do not become indignant if I implore you for an answer, which my jabbering will have discouraged. But I must ask you that, if you should trouble to reply and do me this greatest favor, you focus your answer on specific matters and not on general points that I have already encountered in your writings when my friend and I happily experienced them together—you would certainly be pleased with him, for his character is upright, his heart is good and his mind deep and besides that fortunate enough to fit into this world. And he is self-sufficient and strong enough to abstain from everything, and that is why I am confident I can tear myself away from him. Do guard your health, for you still have much to give to the world. Would that I were God and could reward you for what you have done for us. I am with deepest respect and truly, reverently,

MARIA HERBERT

From J. B. Erhard, January 17, 1793

- 557 - VOL. XI, *pp. 407–8*

[Erhard responds to Kant's inquiry as to how his letter affected Maria von Herbert.]

. . . I can say little of Miss Herbert. I had expressed my opinion of her actions to a few of her friends in Vienna, thereby spoiling our friendship so that she won't even speak to me. She takes me to be a man of no moral scruples, who judges only according to prudential rules. I do not know whether she is better off now. She has capsized on the reef of romantic love, which I have managed to escape (more by luck than by desert). In order to realize an idealistic love, she gave herself to a man who misused her trust; and then, to achieve such a love with a second person, she told her new lover about the other one. That is the key to her letter. If my friend Herbert had more delicatesse, she could still be saved. Her present state of mind is briefly this: her moral feeling is totally severed from prudence and therefore is united with the finer sensibility of fantasy. I find something moving about this state of mind, and I pity people of that sort more than actual maniacs. Unfortunately this state of mind appears to be common among people who escape fanaticism and superstition. They escape only by embracing oversensitivity, private deceptions, and dreams (the steadfast determination to realize one's own chimeras, which one takes for ideas), and they think they do truth a service thereby. . . .

ERHARD

To Elisabeth Motherby,[1] February 11, 1793

- 559 - VOL. XI, *pp. 411–12*

I have numbered the letters [2] which I have the honor of passing on to you, my dear mademoiselle, according to the dates I received them. The ecstatical young lady did not remember to date them. The third letter, from another source,[3] is included because part of it provides an explanation of the lady's curious mental derangements. A number of expressions, especially in the first letter, refer to writings of mine that she read and are difficult to understand without an explanation.

You have been so fortunate in the upbringing you have received that I do not need to commend these letters to you as an example of warning, to guard you against the errors of a sublimated fantasy. Nevertheless they may serve to make your perception of that good fortune all the more lively.

With the greatest respect, I am

My honored lady's obedient servant,
I. KANT

---

[1] Daughter of Kant's friend Robert Motherby, an English merchant in Königsberg.
[2] From Maria von Herbert.
[3] J. B. Erhard to Kant, January 17, 1793 [557].

To C. F. Stäudlin,[1] May 4, 1793

- 574 - VOL. XI, pp. 429-30

. . . The plan I prescribed for myself a long time ago calls for an examination of the field of pure philosophy with a view to solving three problems: (1) What can I know? (metaphysics). (2) What ought I to do? (moral philosophy). (3) What may I hope? (philosophy of religion). A fourth question ought to follow, finally: What is man? (anthropology, a subject on which I have lectured for over twenty years). With the enclosed work, *Religion within the Limits [of Reason Alone]*, I have tried to complete the third part of my plan. In this book I have proceeded conscientiously and with genuine respect for the Christian religion but also with a befitting candor, concealing nothing but rather presenting openly the way in which I believe that a possible union of Christianity with the purest practical reason is possible.

The biblical theologican can oppose reason only with another reason or with force, and if he intends to avoid the criticism that attends the latter move (in the current crisis, when freedom of public expression is universally restricted, the appeal to force is much to be feared), he must show our rational grounds to be weak, if he thinks ours are wrong, by offering other rational grounds. He must not attack us with anathemas launched from out of the clouds over officialdom. This is what I meant to say in my Preface on page xix. The complete education of a biblical theologian should unite into one system the products of his own powers and whatever contrary lessons he can learn from philosophy. (My book is that sort of combination.) By assessing his doctrines from the point of view of rational grounds, he shall be armed against any future attack.

Perhaps you will be alienated by my Preface, which is in a way rather violent. What occasioned it was this: the whole book was supposed to appear in four issues of the *Berliner Monatsschrift,*

---

[1] Carl Friedrick Stäudlin (1761-1826), professor of theology in Göttingen. Kant dedicated his *Der Streit der Fakultäten* ("Strife of the Faculties" [1798]) to Stäudlin.

with the approval of the censor there. The first part, "On the Radical Evil in Human Nature," went all right; the censor of philosophy, Mr. Privy Counselor Hillmer, took it as falling under his department's jurisdiction. The second part was not so fortunate, since Mr. Hillmer thought that it ventured into the area of biblical theology (for some unknown reason he thought the first part did not), and he therefore thought it advisable to confer with the biblical censor, *Oberconsistorialrath* Hermes, who then of course took it as falling under his own jurisdiction (when did a mere priest ever decline any power?), and so he expropriated it and refused to approve it. The Preface therefore tries to argue that if a censorship commission is in doubt over which sort of censor should judge a book, the author ought not to let the outcome depend on the commission's coming to an agreement but should rather submit the question to a domestic university. For while each individual faculty is bound to maintain its own authority, there is an academic senate that can decide disputes of this kind. To satisfy all the demands of justice, therefore, I presented this book in advance to the theological faculty, asking them to decide whether the book invaded the domain of biblical theology or whether it belonged rather to the jurisdiction of the philosophical faculty, which is how it turned out.

I am moved to disclose this incident to you, sir, so that you will be able to judge whether my actions are justified in case a public quarrel should arise over the case. I am, with genuine respect,

Your most obedient servant,
I. KANT

From J. G. C. Kiesewetter, June 15, 1793

- 580 - VOL. XI, *pp. 436–37*

[Kiesewetter thanks Kant for sending a copy of Kant's *Religion within the Limits of Reason Alone*. It can bring endless benefits, if properly understood, at least by putting an end to the current intolerance of dissent. Kiesewetter is eager to hear what the theologians and especially the inquisitors will say to it, since they have been unable to prevent its publication.]

Mr. Tilling[1] of Courland, who brought me regards from you, gave me great pleasure with the news that you are feeling quite well. So now we can hope that your [metaphysics of] moral[s] will soon appear—no book is awaited more eagerly by so many people. The majority of thinking people have been persuaded of the correctness of the formal principle of morality, as could easily have been predicted; but the deduction of a system of duties and of various rights (for example, the right of property) is so frought with difficulties, not successfully solved by any previous system, that everyone is truly anxious to see your system of morality appear, and all the more so just now since the French Revolution has stimulated a mass of such questions anew. I believe that there are many interesting things to be said about the rationality of the basic principles on which the French Republic bases itself, if only it were prudent to write about such things. It is the topic of every conversation around here and the subject of every argument, though the disputes all tend to stray from the point at issue, either because people confuse the question [of republicanism] with questions about the merits of the current representatives of the institution or else because they try to establish and refute the validity of the ideas by appeal to experience or they demand the impossible.

[Kiesewetter tells of his career as tutor to the royal children. He teaches 15 hours a week and receives 600 thalers a year. He gives public lectures, without pay, on logic; the king has promised him a salary. The war (first coalition war, 1792–95, ended by the Peace of Basel) makes it unlikely that he will receive any more money, but Kiesewetter hears from a reliable source that the king is inclined to make peace before the year is over.]

To J. S. Beck, August 18, 1793

- 584 - VOL. XI, p. 441

I am sending you the essay I promised you, dearest sir. It was supposed to be a preface to the *Critique of Judgment*, but I discarded it because it was too long. You may use it as you see fit,

---

[1] Nicholaus Tilling, theology student in Mitau and Jena (1769–1823).

in your summary of that book. I am also enclosing the proof sheets sent to me by Mr. Court Preacher Schultz.

The essential theme of this preface (which might cover half the manuscript) concerns a unique and unusual presupposition of our reason: [it is almost] as if nature, in the diversity of its products, were inclined to make some accommodation to the limitations of our power of judgment, in the simplicity and noticeable unity of her laws and the presentation of the infinite diversity of her species in accordance with a certain law of continuity that makes it possible for us to organize them under a few basic concepts; . . . as if nature acted arbitrarily and for the sake of our comprehension, sensing that we do not recognize this purposiveness as necessary but that we need it and hence are justified in assuming it a priori and in using the assumption as far as we can.

You will be kind enough to forgive me, at my age and with all my work, for not having had time to look at the proof sheets so as to give you any sound judgment about them. I can trust your own examination to do this. . . . .

Your servant,
I. KANT

From J. E. Biester,[1] October 5, 1793

- 596 -   VOL. XI, *pp. 456–57*

Finally I am able to send you the new issue of the *Berliner Monatsschrift,* most worthy friend. I do so with the deepest gratitude for your excellent September essay.[2] As you wished, it has been printed all in one piece, in a single issue. How abundantly full of significant lessons it is! The second section was especially pleasing to me, on account of its new, masterful way of representing and developing the concepts. To speak quite openly, it pleased me all the more since it refuted the rumor (which I

---

[1] Johann Erich Biester (1749–1816), secretary to Minister von Zedlitz (to whom Kant dedicated the *Critique of Pure Reason*), librarian of the Royal Library in Berlin, publisher of the *Berliner Monatsschrift.*

[2] *Über den Gemeinspruch: "Das mag in der Theorie richtig sein, taugt aber nicht für die Praxis"* ("On the Common Saying: 'That May Be True in Theory but Not in Practice' " [1793]).

suspected from the start) that you had come out in favor of the ever increasingly repulsive French Revolution, in which the actual freedom of reason and morality and all wisdom in statecraft and legislation are being most shamefully trampled under foot—a revolution that even shatters and annuls the universal principles of constitutional law and the concept of a civil constitution, as I now learn from your essay. Surely it is easier to decapitate people (especially if one lets others do it) than courageously to discuss the rational and legal grounds of opposition with a despot, be he sultan or despotic rabble. Till now, however, I see only that the French have mastered those easier operations, performed with bloody hands; I do not see that they have the power of rational examination.

In view of the purpose of your first section, I wish you would look at Schiller's essay,[3] *Über Anmuth und Würde* ["On Grace and Dignity"],[4] and notice what he says, quite speciously, about your moral system, viz., that the hard voice of duty sounds too strongly therein (duty being a law prescribed by reason itself but nevertheless in a way a foreign law) and that there is too little attention to *inclination*.

BIESTER

Berlin

From J. G. C. C. Kiesewetter, November 23, 1793
- 605 - VOL. XI, pp. 468–70

Esteemed professor,

I took the liberty of sending you a little tub of Teltow turnips [1] about two weeks ago and I would have informed you sooner had I not wished to include the first issue of the *Philoso-*

[3] In a footnote to *Religion within the Limits of Reason Alone* Kant calls Schiller's essay a "masterful treatise" and explains how he agrees and disagrees with Schiller. See Kant's *Werke*, VI, 23 f., or the translation by T. M. Greene and H. H. Hudson (New York: Harper & Bros., 1960), 18 f.

[4] In *Thalia* (1793), second issue, published separately.

[1] Kant was enormously fond of these turnips. Kiesewetter kept him regularly supplied for a number of years. Some of Kant's last letters deal with Teltow turnips, requesting more and discussing the proper way to cook them.

phische Bibliothek,[2] which Professor Fischer and I are publishing jointly. But since it is being printed outside Prussia and this will take a while longer, I decided to send it to you later on, so that the turnips will not arrive unannounced. I do hope they meet with your approval. I made sure that they really did come from Teltow. You may wonder why the *Philosophische Bibliothek* is being published abroad. Mr. Hermes[3] thought it dangerous to publish an extract from Heidenreich's *Natürliche Religion.*[4] On the first page of it Hermes made so many corrections that I was forced to decide in favor of foreign publication. His corrections are masterpieces; they would deserve to be printed as an official document of the Berlin Censorship Commission if I were not so lazy. He will not allow that God is an individual, and he says that one does not become worthy of blessedness through virtue but rather *capable* of blessedness, and other such stuff. I am waiting to see whether he will condemn the book. If so, I am determined to fight him. He has still been treating me with indulgence, but Professor Grillo,[5] a man of 60, wanted to publish a summary of your *Religion within the Limits of Reason* and Hermes treated him like a schoolboy, writing doggerel in the margins of his manuscript. If only Grillo were not so peace-loving.

You see, we have hard taskmasters. Hermes himself said to my publisher that he is only waiting for the war[6] to be over before issuing more cabinet orders, which he has in his desk. These gentlemen are now visiting schools and investigating the children. Among other things, people are talking about an examination that von Woltersdorf[7] gave in the school of the Grey Convent. It was really remarkable. It would be a waste of time to tell you the whole story, but here are the first two questions—WOLTERSDORF: How old are you, my son? CHILD: Nine years old. W: And where were you ten years ago, then?—! The story is absolutely true and not something somebody made up.

The new law code[8] is now being introduced, but with four changes, one of which I forget. First, in the preface, the commen-

---

[2] *Neue philosophische Bibliothek,* first (and last) issue, Berlin, 1794.

[3] Hermann Daniel Hermes (1731–1807), member of the Censorship Commission on Spiritual Affairs in Berlin.

[4] Karl Heinrich Heydenreich's *Betrachtung über die Philosophie der natürlichen Religion* (2 vols.; Leipzig, 1790/91) followed Kant's moral theology.

[5] Friedrich Grillo (1739–1802).

[6] The first coalition war (French Revolutionary Wars), 1792–95.

[7] Woltersdorf was another member of the Censorship Commission.

[8] *Allgemeine Landrecht,* in effect July 1, 1794.

dation of monarchy as the best form of government is omitted, for the reason that it is supposed to be self-evident. Second, the article on legally recognized concubinage [*Ehe an der linken Hand*] is taken out, and third, the article on the punishment of exorcists is removed.

Nobody knows how the war will go. I heard yesterday that we are demanding 45 million from Austria, in exchange for which we would prosecute the war by ourselves. It is certain that at the beginning of the war we made many loans to Austria, because they are not as efficient as we are. A special envoy from Austria is awaited. The princes are expected in a week and so is the king, who is now in Potsdam. Lucchesini,[9] Bischoffwerders'[10] brother-in-law, is going to Vienna as ambassador. Everyone longs for peace. . . .

Your grateful pupil,
J. G. C. KIESEWETTER

To K. L. Reinhold, March 28, 1794

- 620 - VOL. XI, *pp. 494–95*

Esteemed sir, dearest friend,

[Kant extends his best wishes on Reinhold's decision to accept another position, in Kiel. He apologizes for not writing to offer his opinion of Reinhold's book on natural right, but says he was unable to do so.]

. . . For the past three years or so, age has effected my thinking —not that I have suffered any dramatic change in the mechanics of health, or even a great decline (though a noticeable one) in my mental powers, as I strive to continue my reflections in accordance with my plan. It is rather that I feel an inexplicable difficulty when I try to project myself into other people's ideas, so that I seem unable really to grasp anyone else's system and to form a mature judgment of it. (Merely general praise or blame does no one any good.) This is the reason why I can turn out essays of my own, but, for example, as regards the "improvement" of the critical philoso-

---

[9] Girolamo Lucchesini (1752–1825), an Italian in the Prussian diplomatic service.

[10] Johann Rudolf von Bischoffswerder (1741–1803), a favorite of Friedrich Wilhelm II's.

phy by Maimon [1] (Jews always like to do that sort of thing, to gain an air of importance for themselves at someone else's expense), I have never really understood what he is after and must leave the reproof to others.

I infer that this problem is attributable to physical causes, since it dates from the time, three years ago, when I had a cold that lasted a week. A mucus made its appearance then, and after the cold was better, this material seems to have moved into the sinuses. It clears up momentarily when I am fortunate enough to sneeze but returns soon after, fogging my brain. Otherwise I am quite healthy, for a man of 70.

I hope that this explanation, which would be pointless to relate to a doctor, since they can do nothing about the consequences of ageing, will serve to assure you of my friendship and devotion.

Now as to our friends—[Kant inquires about J. B. Erhard,[2] who was duped by a confidence man into cashing a large check and accepting a non-existent position as surgeon with the American army.] . . .

To J. E. Biester, April 10, 1794

- 621 - VOL. XI, pp. 496–97

Here is something [1] for your [Berliner Monatsschrift, dearest friend, which may serve, like Swift's Tale of a Tub, to create a momentary diversion from the constant uproar over the same problem. Mr. Rehberg's essay "On the Relation of Theory to Practice" [2] arrived only yesterday. In reading it, I found that, as regards the infinite disparity between rationalist and empiricist

---

[1] Solomon Maimon. See letters April 7, 1789 [352], May 26, 1789 [362], and September 20, 1791 [486].

[2] See the letter to J. B. Erhard of December 21, 1792 [552], n. 1.

[1] "Etwas über den Einfluss des Mondes auf die Witterung" (1794).

[2] "Ueber das Verhältnis der Theorie zur Praxis," in the Berliner Monatsschrift (1794), by August Wilhelm Rehberg (1757–1836), author and statesman. Rehberg claimed that Kant's proof of the highest principle of morality was valid but that it was impossible to derive any specific moral knowledge from it, since the formal law has no content and does not indicate any specific purpose at which man's activity should aim. The principle needs to be supplemented with empirical knowledge. See also Kant's letter to him of around September 25, 1790 [448].

interpretations of the concept of right, the answering of his objections would take too *long;* with regard to his principle of right grounded on power as the highest source of legislation, the answering would be too *dangerous;* and in view of his already having decided in favor of the powers that be (as on page 122),[3] the answering would be in *vain.* It can hardly be expected that a man of 70 would occupy himself with tasks that are burdensome, dangerous, and in vain.

Mr. Rehberg wants to unite the actual *lawyer* [*Juristen*] (who puts a sword onto the balance scales of justice on the side of rational grounds) with the *philosopher of right,* and the inevitable result is that the *application* [*Praxis*] extolled as so necessary in order to render the theory adequate (so they pretend, though actually they want to substitute application for theory) will turn out to be *trickery* [*Praktiken*]. As a matter of fact, an essay of that sort forbids one at the outset to say anything against it. That injunction presumably will soon be felt with its full force, since Mr. Hermes [4] and Mr. Hillmer [5] have taken their positions as overseers of secondary schools and have thereby acquired influence on the universities with respect to how and what is supposed to be taught there.

The essay I will send you soon is entitled "The End of All Things." It will be partly doleful and partly jolly to read.

Your devoted servant and friend,
I. KANT

From *J. S. Beck, June 17, 1794*

- 630 - VOL. XI, *pp. 509–11*

[Beck asks Kant's opinion of the proposed third volume, Beck's "On the Critical Philosophy." It is the work that appeared in 1796,

---

[3] Rehberg claimed that the principle that man must be treated as an end in himself is invalid. It holds only for man *qua* rational being, but in fact man is also a natural being, not governed by reason, and can therefore be treated as an object.

[4] Hermann Daniel Hermes (1731–1807), member of the Censorship Commission on Spiritual Affairs from 1791.

[5] Gottlob Friedrich Hillmer (1756–1835), *Oberconsistorialrath* and member of the same censorship commission.

entitled *Einzig möglicher Standpunkt, aus welchem die critische Philosophie beurtheilt werden muss* ("Only Possible Standpoint from Which the Critical Philosophy Must Be Judged.")]

In your *Critique of Pure Reason* you lead your reader gradually to the highest point of the transcendental philosophy, viz., to the synthetic unity. First, you draw his attention to the consciousness of a given, then make him attentive of concepts by means of which something is thought; you present the categories initially also as concepts, in the ordinary sense, and finally bring him to the insight that these categories are actually the activity of the understanding through which it *originally* creates for itself the concept of an object and produces the *"I think an object."* I have become used to calling this production of the synthetic unity of consciousness "the original activity" (*Ursprüngliche Beylegung.*) It is this activity, among others, that the geometer postulates when he starts his geometry from the proposition "Conceive of space"; and no discursive representation whatsoever could take its place for this purpose. As I see the matter, the postulate "To conceive of an object by means of the original activity" is also the highest principle of philosophy as a whole, the principle on which both general pure logic and the whole of transcendental philosophy rests. I am therefore strongly convinced that this synthetic unity is just the standpoint from which, if one has once mastered it, one can truly understand not only the meaning of "analytic" and "synthetic" judgment but what is actually meant by "a priori" and "a posteriori," what the *Critique* means when it attributes the possibility of geometric axioms to the purity of the intuition on which the axioms are based, what it really is that affects us—whether it is the thing-in-itself (or whether this expression only means a transcendental Idea) or, instead, the object of empirical intuition itself, that is, appearance—and whether the *Critique* argues circularly when it makes the possibility of experience into the principle of synthetic a priori judgments and yet conceals the principle of causality in the concept of this possibility. I say that one can only have a full understanding of all these things, and even of the discursive concept "possibility of experience" itself, when one has fully mastered this standpoint. So long as one still thinks of this "possibility of experience" purely discursively and does not follow up the original activity in just such an activity as this, one has insight into virtually nothing, having merely substituted one incomprehensible thing for another. Your *Critique,* however, leads your reader only gradually, as I say, to this standpoint, and thus, according to its method, it cannot clear up the matter right at the beginning, that is, in the Introduction. The difficulties that reveal themselves along the way ought to encourage the thoughtful reader to be persistent and patient. But since only a very few readers know how to master this highest standpoint, they attribute the difficulties to the style of the work and doubt that they can stick to it. Their difficulties would certainly be overcome, if they were once in a position to consider the challenge: produce the synthetic unity of consciousness. But a proof that even the friends of the *Critique* don't know what they are about is that they don't know where they ought to locate the object that produces sensation.

I have decided therefore to pursue this subject, truly the most important in the whole *Critique,* and am working on an essay in which the method of the *Critique* is reversed. I begin with the postulate of the original activity, locate this activity in the categories, try to get the reader right into this activity itself, as it discloses itself originally in the material of time representation. —Once I think I have the reader completely in the framework in which I want him, I shall then lead him to the review of the *Critique of Pure Reason,* through the Introduction, Aesthetic, and Analytic. Then I shall let him evaluate the most important criticisms of it, especially those of the author of *Aenesidemus.*[1]

What do you think of this? Your age oppresses you, and I shall not ask you to answer me, though I must confess that your letters are most treasured gifts to me. But I do beg you to be kind enough to give your true opinion about this work to my publisher, for he shall base his decision on that. Of course I desire only that you tell him exactly what you think of the project, whether such a work of mine would be useful to the public.

Please excuse me if I seem too assertive. I must send this letter to Hartknoch, and the mail is leaving; so I have had to write somewhat glibly. May you remain well disposed toward

Your most respectful
BECK

[1] See letter of December 4, 1792 [549], n. 1, for further details about *Aenesidemus.*

To J. S. Beck, July 1, 1794

- 634 - VOL. XI, pp. 514-16

Aside from remarking on the pleasure that your letters always give me, I have only the following little remarks to make concerning your proposed book on the "original activity" [*Ursprüngliche Beylegung*] (the relating of a representation, *qua* determination of the subject, to an object distinguished from it, by which means it becomes a cognition and is not merely a feeling):

1. Could you also make clear what you mean by the word *Beylegung* in Latin? Furthermore, one cannot actually say that a representation *befits* another thing but only that, if it is to be a cognition, a *relation* to something else (something other than the subject in which the representation inheres) *befits* the representation, whereby it becomes *communicable* to other people; for otherwise it would belong merely to feeling (of pleasure or displeasure), which in itself cannot be communicated. But we can only understand and communicate to others what we ourselves can *make*, granted that the manner in which we intuit something, in representing this or that, can be assumed to be the same for everybody. That alone is the representation of a *composite*. For—

2. The synthesizing itself is not given; on the contrary, it must be done by us: we must *synthesize* if we are to represent anything as *synthesized* (even space and time). We are able to communicate with one another because of this synthesis. The grasping (*apprehensio*) of the given manifold and its reception in the unity of consciousness (*apperceptio*) is the same sort of thing as the representation of a composite (that is, it is only possible through synthesis), if the synthesis of my representation in the grasping, and its analysis insofar as it is a concept, yield one and the same representation (reciprocally bring forth one another). This agreement is applied to something that is valid for everyone, something distinguished from the subject, that is, an object, since it lies exclusively neither in the representation nor in consciousness but nevertheless is valid (*communicable*) for everyone.

I notice, as I am writing this down, that I do not even entirely understand myself and I shall wish you luck if you can put this simple, thin thread of our cognitive faculty under a sufficiently bright light. Such overly refined hair-splitting is no longer for me; I cannot even make Professor Reinhold's work clear to me. I need not remind a mathematician like you, dear friend, to stay within the boundaries of clarity, both by using the most ordinary expressions and by furnishing easily grasped examples. —Mr. Hartknoch will be very pleased with your projected book. Hold me dear as

Your respectful friend and servant,
I. KANT

To Friedrich Wilhelm II [1] [after October 12, 1794]

- 642 - VOL. XI, pp. 527–30

Your Royal Majesty's order of October 12 enjoins me as follows.[2] First, on account of my misuse of philosophy in distorting and depreciating many of the basic teachings of Holy Scripture and of Christianity, namely, in my book *Religion within the Limits of Reason Alone*[3] and in other smaller essays, and because I am guilty of overstepping my duty as an educator of the youth and guilty of opposing the very highest intentions of our sovereign, intentions that are supposedly well known to me, I am therefore duty-bound to bring forward my conscientious vindication of my conduct. Second, I am not to repeat this sort of offense in the future. In regard to both of these obligations and with profound submissiveness I hope to show Your Royal Majesty sufficient proof of my previously demonstrated and further to be demonstrated obedience.

As for the complaint against me, that I have misused my philosophy to depreciate Christianity, my conscientious self-vindication is as follows:

1. As an educator of the youth, in academic lectures, I have never been guilty of this sort of thing. Aside from the testimony of my listeners, to which I appeal, this is sufficiently demonstrated by

[1] This letter appears as well in the Preface to Kant's *Strife of the Faculties* (*Streit der Facultäten* [1798]).

[2] The *Cabinetsordre* was signed by Woellner and dated October 1, 1794. It also appears in the Preface of *Strife of the Faculties*.

[3] On October 14, 1795, the King, or rather his ministers Woellner and Hillmer, issued an order to the academic senate in Königsberg forbidding all professors to lecture on Kant's book. (Schultz had announced a course of lectures.) *Werke*, XIII, 371.

the fact that my pure and merely philosophical instruction has conformed to A. G. Baumgarten's textbooks, in which the subject of Christianity does not even occur, nor can it occur. It is impossible to accuse me of overstepping the limits of a philosophical investigation of religion in my teaching.

2. Nor have I, as an author, for example, in my *Religion within the Limits* . . . , opposed the highest purposes of the sovereign that were known to me. For since those purposes concern the state religion, I would have had to write as a teacher of the general public, a task for which this book along with my other little essays is ill-suited. They were only written as scholarly discussions for specialists in theology and philosophy, in order to determine how religion may be inculcated most clearly and forcefully into the hearts of men. The theory is one of which the general public takes no notice and which requires the sanction of the government only if it is to be taught to schoolteachers and teachers of religion. But it is not against the wisdom and authority of the government to allow academic freedom. For the official religious doctrines were not thought up by the government itself but were supplied to it from these scholarly sources. The government would rather be justified in demanding of the faculty an examination and justification of religious doctrines, without prescribing what it is to be.

3. I am not guilty of depreciating Christianity in that book, since it contains no assessment of any actual revealed religion. It is intended merely as an examination of rational religion [*Vernunft-religion*], an assessment of its priority as the highest condition of all true religion, of its completeness and of its practical aim (namely, to show us what we are obligated to do) as well as of its incompleteness from the standpoint of the theoretical [reason] (an incompleteness that is the source of evil, just as the latter is the source of our transition to the good or the reason the certainty that we are evil is possible, and so on). Consequently the need for a revealed doctrine is not obscured, and rational religion is related to revealed religion in general, without specifying which one it is (where Christianity, for example, is regarded as the mere idea of a conceivable revelation). It was, I maintain, my duty to make clear the status of rational religion. It should have been incumbent on my accusers to point out a single case in which I depreciated Christianity either by arguing against its acceptance as a revelation or by showing it to be unnecessary. For I do not regard it as a depreciation of a revealed doctrine to say that, in relation to its

practical use (which constitutes the essential part of all religion), it must be interpreted in accordance with the principles of pure rational faith [*Vernunftglaubens*] and must be urged on us openly. I take this rather as a recognition of its morally fruitful content, which would be deformed by the supposedly superior importance of merely theoretical propositions that are to be taken on faith.

4. My true respect for Christianity is demonstrated by my extolling the Bible as the best available guide for the grounding and support of a truly moral state religion, perennially suitable for public instruction in religion. Therefore I have not allowed myself any attacks or criticisms of the Bible based on merely theoretical beliefs (though the faculties must be allowed to do this). I have insisted on the holy, practical content of the Bible, which, with all the changes in theoretical articles of faith that will take place in regard to merely revealed doctrines, because of their coincidental nature, will always remain as the inner and essential part of religion. The essential, practical essence of religion can always be recovered in its purity, as it was after Christianity had degenerated in the dark ages of clericalism.

5. Finally, I have always insisted that anyone who confesses a revealed faith must be conscientious, viz., he must assert no more than he really knows, and he must urge others to believe only in that of which he himself is fully certain. My conscience is clear: I have never let the Divine Judge out of my sight, in writing my works on religion, and I have tried voluntarily to withdraw not only every error that might destroy a soul but even every possibly offensive expression. I have done this especially because, in my 71st year, the thought necessarily arises that I may soon have to give an accounting of myself before a judge of the world who knows men's hearts. Therefore I have no misgivings in offering this vindication now to the highest authority in our land, with full conscientiousness, as my unchangeable, candid confession.

6. Regarding the second charge, that I am not to be guilty of such distortion and depreciation of Christianity (as has been claimed) in the future, I find that, as Your Majesty's loyal subject,[4] in order not to fall under suspicion, it will be the surest course for

---

[4] Kant later interpreted this phrase as committing him to silence only insofar as he was a subject of Friedrich Wilhelm II. He therefore felt himself not in violation of his promise when he published on religious topics after the death of that monarch.

me to abstain entirely from all public lectures on religious topics, whether on natural or revealed religion, and not only from lectures but also from publications. I hereby promise this.

I am eternally Your Royal Majesty's most submissive and obedient subject.

From J. E. Biester, December 17, 1794

- 646 - VOL. XI, pp. 535–36

. . . If your muse should permit it, you know how grateful all your readers would be for another essay.

I have had the opportunity of reading your defense submitted to the Department of Spiritual Affairs, concerning the accusation against your *Religion within the Limits of Reason*.[1] It is noble, manly, meritorious, thorough. But everyone will regret your voluntary promise not to discuss positive and natural religion any more. You thereby prepare a great triumph for the enemies of the Enlightenment, and the good cause suffers a great loss. It seems to me that you did not need to make this promise. You could have continued to write on the topics in question, in the philosophical and respectable way you always have, which you justify so excellently. Granted, you would then perhaps have had to defend yourself again on specific points. Or you could even have remained silent for the rest of your life but without giving these people the satisfaction of being released from the fear of your words. I say, for the rest of your life; for people will in any event continue to work on the great philosophical and theological enlightenment that you have so happily begun, and we may hope that at least our descendants may someday (perhaps it will be soon) read these works and use them—of that we are all convinced, out of our love for reason and morality.

Be well, excellent man, and be for us ever an example of how a wise and noble person can maintain his calm and inner peace, even when reason is threatened by storms.

BIESTER

[1] See Kant's letter of sometime after October 12, 1794 [642], to Friedrich Wilhelm II.

To Friedrich Schiller,[1] March 30, 1795

- 656 - VOL. XII, pp. 10–11

Esteemed sir,

I am always delighted to know and engage in literary discussions with such a talented and learned man as you, my dearest friend. I received the plan for a periodical that you sent me last summer and also the two first monthly issues. I found your *Letters on the Aesthetic Education of Mankind* splendid, and I shall study them so as to be able to give you my thoughts about them.

The paper on sexual differences in organic nature, in the second issue, is impossible for me to decipher, even though the author seems to be an intelligent fellow.[2] There was once a severely critical discussion in the *Allgemeine Literaturzeitung* about the ideas expressed in the letters of Mr. Hube of Thorn[3] concerning a similar relationship extending throughout nature. The ideas were attacked as romantic twaddle [*Schwärmerei*]. To be sure, we sometimes find something like that running through our heads, without knowing what to make of it. The organization of nature has always struck me as amazing and as a sort of chasm of thought; I mean, the idea that fertilization, in both realms of nature, always needs two sexes in order for the species to be propagated. After all, we don't want to believe that providence has chosen this arrangement, almost playfully, for the sake of variety. On the contrary, we have reason to believe that propagation is not possible *in any other way*. This opens a prospect on what lies beyond the field of vision, out of which, however, we can unfortu-

---

[1] Friedrich Schiller (1759–1805), the great poet and essayist, wrote to Kant, June 13, 1794, asking Kant to contribute an essay to a new literary magazine, *Die Horen* (12 vols., 1795–97). He assures Kant of his devotion to Kant's moral system and expresses profuse gratitude to Kant for illuminating his spirit. On March 1, 1795, Schiller wrote again, repeating his request and sending two issues of *Die Horen*. He confesses that he is the author of the *Letters on the Aesthetic Education of the Human Race,* a work he believes to be an application of Kant's philosophy and hopes that Kant will like it.

[2] The article was by Wilhelm von Humboldt: "Ueber den Geschlechts unterschied und dessen Einfluss auf die organische Natur."

[3] Johann Michael Hube (1737–1807), director and professor at the military academy in Warsaw, author of a book on natural science (*Naturlehre*).

nately make nothing, as little as out of what Milton's angel told Adam about the creation: "Male light of distant suns mixes itself with female, for purposes unknown." [4] I feel that it may harm your magazine not to have the authors sign their names, to make themselves thus responsible for their considered opinions; the reading public is very eager to know who they are.

For your gift, then, I offer my most respectful thanks; with regard to my small contribution to this journal, your present to the public, I must however beg a somewhat lengthy postponement. Since discussions of political and religious topics are currently subject to certain restrictions and there are hardly any other matters, at least at this time, that interest the general reading public, one must keep one's eye on this change of the weather, so as to conform prudently to the times.

Please greet Professor Fichte and give him my thanks for sending me his various works. I would have done this myself but for the discomfort of ageing that oppresses me, with all the manifold tasks I still have before me, which, however, excuses nothing but my postponement. Please give my regards also to Messrs. Schütz and Hufeland.

And so, dearest sir, I wish your talents and your worthy objectives the strength, health, and long life they deserve, and also the friendship, with which you wish to honor one who is ever

Your most devoted, loyal servant,
I. KANT

From Maternus Reuss,[1] April 1, 1796

- 699 - VOL. XII, pp. 68–69

[Reuss writes from Würzburg to tell Kant of the progress of Kant's philosophy in Catholic, that is, southern Germany. . . .]

[4] The correct quotation is as follows:
and other suns perhaps
With their attendent moons thou wilt descry
Communicating male and female light,
Which two great sexes animate the world,
Stor'd in each orb perhaps with some that live.
[Paradise Lost, Book VIII, vss. 148–52]

---

[1] Maternus Reuss (1751–98), Benedictine, professor of philosophy in Würzburg, a disciple of Kant's.

I continue to expound both theoretical and practical philosophy according to your principles, without any opposition. Professor Andres [2] is teaching your aesthetics. Almost all the professors of theology and jurisprudence are modeling at least their approaches if not the content of their teachings on your principles, and even in religious instruction these principles are used to teach catechism and sermons. Many foreigners come here just to hear my lectures on the Kantian philosophy, and my prince [3] relieved me of all my other duties so that I could devote myself to philosophy.

The prospects are not quite so bright in colleges in Bamberg, Heidelberg, and other Catholic schools, and the situation is even more bleak in Bavaria, Swabia, and the Catholic part of Switzerland. I traveled through these three countries, and I hope I did some good. Since their schools are largely run by monks who are strictly forbidden to use a German textbook and certainly not a Protestant one, I wrote a textbook of theoretical philosophy in Latin for the sake of these schools. However, it has not been printed yet. In the Italian and French parts of Switzerland, they also want a Latin exposition of Kant's philosophy. Professor Ith [4] in Bern asked me to give him one.

I cannot convey to you the enthusiasm for your ideas, even among people who used to oppose them, and even the ladies here are taken with you, since we read in a number of newspapers that you have been called to France to act as lawgiver and patron of peace and that your king has given you his consent. I myself am receiving many a friendly glance from the ladies now, more than before.

I asked Court Preacher Schultze to tell me whether the news is correct, since I know you have no time to write.

Your devoted servant,

REUSS, *Professor*

Mr. Stang sends his best regards.[5]

[2] Johann Bonaventura Andres (1743–1822), professor of philosophy in Würzburg.
[3] Georg Carl, Freiherr von Fechenbach.
[4] Johann Samuel Ith (1747–1813), professor of philosophy in Bern.
[5] Conrad Stang. See the letter of October 2, 1796 [715].

From Conrad Stang,[1] October 2, 1796

- 715 - VOL. XII, *pp. 97–100*

. . . For a while I studied law, but I found it unbearably dry. I returned to philosophy, a more rewarding subject, which I had always loved. Granted, it is an unusual thing in a Catholic country, where people are used to leaving this auxiliary science to the clerics and no one really appreciates it as valuable in itself. But I also had to become a Mason (a synonym for Jacobin in this country as in other Catholic lands), and many people have busied themselves with warning me, pitying me, or even viewing me as dangerous. But I can laugh at them all, for I am wholly at peace, pursuing my philosophical studies of your works and finding truth in them and the feeling that you are with me as I read them. I enjoy practical philosophy most. And why not? For your tone here is so stirring, so moving, and this subject concerns the most important part of our lives.

Your system has been totally triumphant here, and no one dares to attack it. You know already how they used to intrigue against it, as Prof. Reuss wrote you earlier.[2] Last year I made a trip to Vienna, returning by way of Salzburg and Munich. The many people I met enabled me to get an adequate picture of the condition of philosophy. The critical philosophy is regarded as an enemy in the Austrian monarchy, and woe to him who wants to teach it. The Emperor[3] is totally against it. When Mr. von Birkenstock, the director of education in Vienna, told him about the critical system, the Emperor turned and said, "Once and for all, I don't want to hear any more of this dangerous system." In Vienna I heard about a Mr. von Delling, who lost his professorship in Fünfkirchen, because he lectured on the principles of the critical philosophy. For three years they intrigued against him but he remained firm, but last summer the entire clergy of Hungary attacked him and he lost his position. The decree firing him

---

[1] Conrad Stang, Benedictine from Würzburg. Nothing further is known of him.

[2] See the letter of April 1, 1796 [699].

[3] Joseph II.

charged him, among other things "*propter perniciosum Sistema ad Scepticism ducens.*" Other accusations were that he had tried to answer the charge (and they had actually asked him to defend himself) and had published a defense of the critical philosophy. Finally they said he had to be removed since, as his defense made clear, it was impossible to cure him of his allegiance to the critical principles. Nevertheless, the cause of the critical philosophy grows secretly as the Hungarian Protestants who study in Jena and Halle bring the new principles home with them. Also in Vienna I met the rector of philosophy from Grätz, Mr. von Albertini,[4] who had lost his position for defending the critical philosophy. People assure me that there are many in the Austrian monarchy who favor the new system. But nothing much can happen in Vienna, where there is a total lack of community among scholars, and the professors at the university do not know each other. Only by accident do they ever meet. The situation is better in Salzburg, where the worthy regent[5] of the seminary favors the critical philosophy. But many are still opposed, and not till Würzburg does one find a decent intellectual climate. The prince[6] has a hobbyhorse there; he wants to be known abroad as enlightened. That provides the aegis of the critical philosophy in Salzburg, which it will lose, however, when he dies. Munich is impossible for critical philosophy, since Stattler[7] lives and reigns there. Nevertheless there are individuals who study and try to make use of the Critical philosophy in secret. Your books are contraband there as in Austria, but especially your work on religion. Alas, why must truth have to battle against so many enemies before its voice is half heard! But if the men are struggling so vigorously against the critical Philosophy, its fortunes are somewhat better among the women. You can't guess how enthusiastically young ladies and women are taken with your system and how eager they all are to learn about it. There are many women's groups here in Würzburg, where each one is eager to outdo the others in showing a knowledge of your system: it is the favorite topic of conversation. Yes, remarkable as it seems, they do not restrict themselves to practical philosophy but even venture into the theoretical part. . . .

[4] Johann Baptist Albertini (1742–1820). He had actually been rector of philosophy in Innsbruck, not Grätz.
[5] Matthäus Fingerlos (1748–1817).
[6] Hieronymous Joseph Franz de Paula, Count of Colloredo (1732–1812).
[7] Benedikt Stattler (1728–97), author of *Antikant* (2 vols.; Munich, 1788).

To J. A. Schlettwein,[1] May 29, 1797

- 752 - VOL. XII, pp. 367-68

In a letter dated Greifswald, May 11, 1797, a letter recently made public, which is distinguished by its singular tone, Mr. Johann August Schlettwein demands that I engage in an exchange of letters with him on the critical philosophy. He indicates that he already has various letters prepared on the subject and adds that he believes himself to be in a position to overthrow completely my whole philosophical system, both its theoretical and its practical parts, an event that should be pleasing to every friend of philosophy. But as for the proposed method whereby this refutation is to be carried out, namely, in an exchange of letters, either handwritten or printed, I must answer curtly: Absolutely not. For it is absurd to ask a man in his seventy-fourth year (when the *sarcinas colligere* ["packing one's bags"] is really of the highest importance) to engage in a project that would take many years, just to make even tolerable progress with the criticisms and rejoinders. But the reason why I am making this declaration (which I have already sent to him) public is that his letter clearly had publicity as

---

[1] Johann August Schlettwein (1731–1802), prominent German physiocrat. This letter is a reply to an open letter to Kant, published by Schlettwein in the *Berlinische Blätter*, September, 1797 (751, in Kant's *Werke*, XII, 362–66.) Schlettwein's letter is incredibly insulting, accusing Kant of contempt for his great predecessors and contemporaries, of pride, self-love, and self-seeking, the arrogant claim of infallibility and originality, and so on. He calls it a scandal that so-called critical philosophers dispute the sense and spirit of Kant's works and asks Kant to say which one of his disciples has understood him correctly. Schlettwein claims to have a refutation of Kant ready but does not in fact state any arguments. A hint of his own position is given in the assertion that "true philosophy teaches the incontrovertible doctrine of the reality of an infinite power, the forces of nature, and the marvelous and sublime properties and capacities of physical and spiritual man." He states that philosophy, in its practical part, should seek to bring people ever closer to God, "not by means of a loveless, despotic categorical imperative, contrary to the very nature of reason, but through the gentle, all-powerful tie of love that animates all things" (p. 366).

Kant's answer appeared in the *Allgemeine Literaturzeitung* on June 14, 1797. Schlettwein responded with another open letter (753, *Werke*, XII, 368–70), which is uninteresting. A lost letter of Kant's, May 19, 1797, is alluded to in it.

its object, and since his attack may be broadcast by word of mouth, those people who are interested in such a controversy would otherwise be left waiting empty-handed. Since Mr. Schlettwein will not let this difficulty halt his projected overthrow of my system (probably with a massive assault, since he appears to rely on allies as well), and my declaration will make him regard me as his archenemy, he wisely has the foresight to ask "which one of the disputants [2] has really interpreted at least the main points of my system *in the way I want them to be interpreted.*" My answer is, Unquestionably the worthy court preacher and professor of mathematics here, Mr. Schultz, whose book on the critical system, entitled *Prüfung* [*der Kantischen Kritik der reinen Vernunft* (1789/92)], should be examined by Mr. Schlettwein.

I would only add the qualification that Mr. Schultz's words are to be taken literally and not according to some spirit ostensibly expressed in them (which would enable anyone to add any interpretation he pleases). Whatever ideas anyone else might have associated with the same expressions are of no interest to me or to the learned man to whom I commit myself. The sense that he attaches to those expressions is unmistakable in the context of the book as a whole. So now the feud may continue forever, with never a shortage of opponents for every disputant.

I. KANT

From J. S. Beck, June 20, 1797

- 754 - VOL. XII, *pp. 162–69*

[Beck is replying to the charge made by Johann Schultz, Kant's favorite expositor, that Beck had totally misrepresented the Kantian philosophy. Beck is convinced that Kant will see his account of the critical philosophy to be correct.]
. . . I remark concerning the categories, *first,* that their logical employment consists in their use as predicates of objects. For instance, we say that a thing *has* size, *has* factuality, that substantiality, causality, and so on, *befit* it. I give evidence of this logical employment of the understanding also in a priori judgments: for

[2] Schlettwein had asked whether Reinhold, Fichte, Beck, or someone else was the correct interpreter.

example, "In all change of appearance, substance persists," "What happens has a cause," and so on. How then is the explanation of this synthesis of concepts to be approached? I notice the original procedure of the understanding in the category; this activity is precisely what produces the synthetic objective unity that determines the sense and meaning of my concept. What is it, I ask, that requires the chemist, in his experiment of burning phosphorous in atmospheric air, to say that that weight by which the phosphorus has become heavier is just that by which the air has become lighter? I answer: His very own understanding, the *experiencing* in him. He becomes aware of this original understanding-experience when I ask him to suspend all the objects in space and, after the passing of 50 years, set up a world again. He will assert that both worlds go together and that no empty time has passed, that is, that he can only conceive of time in connection with something persisting. Attention must be paid to this, in order to lay the ghost of Berkeleian idealism. Just so, if I focus attention on the *experiencing* in me, whereby I arrive at the claim that something has happened, I notice that the cause that I connect with this is simply the determination of the synthesis of perceptions as a succession (the original positing of a something through which the event follows according to a rule). By means of this, the experience of an event is created. In fact the explanation of all a priori synthetic judgments consists in this: the predicate that I connect with the subject, in such judgments, is the original activity of the understanding through which I arrive at the concept of an object. By recognizing this principle, I think I become clearer about the judgment "My representation of the table before me conforms to the table; and this object affects me—it brings forth sensation in me." Everyone else is conscious of this original activity of the understanding, though only in its application, not abstractly. Thus I am certainly convinced that the division of the cognitive faculties —viz., into sensibility, as the subjective faculty (the capacity of being affected by objects) and understanding, the power of thinking objects (of relating the subjective element to an object)—can only be seen with requisite clarity after one has a proper perspective of the categories, as an original activity of the understanding.

Jacobi of Düsseldorf says in his lecture "David Hume," "I must admit that this claim (namely, that objects produce sense impressions) made me hesitate more than a little in my studies of the Kantian philosophy, so that year after year I had to begin the

Critique of Pure Reason once more from the beginning. For I was continuously confused, since *without* that assumption I could not enter the system, and *with* it I could not remain in it." If I were to give my judgment concerning this problem, which is so important to a great many people, and if I were to say what your *Critique* actually means, when, on the first page of the Introduction, it speaks of objects that affect the senses—whether it means by that things-in-themselves or appearances—I should answer that since the object of my representation is appearance, and since it is this representation in which determinations of the object are thought, and since I achieve the representation by means of the original activity of the understanding (for example, by means of the original fixation of my synthesis of perceptions as a successive one, whereby experience of an event becomes possible), the object that affects me must therefore be appearance and not thing-in-itself. But if someone should believe it possible to have an absolute employment of the categories, to regard them absolutely as predicates of things, disregarding the original activity of the understanding that lies in them (as you would say: to believe possible an application of them to objects without the condition of intuition), he would believe himself capable of cognizing things-in-themselves. If I wanted to get a little bit angry with Mr. Schultz, I would say that I have more right to accuse him of thinking he has an intellectual intuition than he has to make this accusation against me. In my view, the only thing of which man is capable is the awareness of the relation of nature in general to a substratum. We are conscious of this in connection with morality, when we recognize that our desires are determinable by means of the mere representation of conformity to law. For in this awareness—it is exactly here that the synthetic practical principles arise, just as those synthetic a priori theoretical judgments arise out of the original activity of the understanding—we lift ourselves above nature and place ourselves outside her mechanism. This is true even if, as men, we are also natural objects and our morality itself is something that begins and thus presupposes natural causes. The mechanism of nature, which is continuous with a corresponding unity of purposes, adjusts us to this condition even more and encourages and strengthens the soul of a morally good man, even though he only knows how to represent this substratum symbolically. The course of human events itself, of such natural events as, for example, the appearance of the Christian religion, concerning which one can say that it carries in itself the principle of its own dissolution, natural events whose ostensible goal is to bring forth the pure moral faith in our species—all of these things lead the understanding to such a relation.

But I sound as if I wanted to tell you something new! . . . I have pointed out to the commentators of your *Critique* who make much of your words that in their mouths it seems to me entirely senseless to speak of a priori concepts. For they, do not want to regard such concepts as innate, the way Leibniz did. I point this out solely to make conspicuous the important distinction between your claim, that the categories are a priori concepts, and the contention that they are innate, and in order to show that these categories are actually the activity of the understanding whereby one arrives at the concept of an object, arrives at the point at which one can say at all, "Here is an object distinct from me." No one can be more convinced of the correctness of his insights than I at this moment. What Mr. Schultz blames me for never occurred to me. It never occurred to me to try to construct an exegesis that would explain away sensibility. As I said, I could not close my eyes to the light I glimpsed when the idea came to me, to start from the standpoint of the categories and to connect what you are especially concerned with in your transcendental aesthetic (space and time) with the categories. Mr. Reinhold had corrected you, when you said: Space is an a priori intuition; his expert opinion was that you ought rather to have said, "The representation of space is an intuition." But I show him that space itself is a pure intuition, that is, the original synthesis of the understanding on which objective connecting (an object has this or that magnitude) rests. It never entered my mind to say that the understanding creates the object: a piece of naked nonsense! How can Mr. Schultz be so unfriendly as to charge me with this. As I said, I wanted not a whit more than to lead people to this point: that we cannot objectively synthesize anything (or judge it—for example, assert "a thing has this or that size, this or that reality, substantiality, and so on) that the understanding has not previously bound together and that herein lies the objective relation. I want to lead everyone to this by the nose. How can one fail to see by this light! The object that here affects my senses is called appearance and not thing-in-itself; of the latter I can only construct the negative concept, a thing to which predicates belong absolutely (entirely apart from this original activity of the understanding)—an Idea, and also the idea of an intuitive understanding, which we get by negating the characteristic of our own understanding. My intention was to bar the concept of the thing-in-itself from theoretical philosophy. Only in the moral consciousness am I led to that unique mode of reality. . . . No one, of all the friends of the critical philosophy, has stressed the distinction between sensibility and understanding more than I have. I do it under the expression: a concept has sense and meaning only to the extent that the original activity of the understanding in the categories lies at its basis—which in fact is the same as your contention that the categories have application only to what is directly experienced. . . .

[The remainder of Beck's letter tries to explain how the phrase "On the advice of Kant" came to appear on the title page of Beck's book. It was supposed to appear only on Beck's summary of Kant, not on his original interpretation in the *Standpoint*. Beck offers to set the matter straight by informing the public that only the summary has Kant's approval. He fears, however, that the "enemies of the critical philosophy" will seize on his announcement, "smelling quarrel and dissention" among Kant's followers. Beck says that he has asked his friend Professor Tieftrunk to write to Kant on his behalf, in order to corroborate his contention that he is loyal to Kant's position.]

From *J. S. Beck, June 24, 1797*

- 756 - VOL. XII, *pp. 173–76*

Esteemed sir,

 . . . You say that the purpose of your letter [1] is the swift and public removal of a disagreement over the fundamental principles of the critical philosophy. And Court Preacher [Schultz] attributes to me the claim that "reality is the original synthesis of the homogeneous in sensation, which proceeds from the whole to its parts." [2] (The question must be yours, sir, when he asks, quite

---

[1] Friedrich Heinrich Jacobi (1743–1819), the well-known "philosopher of faith" who fought Mendelssohn. *David Hume über den Glauben* was published in 1787.

[1] Sometime before June 20, 1797; the letter is not extant.

[2] Beck in fact wrote that *the category* of reality is the original synthesis of the homogeneous, proceeding from the whole to its part. See Kant's *Werke*, XIII, 452, and Beck's explanation in the next paragraph of the present letter.

justifiably, in this connection, "What 'sensation' can mean, if there is no such thing as sensibility, I fail to understand." Surely, excellent sir, if such a thing had ever occurred to me, this nonsense would have made me repulsive to myself); and Schultz also quotes me as saying that "the understanding creates [*erzeugt*] objects." [3] I infer from this that you and Mr. Schultz have been discussing Mr. Fichte's strange invention, since these expressions I quoted sound completely Fichtean to me. All I can do is to remind you of the following things and to offer a proposal that I have in mind.

I assure you, as I am an honest man, that my views are infinitely removed from this Fichtean nonsense. I only thought it essential to focus the attention of philosophers on the categories, as being an original activity of the understanding, to which your entire deduction is directed, since the deduction is an attempt to answer the question of how the categories are applicable to appearances. For I felt sure that disagreements would vanish when people came to see that the understanding cannot combine objectively [*objectiv verknüpfen*] anything that it has not already originally bound together [*verbunden*].[4] When I say that the category of reality is the synthesis of sensation, proceeding from whole to parts (through remission), the only rational interpretation of my claim is this: the objectivity [*Sachheit*] of a thing (the objective aspect [*das Reale*] of the appearance that affects me and that produces this sensation in me) is necessarily an intensive magnitude, and therefore an absolutely objective thing [*Sachheit*] such as Descartes supposes [5]—a thing with no magnitude but nevertheless a material substance, filling space just by its mere existence—would be meaningless. This original activity of the understanding, in the category of reality, converges with the activity in the category of existence, whereby I get beyond my own self and say, "Here is an object that affects me." But a proponent of the transcendental philosophy must distinguish these two aspects of the original activity. I thought it necessary to guide the reader's eye to each particular category. When someone asks me, "Suppose you think yourself away, do you then also remove everything existing outside you?" I will not be so stupid as to say yes to this silly idea. If I

[3] Possibly an interpretation of Beck's claim that "the understanding originally posits a something [*Etwas*]."

[4] Cf. *Critique of Pure Reason* B 130.

[5] *Principles of Philosophy*, I, 53: "We can conceive extension without figure or action."

think myself away, I am still considering myself under temporal conditions, and I can conceive of this passage of time only in relation to something enduring. To *neglect* this original activity of the understanding is not the same as to *abolish* myself. Indeed, I shall say, if I ignore the original synthesis of which I am conscious when I draw a line, I lose all sense of the extensive magnitude that I attribute to an object, and just for that reason the object of my representations is called appearance and not thing-in-itself. Assuredly, excellent sir, if you would only honor me by examining my method, in which I descend from the standpoint of the categories, just as you proceed by ascending to them in your immortal book, you would see the feasibility of what I do. What is required is only that one get to feel at home with the whole system; then it is easy to show anyone who has interest and a bit of talent how to arrive at the true critical principles. I think my method is especially helpful for lectures. Court Preacher Schultz, of whom I am ever fond and whose knowledge and sincerity I respect, has really been unfair to me, and I am depressed that this fine man could believe that I hold such absurd views as that the understanding creates the object. He would not have been able to think such things of me before, when I was his attentive pupil in mathematics.

But I know that Mr. Fichte, who apparently wants disciples, has claimed that I agree with him, even though I strongly denied this in a review I published in Mr. Jakob's *Annalen* [6] and also in my *Standpoint.* When I visited him in Jena last Easter, he really did try to ensnare me. He actually started one conversation by saying, "I know it, you agree with me that the understanding creates the object." He said a number of foolish things, and since I saw through him immediately, he must have been highly perplexed by my friendly answers. I also wanted to say to you that Fichte told me that his new journal [7] will contain a revised version of his *Wissenschaftslehre* ["Theory of Science"] and will, among other things, treat philosophy as a single discipline, without assuming

[6] *Annalen der Philosophie und des philosophischen Geistes von einer Gesellschaft gelehrter Männer* (Halle, 1795).

[7] *Philosophisches Journal einer Gesellschaft Teutscher Gelehrten,* published by Fichte and F. J. Niethammer (Jena and Leipzig, 1797). Fichte praises Beck for "having independently liberated himself from the confusions of the age, in that he has come to see that the Kantian philosophy is a transcendental idealism and not dogmatism, since it maintains that the object is neither wholly nor partly given but rather made. . . ." See Kant's *Werke,* XIII, 452 f., for a slightly fuller quotation.

any distinction between theoretical and moral philosophy, since the understanding, through its absolute freedom, posits every object (A stupid idea! Anyone who talks like that must never have mastered the critical principles); and he says he discusses my *Standpoint* at length there. I have not seen it yet, but I feel sure in advance that it will provide me with an occasion to explain myself, perhaps in Jakob's *Annalen,* so that I can point out, first, that I do not at all agree with him; second, that I believe I have given an accurate exposition of the *Critique* and therefore do not regard myself as deviating from it—for nothing concerns me more than to distinguish sensibility (the faculty of being affected by objects) from the understanding (the faculty of thinking objects, relating this subjective material of sensibility to objects); third, that nevertheless I do not at all intend to compromise the founder of the critical philosophy in the slightest way, since the *Standpoint* is entirely *my own idea,* which anyone is free to compare with your published works and make his own judgment. I don't want to antagonize Fichte personally, and I shall therefore be completely pleasant in discussing him. But in connection with the second point above, I want to express myself in detail and make clear what was badly stated in the *Standpoint*. Do you concur with me? I don't want to start anything until I have your approval. But please don't be vexed with me. I am dedicated to philosophy and would be pained indeed by the thought that I have fallen from your favor.

Your

BECK

To C. G. Schütz, July 10, 1797

- 761 - VOL. XII, *pp. 181–83*

I am inspired by your letter to our mutual friend, the excellent Court Preacher Schultz, to take this opportunity to tell you, dearest sir, how happy I am about your improved health, the rumor of which has been spreading recently. A man of such universal talents deserves a long and joyful life!

I am not offended by your criticism, in the aforementioned letter, of my recently advanced concept of "a person's rights *in rem* over other persons" [*auf dingliche Art persönlichen Rechts*]. For jurisprudence [*Rechtslehre*] based on pure reason accepts the maxim "Entities are not to be multiplied beyond necessity" even more than do the other branches of philosophy. Your suspicion might rather be aroused that I have deceived myself with verbal trickery, begging the question by surreptitiously assuming that what is practicable is also permitted. But no one can be blamed for mistaking a teacher's meaning if a new theory is alluded to without its grounds' being explained in detail. One can easily imagine that one sees errors then, when actually the complaint should only be that there is a lack of clarity.

I only want to touch on the criticisms in your letter and shall develop my comments more explicitly on another occasion.[1]

First: "You cannot really believe that a man makes an object out of a woman just by engaging in marital cohabitation with her, and vice versa. You seem to think marriage no more than a *mutuum adiutorium* ["mutual aid"]." Surely, if the cohabitation is assumed to be *marital*, that is, *lawful*, even if only according to the right of nature [*dem Rechte der Natur*], the authorization is already contained in the concept [of marriage]. But here the question is whether a marital cohabitation is possible, and how. So the discussion should center only on the matter of physical cohabitation (intercourse) and the conditions of its rightness. For the *mutuum adiutorium* is merely the necessary legal consequence of marriage, whose possibility and condition must first be investigated.

Second, you say: "Kant's theory seems to rest simply on a fallacious interpretation of the word, 'enjoyment.' Granted, the *actual* enjoyment of another human being, such as in cannibalism, would reduce a human being to an object; but married people do not become *res fungibiles* ["merely functional objects"] just by sleeping together." It would have been very weak of me to make my argument depend on the word "enjoyment." The word may be replaced by the notion of *using someone* directly (that is, sensuously—a word that has a different meaning here than elsewhere); I mean rendering him or her an *immediately enjoyable* thing. An enjoyment of this sort involves at once the thought of this person as merely *functional* [*res fungibilis*], and that in fact is what the reciprocal use of each other's sexual organs by two people

[1] See Kant's *Anhang erläuternder Bemerkungen zu den metaphysichen Anfangsgründen der Rechtslehre* ("Supplement to the Metaphysical Principles of Right"), in *Werke*, VI, 357 ff.

is. One or the other parties may be destroyed, through infection, exhaustion, or impregnation (a delivery can be fatal), and so the appetite of a cannibal differs only insignificantly from that of a sexual libertine.

So much for the relationship of man to woman. The relation of father (or mother) to child has not been criticized.

Third, you ask, "Does it seem to you a *petitio principii* when Kant tries to show the right of master to servant or domestic to be a person-thing right (it should read, a legal [*dingliche*] right, that is, a formal right) [2] just because one is allowed to catch the runaway domestic servant again? But that is just the question at issue. How can it be shown that this is in fact allowed by the natural law?"

Certainly, this license is only the consequence and the mark of legal possession, when one man holds another as his own, even though the latter is a person. But one man's holding another as his own (that is, as part of his household) signifies a right to possession that may be exercised against any subsequent possessor (*jus in re contra quemlibet hujus rei possessorem*). The right to use a man for domestic purposes is analogous to a right to an object, for the servant is not free to terminate his connections with the household and he may therefore be caught and returned by force, which cannot be done to a hired man paid by the day who quits when his job is only half completed (assuming he takes nothing away with him that belongs to his employer). Such a man cannot be caught and brought back, for he does not belong to the master the way a maid and a servant [*Knecht*] do, since the latter are integral parts of the household. . . .

To J. A. Lindblom,[1] October 13, 1797

- 783 - VOL. XII, *pp.* 205–7

Your Reverence,
Esteemed sir,

Your efforts in the investigation of my genealogy, reverend sir, and your kindness in informing me of your results,

[2] Kant's parenthetical remark.

[1] Jakob Axelson Lindblom (1746–1819), Swedish bishop.

deserve the highest thanks, even though there may be no utility in this work either for myself or for anyone else.

I have known for quite some time that my grandfather, who lived in the Prussian-Lithuanian city of Tilsit, came originally from Scotland, that he was one of the many people who emigrated from there, for some reason that I do not know, toward the end of the last century and the beginning of this one. A large portion of them went to Sweden, and the rest were scattered through Prussia, especially around Memel. The families Simpson, Maclean, Douglas, Hamilton, and others still living there can attest to this. My grandfather was among that group and he died in Tilsit.* I have no living relatives on my father's side (other than the descendants of my brother and sisters). So much for my origin, which your genealogical chart traces back to honest peasants in the land of the Ostrogoths (for which I feel honored) down to my father (I think you must mean my grandfather). Your humanitarian desire to stir me to support my alleged relatives does not escape me, reverend sir.

For it happens that another letter came to me at the same time as yours, from Larum, dated July 10, 1797, with a similar account of my genealogy, but accompanied by a request from one who calls himself my "cousin," a request that I lend him eight or ten thousand thalers for a few years, which would enable him to achieve happiness.

But Your Reverence will acknowledge this and similar demands to be inadmissible when I tell you that my estate will be so diluted by legacies to my nearest relatives—I have one living sister; my late sister left six children; I have a brother, Pastor Kant of Altrahden in Courland, who has four children, one of them a grown son who recently married—that there could hardly be anything left over for a remote relation whose relationship is itself problematic.

With greatest respect I am ever

* [Kant's footote] My father died in Königsberg, with me.

Your Reverence's
KANT

To J. H. Tieftrunk,[1] October 13, 1797

- 784 - VOLS. XIII, *p. 463, and* VOL. XII, *pp. 207–8*

Treasured friend,

I am content with Mr. Beck's decision to announce that his *Standpoint*[2] is not my own position but his. Let me only remark on this point that when he proposes to start out with the categories he is busying himself with the mere form of thinking, that is, concepts without objects, concepts that as yet are without any meaning.[3] It is more natural to begin with the *given,* that is, with intuitions insofar as these are possible a priori, furnishing us with synthetic a priori propositions that disclose only the appearances of objects. For then the claim that objects are intuited only in accordance with the form in which the subject is affected by them is seen to be certain and necessary.

It gave me pleasure to hear of your discussions with Mr. Beck (please convey my respects to him). I hope they may bring about a unanimity of purpose. I am also pleased to learn of your plans for an explanatory summary of my critical writings, and I appreciate your offering to let me collaborate on this work. May I take the opportunity to ask you to keep my hypercritical friends Fichte and Reinhold in mind and to treat them with the circumspection that their philosophical achievements fully merit.[4]

I am not surprised that my *Doctrine of Right* [*Rechtslehre*] has found many enemies, in view of its attack on a number of principles

---

[1] The first paragraph translated here is taken from a draft of this letter, which Kant did not send.

[2] The reference is to J.S. Beck's *Only Possible Standpoint from Which the Critical Philosophy May Be Judged.*

[3] Cf. *Critique of Pure Reason* B 178 = A 139: ". . . Concepts are altogether impossible, and can have no meaning, if no object is given for them. . . ." Kant altered this to "are for us without meaning." See N. Kemp-Smith's translation of the *Critique* (New York: Humanities Press, 1950), p. 181 n.

[4] This often quoted remark, indicative of Kant's disappointment with his erstwhile disciples, seems ironic in tone, but the corresponding lines in Kant's unsent draft do not. There he writes, "I hope your explanatory summary may lead my hypercritical friends back onto the path they once trod; but please do it in a friendly way." *Werke*, XIII, 463.

commonly held to be established. It is all the more pleasant therefore to learn that you approve of it. The Göttingen review (in issue No. 28) taken as a whole is not unfavorable to my system.[5] It induces me to publish a supplement, so as to clear up a number of misunderstandings, and perhaps eventually to complete the system.

Please treat my friend Professor Pörschke [6] kindly, if you should have the opportunity. His manner of speaking is somewhat fierce, but he is really a gentle person. I suppose his fundamental law, "Man, be man!" must mean, "Man, insofar as you are an animal, develop yourself into a moral being, and so on." But he knows nothing about your judgment or anything about my apology for him. . . .

I agree to your proposal to publish a collection of my minor writings, but I would not want you to start the collection with anything before 1770, that is, my dissertation on the sensible world and the intelligible world, and so on. I make no demands with regard to the publisher and I do not want any emolument that might be coming to me. My only request is that I may see all the pieces to be printed before they come out. . . .

It is possible that death will overtake me before these matters are settled. If so, our Professor Gensichen has two of my essays [7] in his bureau; one of them is complete, the other almost so, and they have lain there for more than two years. Professor Gensichen will then tell you how to make use of them. But keep this matter confidential, for possibly I shall still publish them myself while I live. . . .

Your most devoted servant,

I. KANT

---

[5] See Kant's *Werke*, VI, 356 ff. and 519. The review, which was published in the *Göttingische Anzeigen*, February 18, 1797, was by Friedrich Bouterwek (1766–1828), a philosopher who also corresponded with Kant.

[6] K. L. Pörschke (1751–1812), professor of poetry in Königsberg, wrote *Vorbereitungen zu einem populären Naturrechte* (1795). He asks, "How is natural right possible?" and answers, "Man ought to be, and has to be no more than, man; he is an animal and a rational being, and that he should remain." The principle, "Man, be man!" is the rational foundation of all duties, according to Pörschke.

[7] *Der Streit der Fakultäten* ("Strife of the Faculties"), Pts. I and II; the work was in fact published in 1798. Johann Friedrich Gensichen (1759–1807) was one of Kant's dinner companions. He was professor (extraordinarius) of mathematics.

From J. H. Tieftrunk, November 5, 1797

- 787 - VOL. XII, *pp. 212–19*

. . . But it is possible to become aware of the fact that the original, pure apperception exists of itself and exists independently of all that is sensible, a unique function of the mind, indeed its highest function, from which all our knowledge begins, though it does not produce out of itself *everything* that belongs to our knowledge. The specific feature of the category of magnitude[1] (the feature that distinguishes it from space and time, the form of sensibility) is the activity of unifying [*Actus der Einheit*] (*synthesis intellectualis*) that which is manifold but homogeneous. The fundamental condition of this activity of unification is synthesis into unity; thereby the synthesis of what *is* a unity *into* a unity becomes possible, that is, the synthesis of the many [*des Vielen*] and again of binding the many into a unity is totality [*Alles*]. So far there is no reference to space and time or any actual quantum. We have merely noted the rule or condition under which alone a quantum could be apperceived, viz., it must be possible to synthesize a homogeneous manifold into a unity, plurality [*Vielem*], or totality.

The greatest difficulty appears in connection with the category of quality, for it takes the most subtle thinking to distinguish the pure from the empirical here. Some people suppose that sensation and reality are the same thing and therefore believe that all [objects of] sensation, for example, even air and light, could be deduced a priori. Fichte does that. Other people hold these things to be wholly empirical, so that the category of reality is just the same thing as the production of the empirical. Mr. Beck is an example. My view differs from both of these, and I think the *Critique of Pure Reason* must be interpreted otherwise as well. Here is my statement; I wish you would tell me whether it satisfies you and the problem and whether it is sufficiently clear.

Every sensation as such (as empirical consciousness) has two parts, one subjective, the other objective. The subjective part

---

[1] Tieftrunk may be thinking of the axioms of intuition, since magnitude is not one of Kant's categories. See *Critique of Pure Reason* A 162 = B 202 ff.

belongs to sense [*Sinne*] and is the empirical aspect of the sensation (in the strongest sense of "empirical"); the objective part belongs to apperception and is the pure aspect of the sensation (in the stronger sense of "pure"). Now, then, what precisely is it that apperception as such contributes to every sensation? I answer that it is that whereby the sensation is a *quale* at all. [At this point in Tieftrunk's letter, Kant wrote in, "sensation not mere intuition" (*Empfindung nicht blos Anschauung*).] The function of self-consciousness referred to under the title "Quality" consists in positing [*setzen*]. The act of positing is the a priori condition of apperception and consequently the condition of the possibility of all empirical consciousness. Positing, as a function of mind, is spontaneity and, like all functions of self-consciousness, is a spontaneous *synthesis* [*Zusammensetzen,* literally, "positing-together"] and therefore a function of *unity*. The unity in positing is only possible because apperception may *determine* its positing. The determination of positing is [a?] condition of the possibility of the unity of positing. The function of determination of positing consists, however, in the uniting [*Verknüpfung*] of positing and non-positing [*Nichtsetzens*] into a single concept (as act of spontaneity), that is, the determination of a degree [*Gradesbestimmung*] (gradation). The determined positing is thus the same as the determination of degree, and just as positing is [an?] original function of apperception, so the determination of degree (gradation, limitation, uniting of positing and non-positing into a single concept) is the a priori condition of the unity of positing. The function of unity of this positing is called "determination of degree" (intension), and its product is a determined real (intensive magnitude). The unity produced in this manner is not the unity of a collection [*Menge*], by means of the synthesis of parts into a whole, but rather an absolute unity, achieved by the self-determining apperception in its act of positing. But this unity springs from the unification of positing (=1) and non-positing (=0) into a *single* concept. Since there are an infinite number of determinations of positing and non-positing into unity, between 0 and 1, so there are an infinite number of degrees between 0 and 1, each of which must be, and must depend on being, a unity, and each of these is determined by apperception in accord with its positing, which conforms to an a priori necessary rule (of gradation). All existence [*Dasein*] is therefore based on this original positing, and existence is actually nothing else than this being-posited [*Gesetztsein*]. Without the original, pure act of spontaneity (of apperception), nothing *is* or exists. The determination of degree in apperception is thus the principle of all experience, and so on. . . .

But whence comes the manifold of sensation, the *merely empirical* aspect of sensation? Apperception yields nothing but the *degree,* that is, the unity in the synthesis of perception, which therefore rests on spontaneity and which is the *determination* of the material of sensibility, according to a rule of apperception. Whence the material? Out of sensibility. But whence did sensibility obtain it? From the objects that affect it? But what are these objects that affect sensibility? Are they things in themselves or—?

One wrestles with endless questions here, and some of the answers are highly absurd. For me, there is no perplexity, since once the question becomes understood, the answer is obvious. However, it matters greatly how one understands the question, for ambiguities tend to creep in. Let me tell you briefly how I meet the difficulties.

The central thesis of the *Critique,* of which one must not lose sight, is this: a regression to discover the nature and conditions of our cognitive faculty is not a search for anything outside that faculty; it is not a playing with mere concepts but a presentation of how those elements of our cognitive faculty, as grasped in the act of cognizing [*Erkennens*], can inform us about the essential problems of reason. It is a fact of consciousness that there are two distinct sources of knowledge: receptivity and spontaneity. It is absurd to prove their reality, since they are fundamental [*ursprünglich*]. One can only become aware of them and make them evident to oneself. Though they are two distinct, basic sources, nevertheless they belong to one and the same mind, and therefore they correspond to each other. Just as we assert that the representations of the understanding come into existence through spontaneity, so we assert that the representations of sensibility come to be through receptivity.

Sensibility *gives* representations, because it (or the mind whose faculty it is) is *affected*. When I say that the mind is affected, I subsume the existence [*das Sein*] (that is, the fact that certain representations are posited) under the category of causality; I assert a relationship of the mind to itself, viz., receptivity, which relationship is distinct from others that the mind has to itself, for example, those in which the mind regards itself as spontaneous. If

I ask further, What is it that affects the mind? I must answer, It affects itself since it is both receptivity and spontaneity.

The mind's spontaneity, however, imposes its conditions of synthesis (the categories) on the mind's receptivity, and the sense-representations as such thereby acquire determination by the unity of apperception, that is, they acquire intellectual form, quantity, quality, relation, and so on. But whence does sensibility receive that which it gives out of itself? Whence the material and the empirical as such, if I abstract from that into which it has been transformed as a result of the influence of spontaneity and the forms of sensibility? Does sensibility produce this material out of its own stock, or is it perhaps produced by things in themselves, distinct and separate from sensibility? I answer: *Everything* given by sensibility (matter and form) is determined by its nature to be for us nothing but what it is for us. The properties of being *within* us or *external* to us are themselves only ways in which sensible representing takes place, just as identity [*das Einerlei*] and *difference* are only manners of intellectual representing. If sensibility and the understanding were ignored, there would be no "internal" and "external," no "same" and "different." But since one cannot help but ask which of all the conditions of our sensibility (as to form and matter) is the ultimate condition, the ground of representations that is independent of apperception, the answer is this: that ultimate ground is, for our understanding, nothing more than a thought with negative meaning, that is, a thought without any corresponding object, though, as a mere thought, it is permissible and even necessary, since theoretical reason is not absolutely restricted, in its thinking, to that which is a possible experience for *us* and practical reason can offer grounds for admitting the reality (though only from the practical point of view) of such ideas. We cannot say of things in themselves (of which we have only a negative idea) that they *affect* us, since the concept of affection asserts a real relation between knowable entities, and therefore this concept can only be used when the related things are given and positively determined. Therefore it is also impossible to say that things in themselves transfer representations from themselves into the mind, since the problematic concept of "things-in-themselves" is itself only a point of reference for representations in the mind, a figment of thought [*Gedankending*]. Our knowledge is thus exclusively of appearances; yet while we realize this, we posit in thought a something that is not appearance and thus leave open a space (by means of mere logical supposition) for practical knowledge. The chapter in the *Critique,* pages 294 ff., makes the true view unmistakable.[2] . . .

How is *intuition* distinguished from thinking? "The former is the representation that can be given prior to all thinking," says the *Critique.* . . . Thinking (as transcendental function) is the activity of bringing given representations under a consciousness in general, and it is prior to all intuition, a fact that accounts for the dignity of cognition.

One would like intuition and thinking to be one and the same thing, transcendentally speaking. Indirectly, it can be said that if intuition and thinking were one, there would be no such thing as transcendental logic and aesthetic; all concepts would be *absolutely* restricted to experience. But this is contradicted by apperception. I can at least form the negative concept of an experience that is not human experience, that is, form the concept of an *intuitive* understanding. But even this merely problematic concept would be impossible if the categories in and of themselves constituted experience. I could not transcend experience by means of experience; yet I do this in fact by means of the concept of unity of synthesis in general (in relation to the experiences that are possible and impossible for us to have.) Moreover, if the understanding (in its categories) were of itself capable of experiencing, the transition to the practical realm would be impossible, for there it is by means of mere thought, without intuition, that laws, concepts, and objects are determined by the will.

One tends to confuse the sphere of application of the categories with the sphere of their functions as pure forms of apperception in general. People suppose that because we become *aware* of the categories only by applying them in experience (where they are first put to use, which is possible only in experience, in empirical consciousness) that therefore they cannot be elevated beyond the sphere of their application.

Your friend and servant,

J. H. TIEFTRUNK

[2] "The Ground of the Distinction of All Objects in General into Phenomena and Noumena," Bk. II, Chap. III, B 294 ff. = A 235 ff.

To J. H. Tieftrunk, December 11, 1797

- 790 - VOL. XII, pp. 222–25

Treasured friend,

Though I am distracted by a multitude of tasks that interrupt one another while I think constantly of my final goal, the completion of my project before it is too late, I am anxious to clarify the sentence in the *Critique of Pure Reason* that you mentioned in your kind letter of November 5, the sentence that occurs on page 177 [A 138 = B 177, "The Schematism of the Pure Concepts of Understanding"] and deals with the application of the categories to experiences or appearances. I believe I now know how to satisfy your worry and at the same time how to make this part of the system of the *Critique* more clear. My remarks here, however, must be taken as mere raw suggestions. We can make the discussion more elegant after we have exchanged ideas on it again.

The concept of the *synthesized* in general [*des Zusammengesetzten überhaupt*] is not itself a particular category. Rather, it is included in every category (as *synthetic* unity of apperception). For that which is synthesized [that is, complex] cannot as such be *intuited;* rather, the concept or consciousness of *synthesizing* (a function that, as synthetic unity of apperception, is the foundation of all the categories) must be presupposed in order to think the manifold of intuition (that is, of what is given) as unified in one consciousness. In other words, in order to think the object as something that has been synthesized, I must presuppose the function of synthesizing; and this is accomplished by means of the schematism of the faculty of judgment, whereby *synthesiz*ing is related to inner sense, in conformity with the representation of time, on the one hand, but also in conformity with the manifold of intuition (the given), on the other hand. All the categories are directed upon some material synthesized a priori; if this material is homogeneous, they express mathematical functions, [and] if it is not homogeneous, they express dynamic functions.[1] Extensive

---

[1] See *Critique of Pure Reason* B 110.

magnitude [2] is a function of the first sort, for example, a one in many [*Eines in Vielen*]. Another example of a mathematical function is the category of quality or intensive magnitude, a many in one [*Vieles in Einem*]. An example of extensive magnitude would be a *collection* [*Menge*] of similar things (for example, the number of square inches in a plane); an example of intensive magnitude, the notion of *degree* [*Grad*] [3] (for example, of illumination of a room). As for the dynamic functions, an example would be the synthesis of the manifold insofar as one thing's *existence* [*Dasein*] is subordinate to another (the category of causality) or one thing is coördinated with another to make a unity of experience (modality as the necessary determination of the existence of appearances in time).

Mr. Beck (to whom I beg you to send my regards) could thus also quite correctly develop his "standpoint" on this basis, passing from the categories to appearances (as a priori intuitions). Synthesis [*die Synthesis der Zusammensetzung*] of the manifold requires a priori intuitions, in order that the pure concepts of the understanding may have an object, and these intuitions are space and time.[4] But in thus changing his standpoint, the concept of the synthesized, which is the foundation of all the categories, is in itself an empty concept [*Sinnleer*], that is, we do not know whether any object corresponds to it. [So, too, are the categories:] For example, is there anything that is an extensive magnitude while also having intensive magnitude, that is, reality; or in the dynamic categories, is there anything corresponding to the concept of causality (a thing so situated as to be the ground of the existence of another thing) or anything corresponding to the category of *modality,* that is, any object of possible experience that could be *given?* For the categories are mere forms of synthesis [*Formen der Zusammensetzung*] (of the synthetic unity of the manifold in general) and they belong to thinking rather than to intuition.

Now there are in fact synthetic a priori propositions, and it is a priori intuition (space and time) that make these propositions possible) and therefore they have an object, the object of a non-

---

[2] See "Axioms of Intuition," *Critique of Pure Reason* A 162 = B 202 ff.

[3] See *Critique of Pure Reason* A 166 = B 206 ff. and the section on anticipations of perception that follows.

[4] In another draft, Kant writes "in space and time" here rather than "space and time."

empirical representation, corresponding to them. (Forms of intuition can be supplied for the forms of thought, thus giving sense and meaning to the latter.) But how are such propositions possible? The answer is not that these forms of the synthesized present the object in intuition as that object is in itself. For I cannot use my concept of an object to reach out a priori beyond the concept of that object. So the [synthetic a priori] proposition is only possible in the following way: The forms of intuition are merely subjective, not immediate or objective, that is, they do not represent the object as it is in itself but only express the manner in which the subject is affected by the object, in accordance with his particular constitution, and so the object is presented only as it *appears* to us, that is, indirectly. For if representations are limited by the condition of conformity to the manner in which the subject's faculty of representation operates on intuitions, it is easy to see how synthetic (transcending a given concept) a priori judgments are possible. And it is easy to see that such a priori ampliative judgments are absolutely impossible in any other way.

This is the foundation of that profound proposition: We can never know objects of sense (of outer sense and of inner sense) except as they appear to us, not as they are in themselves. Similarly, supersensible objects are not objects of theoretical knowledge for us. But since it is unavoidable that we regard the idea of such supersensible objects as at least problematic, an open question (since otherwise the sensible would lack a non-sensible counterpart, and this would evidence a logical defect in our classification), the idea belongs to pure practical knowledge [*practischen Erkenntniss*], which is detached from all empirical conditions. The sphere of non-sensible objects is thus not quite empty, though from the point of view of theoretical knowledge such objects must be viewed as transcendent.

As for the difficult passage on pages 177 ff. in the *Critique,* the explanation is this: The *logical* subsumption of a concept under a higher concept occurs in accordance with the rule of identity—the subsumed concept must be thought as *homogeneous* with the higher concept. In the case of *transcendental* subsumption, on the other hand, since we subsume an empirical concept under a pure concept of the understanding by means of a mediating concept (the latter being that of the synthesized material derived from the representations of inner sense), this subsumption of an empirical concept under a category would seem to be the subsumption of something heterogeneous in content; that would be contrary to logic, were it to occur without any mediation. It is, however, possible to subsume an empirical concept under a pure concept of the understanding if there is a mediating concept, and that is what the concept of something *synthesized* out of the representations of the subject's inner sense is, insofar as such representations, in conformity with time conditions, present something synthesized a priori according to a universal rule. What they present is homogeneous with the concept of the synthesized-in-general (as every category is) and thus makes possible the subsumption of appearances under the pure concept of the understanding according to its synthetic unity (of synthesizing). We call this subsumption a *schema*. The examples of schematism that follow [in the *Critique*] make this concept quite clear.*

And so, estimable sir, I close now, so as not to miss the post. I enclose a few remarks on your projected collection of my minor writings. . . .

I. KANT

From Marcus Herz, December 25, 1797

- 791 - VOL. XII, *pp.* 225–26

Esteemed teacher,

The great and well-known Meckel asks to be commended to the great, all-knowing Kant, via me, so little known, so little knowing. I would hesitate greatly to satisfy this superfluous desire, were it not an opportunity, long coveted, to call up in the mind of my unforgettable mentor and friend the name of Herz and to tell him once more how much the memory of those early years of my education under his guidance still spreads joy over my whole being and tell him how burning is my desire to see him again and to embrace him again while there is still time. Why am I not a great obstetrician, a cataract specialist, or healer of cancer, that I might be summoned to Königsberg by some Russian aristocrat? Alas, I have learned absolutely nothing! The little skill I possess can be found tenfold in any village in Kamchatka, and thus I must

---

* [Kant's footnote] You will notice my haste and brevity here, which might be remedied in another essay.

stay in Berlin, moldering, and abandon forever the thought of seeing you again before one or the other of us leaves this earth.

All the more consoling, therefore, is every little bit of news I get of you from travelers, every greeting passed on to me from letters to a friend. Revive me often, therefore, with this refreshment and preserve your health and your friendship for me.

Your devoted,
MARCUS HERZ

To J. H. Tieftrunk, April 5, 1798

- 805 - VOL. XII, *pp. 240–41*

I read your letter with pleasure, dearest friend, and I am especially pleased at your determination to support the cause of the *Critique* in its purity, to explain it and to defend it resolutely, a decision that, as your success will show, you will never have occasion to regret. I would be happy to write a preface to my minor essays [*kleine Schriften*], one that would express my approval not only of your bringing the book out but also of any commentary you might be adding. I could do this if it were possible for me to see the book before it is put together or published. . . .

Several years ago I planned to publish a work under the title "The Strife of the Faculties, by I. Kant." However, it fell under the censorship of Hermes and Hillmer and had to be abandoned. But now the way lies open for it. Alas, another unpleasantness has come in the way of the birth of my genius, namely, a recent book entitled "A New Inquiry as to Whether the Human Race Is Capable of Continual Progress" ["Erneuerte Frage, ob das menschliche Geschlecht im beständigen Fortschreiten zum Bessern sey"], which I sent to the librarian Biester to be published in his *Berliner Blätter*, has been presented to Stadtpräsident Eisenberg for censorship. This was done on October 23, 1797, that is, while the late king was still alive, and the book was denied the censor's imprimatur. It is incomprehensible to me that Mr. Biester waited until February 28, 1798, to report this incident to me. Everyone knows how conscientiously I have kept my writings within the limits of the law; but I am not willing to have the products of my careful efforts thrown away for no reason at all. Therefore I have decided, after inquiring of a lawyer, to send this work, together with the one censored by Eisenberg, to Halle, via my publisher Nicolovius, and to ask you to be so kind as to have it submitted to the censor there. I am sure it will not be condemned, and I shall try to write the Introduction to it in such a way that the two parts will compose one book. If you like, you may then publish the latter in your collection of my minor essays.

What do you think of Mr. Fichte's *Wissenschaftslehre?* He sent it to me long ago, but I put it aside, finding the book too long winded and not wanting to interrupt my own work with it. All I know of it is what the review in the *Allgemeine Literaturzeitung* said. At present I have no inclination to take it up, but the review (which shows the reviewer's great partiality for Fichte) makes it look to me like a sort of ghost that, when you think you've grasped it, you find that you haven't got hold of any object at all but have only caught yourself and in fact only grasped the hand that tried to grasp the ghost. The "mere self-consciousness," indeed, the mere form of thinking, void of content, therefore, of such a nature that reflection upon it has nothing to reflect about, nothing to which it could be applied, and this is even supposed to transcend logic—what a marvelous impression this idea makes on the reader! The title itself arouses little expectation of anything valuable—*Theory of Science*—since *every* systematic inquiry is science, and "theory of science" suggests a *science of science,* which leads to an infinite regress. I would like to hear your opinion of it and also find out what effect it is having on other people in your territory.

Fare you well, dearest friend.

I. KANT

To Christian Garve, September 21, 1798

- 820 - VOL. XII, *pp. 256-58*

I hasten to report my receipt, on September 19th, of your book [1] and letter,[2] so full of kindness and fortitude. . . . The description

[1] *Uebersicht der vornehmsten Principien der Sittenlehre* (1798).

[2] In his letter to Kant, September 1798 [819], Garve movingly depicts his agonizing illness, a malignant tumor of the face, and expresses his astonish-

of your physical suffering affected me deeply, and your strength of mind in ignoring that pain and continuing cheerfully to work for the good of mankind arouses the highest admiration in me. I wonder though whether my own fate, involving a similar striving, would not seem to you even more painful, if you were to put yourself in my place. For I am as it were mentally paralyzed even though physically I am reasonably well. I see before me the unpaid bill of my uncompleted philosophy, even while I am aware that philosophy, both as regards its means and its ends, is capable of completion. It is a pain like that of Tantalus[3] though not a hopeless pain. The project on which I am now working concerns the "Transition from the metaphysical foundations of natural science to physics." It must be completed, or else a gap will remain in the critical philosophy. Reason will not give up her demands for this; neither can the awareness of the possibility be extinguished; but the satisfaction of this demand is maddeningly postponed, if not by the total paralysis of my vital powers then by their ever increasing limitation.

My healthiness, as others will have informed you, is not that of a scholar but of a vegetable—eating, seeing, sleeping. And this so-called health, now that I am in my 75th year, is not enough for me to be able to follow your kind suggestion that I compare my present philosophical insights with those ideas of yours that we once disputed in a friendly fashion, unless my health should improve somewhat. I have not abandoned all hope of that since my present state of disorganization began, about a year and a half ago, with a head cold.

If there should be an improvement, it will be one of my pleasantest tasks to try such a unification—I won't say of our intentions, for those I take to be unanimous, but of our approaches, where perhaps we only misunderstood each other. I have made a start by carefully reading your book.

---

ment that he is still living and thinking. Indeed, his thoughts are exalted. "Never have I perceived the beauty of a poem, the validity of an argument, and the charm of a story more clearly and pleasurably. Yet how little all this compensates for the pain I feel from time to time, and I ask myself how long this battle must yet be fought."

Earlier Garve asks Kant for his opinion of Garve's book, and wonders why Kant refuses to speak out his opinion of his pupils, especially Fichte.

[3] In Greek mythology, Tantalus was a wealthy king who, for revealing the secrets of Zeus, was punished by being made to stand in water that receded when he tried to drink and under branches laden with fruit too far away for him to reach.

On skimming it, I came upon a note, page 339, to which I must protest. It was not the investigation of the existence of God, immortality, and so on, but rather the antinomy of pure reason—"the world has a beginning; it has no beginning, and so on," right up to the 4th [*sic*]: "There is freedom in man, versus there is no freedom, only the necessity of nature"—that is what first aroused me from my dogmatic slumber and drove me to the critique of reason itself, in order to resolve the scandal of ostensible contradiction of reason with itself.

With greatest affection and respect, I am

Your loyal, most devoted servant,
I. KANT

To J. G. C. C. Kiesewetter, October 19, 1798

- 821 - VOL. XII, *pp. 258–59*

Your informative letters certainly occasion many pleasant memories of our lasting friendship, dearest friend. Allow me to mention now my periodic recollection of Teltow turnips, a winter's supply of which you will, I hope, be kind enough to secure for me, though I would be happy to take care of any expenses you will incur.

The state of my health is that of an old man, free from illness, but nevertheless an invalid, a man above all who is superannuated for the performance of any official or public service, who nevertheless feels a little bit of strength still within him to complete the work at hand; with that work the task of the critical philosophy will be completed and a gap that now stands open will be filled. I want to make the *transition* from the metaphysical foundations of natural science to physics into an actual branch of natural philosophy, one that must not be left out of the system.

You have steadfastly remained loyal to the critical philosophy, and you will not regret it. Although others who had also once dedicated themselves to it, motivated in part by a ridiculous fondness for innovation and originality, now seek to lay a trap out of sand and raise a cloud of dust all about them, like Hudibras,[1] it will all subside in a little while.

[1] Samuel Butler, *Hudibras*, Pt. I, Canto I, v. 157 ff.

I have just received the news (though not yet sufficiently authenticated) that Reinhold has recently changed his mind again, abandoned Fichte's principles and been reconverted.[2] I shall remain a silent spectator to this game and leave the scoring to younger more vigorous minds who are not taken in by ephemeral productions of this sort.

It would delight me to be regaled with news from your city, especially on literary matters. I am, with greatest friendship, respect and devotion,

Your

I. KANT

Open letter on Fichte's Wissenschaftslehre, August 7, 1799

Public Declarations, No. 6; VOL. XII, pp. 370–71

. . . I hereby declare that I regard Fichte's *Theory of Science* [*Wissenschaftslehre*] as a totally indefensible system. For the pure theory of science is nothing more or less than mere logic, and the principles of logic cannot lead to any material knowledge. Since logic, that is to say, *pure logic,* abstracts from the content of knowledge, the attempt to cull a real object out of logic is a vain effort and therefore a thing that no one has ever done. If the transcendental philosophy is correct, such a task would involve metaphysics rather than logic. But I am so opposed to metaphysics, as defined according to Fichtean principles, that I have advised him, in a letter, to turn his fine literary gifts to the problem of applying the *Critique of Pure Reason* rather than squander them in cultivating fruitless sophistries. He, however, has replied politely by explaining that "he would not make light of scholasticism after all." Thus the question whether I take the Fichtean philosophy to be a genuinely critical philosophy is already answered by Fichte himself, and it is unnecessary for me to express my opinion of its value or lack of value. For the issue here does not concern an object that is being appraised but concerns rather the appraiser or

---

[2] In fact, the rumor was incorrect.

subject, and so it is enough that I renounce any connection with that philosophy.

I must remark here that the assumption that I have intended to publish only a *propaedeutic* to transcendental philosophy and not the actual system of this philosophy is incomprehensible to me. Such an intention could never have occurred to me, since I took the completeness of pure philosophy within the *Critique of Pure Reason* to be the best indication of the truth of my work.

Since some reviewers maintain that the *Critique* is not to be taken literally in what it says about sensibility and that anyone who wants to understand the *Critique* must first master the requisite "standpoint" (of Beck or of Fichte), because Kant's precise words, like Aristotle's, will kill the mind, I therefore declare again that the *Critique* is to be understood by considering exactly what it says and that it requires only the common standpoint that any cultivated mind will bring to such abstract investigations.

There is an Italian proverb: May God protect us from our friends, and we shall watch out for our enemies ourselves. There are friends who mean well by us but who are doltish in choosing the means for promoting our ends. But there are also treacherous friends, deceitful, bent on our destruction while speaking the language of good will (*aliud lingua promptum, aliud pectore inclusum genere,* "who think one thing and say another"), and one cannot be too cautious about such men and the snares they have set. Nevertheless the critical philosophy must remain confident of its irresistible propensity to satisfy the theoretical as well as the moral, practical purposes of reason, confident that no change of opinions, no touching up or reconstruction into some other form, is in store for it; the system of the *Critique* rests on a fully secured foundation, established forever; it will be indispensable too for the noblest ends of mankind in all future ages.

IMMANUEL KANT

Index

Locke, John, 52, 143
Love, 24 ff., 188 ff.

Maimon, Salomon, 26, 133 f., 151–56, 175 ff., 196 ff., 212
Malebranche, Nicolas, 72
Marburg, University of, 122(n.1)
Marital and extramarital relations, Kant's views on, 23 f., 115–18, 235 f.
Mathematics, 8, 11, 52 f., 62–66, 128–31, 135, 140, 145 f., 148, 155, 166–69, 179
Meiners, Christoph, 7, 122(n.1)
Mendelssohn, Moses, 3 n. 4, 7, 8, 9, 10, 15, 16, 21, 22, 54–57, 67–70, 76, 86, 87, 96, 103, 105–8, 120(n.1), 123 f., 124(n.3)
Metaphysical Foundations of Natural Philosophy, 49, 49 n., 119, 170
Metaphysics, 8, 9, 10, 11, 29, 31, 44, 48 ff., 55, 57, 59, 62, 64 f., 71, 95–97, 106, 125, 139, 144, 179, 182
Metaphysics of Morals, 4(n.2), 59, 119, 132, 200, 207, 238
Metaphysik der Sitten. See Metaphysics of Morals
Metaphysische Anfangsgründe der Naturwissenschaft. See Metaphysical Foundations of Natural Philosophy
Mind and body, relation of, 56 f., 79. *See also* Spiritual substances
Montesquieu, Baron de la Brède et de, 38 f., 39 n.
Moral law, 192, 194, 199(n.4)
Motherby, Elizabeth, 25, 204
Motherby, Robert, 83 f.

Necessity, subjective *vs.* objective, 144. *See also* A priori
Newton, Isaac, 11

Nicolai, C. F., 7, 8
Nicolovius, F., 31
Noumena, 13

Objects, 16, 30, 71, 103 n., 106, 183
On a Discovery according to Which All Critique of Pure Reason Is Supposed to Be Obviated by an Earlier One, 19, 142 n.
On the Common Saying, "That May Be True in Theory but Not in Practice," 208(n.2)
On the First Ground of the Distinction of Regions in Space, 11 (n.12)
Only Possible Proof of the Existence of God, 5, 44, 46
Ontology, 125, 182
Opus postumum, 31, 99 n., 252

Pantheismusstreit, 21 ff.
Paton, H. J., 12(n.13)
Phenomena, 65; and noumena, 61
Phenomenology, 59, 66
Philanthropin, 15, 83–85
Platner (or Plattner), Ernst, 78, 126
Plato, 72, 143
Pleasure, 60, 68, 78, 127
Plessing, F. V. L., 17, 23 f., 113–18
Positing (*Setzen*), 241 ff.
Pre-established harmony, 39, 73, 154
Prolegomena to Any Future Metaphysics (Prolegomena zu einer jeden künftigen Metaphysik), 7, 13, 101
Propaedentic discipline: *Critique of Pure Reason* as a, 60, 144; *Critique* as not a, 254
Punishment, 199
Pure concepts. *See* Categories

Thing-in-itself, 16, 26, 27, 29, 30, 103 n., 195, 228 ff., 243 f.
Tieftrunk, J. H., 26, 30, 238–50.
Time, 62–65, 69 f., 75, 148, 198. *See also* Intuition, pure; Space and time
Todes, Samuel J., 9 n.
Träume eines Geistersehers, erläutert durch Träume der Metaphysik. See *Dreams of a Ghost-Seer Explained by Dreams of Metaphysics*
Truth, 144
Turnips, 31, 252

Über den Gemeinspruch: "Das mag in der Theorie richtig sein, taugt aber nicht für die Praxis." See *On the Common Saying, "That May Be True in Theory but Not in Practice"*
Über die Buchmacherei (1798), 8
Über eine Entdeckung, nach der alle neue Kritik der reinen Vernunft durch eine ältere entbehrlich gemacht werden soll. See *On a Discovery According to Which All Critique of Pure Reason Is Supposed To Be Obviated by an Earlier One*
Ulrich, J. A. H., 18, 126(n.8)
Understanding, spontaneity of, 71, 214 f., 228 f., 240–44
Untersuchung über die Deutlichkeit der Grundsätze der natürlichen Theologie und Moral. See *Inquiry into the Distinctness of the Fundamental Principles of Natural Theology and Morals*

Verbinden. See Combine
Verknüpfung. See Synthesis

Vleeschauwer, Herman J. de, 31 (n.35)
Von dem ersten Grunde des Unterschiedes der Gegenden in Raum. See *On the First Ground of the Distinction of Regions in Space*
Vorländer, Karl, 24, 24 n., 32 (n.42), 163(n.4)

Was heisst: Sich im Denken orientiren? See *What Is Orientation in Thinking?*
Wasianski, E. A. C., 32
Weldon, T. D., 12(n.13)
What Is Orientation in Thinking?, 21, 121 n., 123(n.2), 158 n.
Wieland, C. M., 18(n.19), 119 (n.1), 126
Will, 192
Windisch-Graetz, Joseph Nicolaus von, 157(n.1)
Wöllner, J. C., 163(n.4), 173
Wolff (or Wolf), Christian, 17, 47, 51, 62(n.3), 149, 152, 179(n.1)
Wolff, Robert Paul, 12(n.13), 64 (n.5)
Wolke, C. H., 14 f., 83–85
Woltersdorf, T. C. G., 173(n.1), 210
Women, Kant's attitude toward, 25 f., 204. *See also* Kant's letters to Maria von Herbert
Wright, Thomas, 46(n.8)

Zedlitz, K. A. von, 8, 12, 91, 92, 94
Zöllner, J. F., 163(n.3)
Zusammensetzung. See Combination; Synthesis